POLICE MISCONDUCT IN AMERICA

A Reference Handbook

Other Titles in ABC-CLIO's
CONTEMPORARY
WORLD ISSUES
Series

Books in the Contemporary World Issues series address vital issues in today's society such as terrorism, sexual harassment, homelessness, AIDS, gambling, animal rights, and air pollution. Written by professional writers, scholars, and nonacademic experts, these books are authoritative, clearly written, up-to-date, and objective. They provide a good starting point for research by high school and college students, scholars, and general readers, as well as by legislators, businesspeople, activists, and others.

Each book, carefully organized and easy to use, contains an overview of the subject; a detailed chronology; biographical sketches; facts and data and/or documents and other primary-source material; a directory of organizations and agencies; annotated lists of print and nonprint resources; a glossary; and an index.

Readers of books in the Contemporary World Issues series will find the information they need in order to better understand the social, political, environmental, and economic issues facing the world today.

POLICE MISCONDUCT IN AMERICA
A Reference Handbook

Dean J. Champion

T 77605

A B C ☙ C L I O

Santa Barbara, California   Denver, Colorado   Oxford, England

Library of Congress Cataloging-in-Publication Data

Champion, Dean J.
  Police misconduct in America : a reference handbook / Dean J. Champion.
    p. cm. — (ABC-CLIO contemporary world issues series)
  Includes bibliographical references and index.
  ISBN 1-57607-599-0 (hardback : alk. paper)
    1. Police misconduct—United States—Handbooks, manuals, etc.
2. Police brutality—United States—Handbooks, manuals, etc. 3. Police corruption—United States—Handbooks, manuals, etc. I. Title.
II. Contemporary world issues
  HV8141.C44 2001
  363.2'3—dc21
                                        2001003624

This book is also available on the World Wide Web as an e-book. Visit www.abc-clio.com for details.

06 05 04 03 02 01   10 9 8 7 6 5 4 3 2 1

ABC-CLIO, Inc.
130 Cremona Drive, P.O. Box 1911
Santa Barbara, California 93116-1911

This book is printed on acid-free paper ∞
Manufactured in the United States of America

Contents

Preface

*P*olice Misconduct in America: A Reference Handbook examines several forms of police misconduct that have been identified and described since the early 1900s. Encompassing police corruption, police deviance, and excessive force, police misconduct includes a broad array of behaviors exhibited by law enforcement officers that are more or less serious and possibly unlawful digressions from the formal responsibilities and duties that comprise their officer roles.

The reasons for studying police misconduct are several. U.S. society today is highly legalistic. Civil rights issues have immense importance, especially for minorities. Much of the police misconduct that occurs is directed toward minority citizens, although it is not restricted to them. Police officers are expected to adhere to and abide by higher standards than those expected of the general public. Public confidence in police departments is based, in part, upon continued good conduct of the police officers who enforce the law. Police misconduct arises when certain conditions are present; it is important that these conditions are understood to the extent that something can be done to change them.

It is important to examine police misconduct as a concept from the 1900s to the present because it was during the first two decades of the twentieth century that police officers in the United States were targeted for professionalization by forward-thinking police chiefs and educators. New standards of professionalism were espoused and attempts were made to upgrade the recruitment and selection process and increase retention, especially for police officers in the larger cities. Consequently, Peace Officer Standards and Training (POST) programs were established in virtually every state. Training academies for law enforcement officers at both the state and federal levels proliferated from the

1950s through the 1970s, an especially critical period of social and economic turbulence.

Police forces throughout the nation were professionalized for several reasons. In the early years of policing, officers were often selected according to physical agility and strength. Little or no recognition was given to their human relations and educational skills or lack thereof. Thus, police-citizen encounters were often confrontational, and many problems were resolved by physical force rather than by constructive dialogue. Because of the lack of emphasis on educational background, many law enforcement officers did not understand the laws they were enforcing or the means by which the laws should be enforced. The authority of the badge took precedence over citizens' constitutional rights and privileges. Often, police officers in different jurisdictions sought to individualize their treatment of persons being taken into custody. Suspects have died or serious bodily injuries have been sustained as the result of unnecessary force and police officer aggressiveness. More than a few citizens were victimized by police misconduct.

Since 1914, the U.S. Supreme Court has decided numerous cases involving police misconduct. Featured in a majority of these cases has been the Fourth Amendment and the right of citizens to be secure against unreasonable searches and seizures of their persons, homes, and personal effects. The high court articulated the exclusionary rule, a standard whereby evidence against criminal suspects that was illegally seized by police could be excluded in court. The landmark case of *Weeks v. United States* was decided in 1914, and subsequently, all police officers have had to observe increasingly rigorous standards for conducting searches of one's person or premises. The exclusionary rule was broadly applied and the importance of it underscored in 1963 in the case of *Mapp v. Ohio*, in which police misconduct had clearly occurred. Many police officers regarded this decision as a condemnation of effective law enforcement, when in fact the U.S. Supreme Court sought to curtail unconstitutional infringement on human rights.

Subsequent to the *Mapp* case, the U.S. Supreme Court decided *Miranda v. Arizona* in 1966. The *Miranda* case led to the establishment of the Miranda warning, which is routinely given to criminal suspects when they are arrested by law enforcement officers. The major reason for the Miranda warning is that many criminal suspects are not aware of their constitutional rights and that their conversations with police, however innocent, may be misconstrued as inculpatory or indicative of criminality. Furthermore, more than a few police officers have used deceptive and/or aggressively persuasive tactics in extracting confessions from detained suspects. Although the use of coercion or force to obtain a confession is unconstitutional, this does not mean that all police officers follow the Miranda protocol whenever they interrogate suspects. In fact, the U.S. Supreme Court had to readdress the Miranda warning and underscore its significance again in June 2000 in the case of *United States v. Dickerson.* A proliferation of civil lawsuits against the police by injured citizens or their families caused increasing numbers of police departments to reconsider their training procedures and what constitutes acceptable police conduct.

Despite the evolution of law regarding police conduct, pervasive corruption has existed among politicians in cities of all sizes, and political influence has contributed to widespread corruption within police officer ranks at all levels. New York police officer Frank Serpico brought national attention to the malignancy of corruption within the New York Police Department during the 1960s. As a result, the Knapp Commission was formed. The purpose of the Knapp Commission was to investigate police officer corruption and rid New York of it. A similar commission, the Christopher Commission, was established in the 1990s after an incident involving the police beating of Rodney King, a California motorist. These commissions are noteworthy because they attracted media attention to some of the activities of police officers in different jurisdictions and resulted in much unfavorable publicity about how officers conducted their affairs. But these were only two of hundreds of similar commissions and investigations occurring in diverse cities and about which the public is generally unaware. Whenever commissions, such as the Knapp Commission or Christopher Commission, are convened, the media and public officials take fairly predictable actions, such as charging the most corrupt and highly visible officials or dismissing those officers who have clearly engaged in misconduct. These commissions, therefore, temporarily incapacitate the system of corruption so that misconduct is at least reduced. Seldom, if ever, do these commissions eliminate misconduct, however. Despite these commissions and their findings, police misconduct continues unabated.

Police misconduct is not limited to the United States. In Brazil, for example, police squads have operated outside of official lines to exterminate vagabond youths who roam the city streets and exploit tourists. Hundreds of youths have been killed outright by these bands of off-duty police officers. In the interests of tourism, unofficial government sanction has been given to these child murders.

In Canada, the Royal Canadian Mounted Police and provincial police units have stirred considerable controversy concerning their treatment of Canadian minorities, including various Aboriginal tribes whose members have been disenfranchised of their rights as Canadian citizens. Race riots and aggressive police suppression of dissent have also been reported in England, where minorities have been subjected to police torture and even death. Police beatings of minority suspects while in custody are fairly routine in England. In fact, descriptions of how minorities are treated in England parallel closely the treatment of minorities by U.S. police in selected jurisdictions. Similar police misconduct has been reported in Australia, the Netherlands, Germany, France, and Russia. Police excesses against citizens in South Africa are well documented.

In sum, police misconduct is pervasive throughout the world. It is unlikely that it will disappear in the near future. Police departments in virtually every country have immense power through the political forces that perpetuate them and use them to enforce their own vested interests. However, in the United States in recent decades, many attempts have been made to control and prevent misconduct among law enforcement officers. Some of these attempts have included, for example, training programs in which police officers have been confronted with real-life scenarios involving opportunities to engage in misconduct. Solutions are proffered that enable new recruits to work through resolutions of these problems. More officer education results in greater police professionalization. Better relations between police and communities can minimize the incidence of certain forms of police misconduct. Community-oriented policing promotes a cooperative atmosphere within which certain forms of police conduct are discouraged. The various forms of police misconduct provide ample justification for professionalizing the police and continuing to hold them accountable for ensuring that their own conduct is both exemplary and law-abiding.

Dean J. Champion
Texas A & M International University
Laredo, Texas

1

History of Police Misconduct

This chapter provides a historical background for the study of police misconduct in the United States. Police misconduct is defined in the context of a departure from standards that are an integral part of the police mission. In order to understand the nature and extent of police misconduct, we must first explore the empowerment of police officers to make decisions affecting others. This empowerment is the discretionary authority to make decisions. These decisions are related directly to the criminal laws that police officers are obligated to enforce.

Generally, legislatures enact criminal laws that are deemed important for the good of society. Police officers are recruited to enforce these laws in order to preserve societal stability and the moral good. Thus, police officers are expected to perform law enforcement functions largely for the purpose of perpetuating societal values and citizen freedoms. The general standard against which to measure misconduct and its seriousness is the code of conduct that all police officers are sworn to uphold.

Police misconduct is defined in the first section of this chapter. Several different types of police misconduct are listed and explained. Police misconduct originates and persists as an abuse of police discretion. Police discretion is described and different types of police discretion are examined. It is important to understand that misconduct is not limited to rank-and-file uniformed officers. It is found at all administrative levels in a majority of police departments. Furthermore, misconduct extends and applies to all law enforcement agencies at both the state and federal levels. No federal, state, or local agency and its officers are immune from engaging in misconduct in its various forms. Several mechanisms for regulating police discretion are described. The chapter concludes with a historical synopsis of police misconduct, ranging from the colonial period to the present.

Police Misconduct Defined

Police misconduct is any inappropriate behavior on the part of any law enforcement officer that is either illegal or immoral or both. All law enforcement officers are expected to conduct themselves according to a higher standard than that set for ordinary citizens. No law enforcement officer is above the law. When any sworn police officer violates the law or behaves in ways that discredit his or her position, this is police misconduct.

Police misconduct stems from an abuse of discretionary powers vested in the police. Police discretion is autonomy in decision making. It is defined by how the police enforce the law.[1] Police discretion depends upon the nature of decision-making activity, such as street decision making, paper decision making in police department offices, and administrative decision making.[2] Police discretion depends on the role assigned it, such as discretion as the absence of law, as antithetical to law, as a relief from excessive legal regulation, as a supplement to law, or as a form of law.[3] Police discretion is the balancing mechanism between justice that is deserved by an individual and justice as equal treatment.[4] Police discretion is articulated in the general case by policy statements issued by police departments. These statements are often referred to as the police mission.

The Police Mission

A clear definition of police discretion is hampered by the fact that many police departments are unclear about their mission.[5] What are the basic functions of modern police departments and the officers who must interact with citizens in their respective communities throughout the United States? What behaviors are expected from police officers and from police departments and personnel? Because many police departments cannot achieve consensus about their general mission and objectives, it is often difficult for them to define consistent codes of conduct for their police officers. This dilemma is underscored by the fact that many police officers say they experience conflicts between what they ideally ought to do and what they actually do while performing their jobs.[6]

The legal codes of all fifty states have been studied by researchers, indicating that mandated police functions are usually divided into three major categories: law enforcement functions, peacekeeping functions, and service functions.[7] Most states have codes that mandate law enforcement and peacekeeping functions, but few states have service-mandated codes. Among all states examined, little consensus exists about which tasks are the most important ones. Often, police officers must incorporate their own role expectations into what is prescribed and what is preferred. Thus, the roles they actually perform are a blend of legislatively prescribed and personalized role definitions. Considerable role conflict exists among police officers. This role conflict is compounded by neighborhood residents who have different and conflicting expectations of the police and what laws they should enforce. Several reasons for why police discretion is necessary include the following:

1. Statute books are filled with archaic and ambiguous laws.
2. Some laws are never enforced and no one expects them to be enforced.
3. Insufficient numbers of police are around to enforce every law violation; thus, there is a need for police to prioritize the laws they will enforce and the ones they won't enforce.
4. Discretion is important for maintaining good community relations.
5. Diverse community standards exist that influence how police officers enforce laws.[8]

Therefore, there is at least some ambiguity associated with police discretion, and this ambiguity stems, in part, from the differences between public expectations of officers and officer definitions of their own roles.

Types of Police Misconduct

Police officer misconduct is committing a crime and/or not following police department policy guidelines and regulations in the course of one's officer duties. Herman Goldstein (1967) was one of the first modern-day law enforcement experts to note the complex nature of the police function.[9] Goldstein wanted police departments to outline all forms of police misconduct as well as to identify the factors contributing to such misconduct. He was among the first to promote officer training programs to be used for instilling officers with a commitment to their professional responsibilities that would minimize and eventually eliminate misconduct. Further, he wanted to integrate both internal and external review mechanisms as a means of controlling and guiding officer discretion. Several specific types of police misconduct have been described:

1. Accessing police records for personal use
2. Abusing sick leave
3. Lying to supervisors and managers
4. Perjuring on reports and in court
5. Committing a crime
6. Falsifying overtime records
7. Using excessive force
8. Drinking while on duty
9. Being involved in off-duty firearms incidents
10. Failing to complete police reports
11. Accepting gratuities
12. Providing recommendations for an attorney, towing service, or bail bond service
13. Failing to report misconduct of a fellow officer
14. Failing to inventory recovered property or evidence
15. Sleeping on duty
16. Cheating on a promotional examination
17. Sexually harassing or performing other such improprieties.[10]

Although all of these forms of police misconduct are serious, some of these behaviors are more important to citizens than others. For instance, citizens may be most concerned about excessive force used by police officers when making arrests. Police officers who commit perjury in court or who engage in sexual harassment with civilians or other officers are treated more seriously than those who fail to complete reports or sleep on duty.

Ancient Origins of Police Misconduct

Police misconduct is not new. In fact, it is ancient. In early Egypt and Mesopotamia, police forces were charged with maintaining order and resolving community disputes.[11] These were principally civilian forces organized and administered by civilian authorities. These police officers often had reputations for molesting or beating prisoners in custody, although their testimony in court was considered trustworthy. In Roman times, from about 100 B.C. to 200 A.D., centurions were used as either military or paramilitary units for policing purposes. Centurions usually commanded units of one hundred men and were used for both policing and combat. Some evidence indicates that around 100 A.D. the Romans established the first professional criminal investigative units in western history. Known as *frumentarii*, these units had three principal duties: (1) to supervise grain distribution to Rome's needy; (2) to oversee the personal delivery of messages among government officials; and (3) to detect crime and prosecute offenders.[12] Frumentarii reenacted crime scenes, conducted custodial interrogations of criminal suspects, compared statements made to different interrogators, and offered immunity to various criminal accomplices in exchange for incriminating testimony against their confederates. Little indication is given, however, about how these frumentarii interacted with the public in their police work.

Accounts of policing in different parts of the world during the period 100 A.D. to about 800 A.D. are fragmented.[13] Of greatest interest to U.S. policing activities is what transpired in early England at or about the time of the Norman Conquest in 1066. English jurisdictions were divided into shires or counties. The chief law enforcement officers in shires were called reeves. Thus, each shire had a reeve. The shire-reeve subsequently yielded the term, sheriff. Shire-reeves were agents of the king of England and collected taxes besides maintaining the peace. The king also used chancellors and justices of the peace as his agents to settle disputes, such as property boundary issues, trespass allegations, and child misconduct, between neighbors. Together with the chancellors and justices of the peace, reeves would maintain order in their respective jurisdictions or shires.

Because of the decentralized nature of policing during this period, there was little accountability. No boards of review existed to oversee the conduct of shire-reeves, constables, or chancellors. Whatever these persons decided was the law, and they defined illegal conduct according to their own definitions of it. Thus, there was considerable opportunity by many officials to engage in corruption and exploit those accused of crimes. The primary means whereby these officials benefited were through bribes and exploitation of convict labor in collaboration with greedy merchants.

The Norman Conquest and Changing Policing Functions

Policing functions during the Norman Conquest were largely shared by community residents. The Norman Conquest had introduced the frankpledge system, which required loyalty to the king of England and shared law and order responsibilities among the public. The frankpledge system required neighbors to form small groups to assist and protect one another if they were victimized by criminals. These neighborhood groups were commanded by constables appointed by favored noblemen of the king. These constables were the predecessors of contemporary police officers. During the next two hundred years, law enforcement duties became increasingly specialized. During the 1600s, citizens performed day watch or night watch duties. Day and night watches were comparable to modern-day shift work. Watchmen would yell out a hue and a cry in the event that they saw crimes being committed or some other type of public disturbance, such as a fire or flood.

The English system of the administration of justice and law enforcement was informal. Law was uncodified and reeves were often corrupt. They accepted bribes from the relatives of those incarcerated in makeshift jails. Debtor's prisons were increasingly common. Persons imprisoned for any crime in a debtor's prison could not be released unless they could make restitution or pay the fine imposed. However, those imprisoned could perform no labor to earn the money to pay their fines. Many prisoners died in prisons because of this unfair system. But reeves were able to exploit those confined by allocating their manual labor to merchants and businesspersons who wanted cheap labor.

The Colonial Period

U.S. colonial law enforcement in the late 1600s and early 1700s was influenced largely by established English precedents. In the colonies, reeves investigated all sorts of crimes, including poaching, trespass, and a host of other offenses. Elaborate jail facilities did not exist in these early years in most jurisdictions, and therefore, corporal punishment or the infliction of pain for offending was the rule rather than the exception. Colonists copied British customs relating to law enforcement.

Because of the great distance between England and the American colonies, differences in law enforcement and judicial practices began to appear. Colonists created systems whereby sheriffs were elected or appointed and could hire deputies to assist them in their law enforcement tasks. Because most colonial communities were rural, formal policing was unnecessary. Between 1630 and 1790, there were only eight communities with populations of 8,000 or more.[14] Rural, informal policing and reliance on local politicians for appointments to law enforcement positions were ideal breeding grounds for corruption and misconduct among police. Policing positions were often given as rewards to certain persons for their support of local politicians. One result of these types of appointments was that politicians and their friends would benefit through selective law enforcement. The law would apply to some but not to others. Thus, the importance of being connected in some way with a politician was highlighted because it shielded those with connections from occasional encounters with the police. Indeed, it became true that some persons were above the law because they could elude punishment based on their political acquaintances.

In some jurisdictions, such as the colony of New York, shouts and rattles were used. People were equipped with noise-making rattles and were expected to shout and rattle their rattles in the event they observed crimes in progress or fleeing suspects. Rattle watchmen were paid 48 cents per 24-hour shift. This work was undesirable, and most persons sought to avoid it. The wealthy could avoid such service because of their political connections. Thus, watchmen became associated with persons of lower socioeconomic status. Watchman work was so undesirable that sometimes offenders themselves were assigned as rattle watchers as a punishment for committing a crime.[15]

In the early 1700s, cities such as Philadelphia established specific patrol areas supervised by constables who commanded squads of volunteers selected from the public. These policing methods were copied by other colonies throughout the 1700s. During this same time in England, Henry Fielding, a politician, was appointed chief magistrate of Bow Street in London in 1848. He organized small groups of citizens to pursue criminals. These persons were known as thief-takers and were selected, in part, by being fleet of foot. Thief-takers received rewards from victims whenever the thief-taker returned stolen merchandise taken from captured criminals. When Henry Fielding died in 1754, Sir John Fielding succeeded him and converted the thief-takers into the Bow Street Runners, a small group of paid police officers who were also quite successful at apprehending criminals. These activities were copied in the colonies. When the Revolutionary War occurred, English and American political and legal policies were officially separated, although English influence on subsequent policing methods persists.

The Metropolitan Police of London

A significant event of the early 1800s was the establishment of the Metropolitan Police of London in 1829 by Sir Robert Peel, the British home secretary. This development was considered a significant police reform. Earlier, in 1792, an influential London magistrate, Patrick Colquhoun, advanced some relatively new ideas about the functions of police. Colquhoun believed that police should establish and maintain order, control and prevent crime, and set an example of good conduct and moral sense for the public. He believed that existing enforcement methods, at least in London, were outmoded and improper and that some degree of professionalism among officers was necessary and should be independently funded by the particular jurisdiction.[16]

Subsequently, Sir Robert Peel followed through on Colquhoun's ideas and was successful in his efforts to establish the first official law enforcement organization in England. This police force was the result of the Metropolitan Police Act of 1829. Initial hirings included six thousand officers whose primary qualifications included the ability to read and write, be of good moral character, and be physically fit.[17] The Metropolitan Police of London were based on the following principles:

1. To prevent crime and disorder, as an alternative to their repression by military force and severity of legal punishment.
2. To recognize always that the power of the police to fulfill their functions and duties is dependent on public approval of their existence, actions, and behavior; and on their ability to secure and maintain public respect.
3. To recognize always that to secure and maintain the respect and approval of the public means also the securing of the willing cooperation of the public in the task of securing observance of the law.
4. To recognize always that the extent to which the cooperation of the public can be secured diminishes, proportionately, the necessity of the use of physical force and compulsion for achieving police objectives.
5. To seek and preserve public favor, not by pandering to public opinion, but by constantly demonstrating absolutely impartial service to law, in complete independence of policy, and without regard to the justice or injustice of the substance of individual laws, by ready

offering of individual service and friendship to all members of the public without regard to their wealth or social standing; by ready exercise of courtesy and good humor; and by ready offering of individual sacrifice in protecting and preserving life.

6. To use physical force only when the exercise of persuasion, advice, and warning is found to be insufficient to obtain public cooperation to an extent necessary to secure observance of law or to restore order; and to use only the minimum degree of physical force that is necessary on any particular occasion for achieving a police objective.

7. To maintain at all times a relationship with the public that gives reality to the historic tradition that the police are the public and that the public are the police, the police being only members of the public who are paid to give full-time attention to duties that are incumbent on every citizen in the interests of community welfare and existence.

8. To recognize always the need for strict adherence to police-executive functions and to refrain from even seeming to usurp the powers of the judiciary of avenging individuals or the state and of authoritative judging of guilt and punishing the guilty.

9. To recognize always that the test of police efficiency is the absence of crime and disorder and not the visible evidence of police action in dealing with them.[18]

These principles stressed police-community cooperative actions, including obtaining public cooperation in law observance, seeking and preserving public order, using minimal force when arresting alleged criminals, and always maintaining favorable relations with the public in the general process of crime control.

Law enforcement agencies in the United States during the early 1800s were increasingly influenced by this new English police organization and its policing methods. In fact, the New York City Police Department modeled its own organization after the Metropolitan Police of London in 1844. By the late 1850s, many other cities established police forces that copied the London model. These cities included Chicago, Boston, Baltimore, Philadelphia, New Orleans, and Newark.[19] Many other contemporary large-city police departments also pattern their organization after the London model.

Urbanization, Industrialization, and the Professionalization of Policing

Urbanization accompanied by industrialization did much to change the nature of law enforcement, especially in large cities. The sizes of police organizations in city areas expanded considerably. These organizations became increasingly bureaucratic, proliferated with diverse divisions and departments indicating particular areas of specialization. Gradually, state and federal governmental law enforcement agencies evolved and new jurisdictional boundaries were established. With the growth of these organizations and expanded law enforcement interests, police work gradually became more specialized. Some police departments performed probation and parole chores before specific agencies were established for these other purposes.[20]

At the same time that police departments were expanding and providing a greater variety of services, the country was changing as the result of massive immigration. Persons from many foreign countries migrated to the United States and located in the larger cities, where they could find work. However, they brought with them different customs and languages, and cultural enclaves of different citizens emerged. Cultural differences were rejected by established residents of cities and towns, and various forms of discrimination were commonplace. Additionally, ethnic and racial minorities competed with established residents for scarce jobs and were therefore perceived as economic threats. This fact alone intensified frictions between different ethnic and racial groups. Civil disorder was increasingly prevalent. In the South, where slavery flourished, laws were created that imposed curfews on slaves so that they could be arrested for wandering the streets after dark. Citizens and police collaborated to create slave patrols to enforce these laws. Such slave patrols were prominent in North Carolina, South Carolina, and in cities such as St. Louis.[21] The Civil War ended such patrols, but civil unrest continued, especially in the larger cities, such as New York, Detroit, Chicago, and Boston, during the period of Reconstruction.

Despite the Civil War, local law enforcement continued to be largely political, and those who performed law enforcement functions were most frequently appointed by politicians. The police were often used, therefore, as an instrument of social control by the politically and economically powerful interests. Their powers were diffuse, and the public was generally unfamiliar with their specific tasks. Thus, when police officers enforced the law, it was difficult to determine whether they were imposing their own standards on citizens arbitrarily or applying the law in an even-handed fashion. Most citizens acquiesced to police authority, regardless of whether it was proper or improper. Police officers had broad discretionary powers, and it was simply unacceptable to challenge this authority.

In such a discretionary milieu, police misconduct escalated. Corruption in various forms occurred. It related largely to revenues derived from gambling, drinking, and prostitution. Payoffs to police officers were commonplace, and thus, law violations were routinely ignored in exchange for financial gain. Graft among the police officers was so widespread and was perpetuated largely because it was supported by higher-level police administrators who also profited from illegal activities. Rank-and-file police officers would ignore criminal activities in exchange for payoffs. In turn, the officers would share this payoff money with those of higher rank who would condone their actions. The police were often involved in illegal activities directly. Gambling establishments would often send police officers to collect money from those who owed gambling debts. Police corruption and graft became so refined that monthly payoffs were standardized according to one's police rank. In New York in 1900, for instance, the standard monthly payoff for patrol officers ranged from $50 to $300 for protecting houses of prostitution and gambling houses. For officers of higher ranks, the rewards were considerably more lucrative. In fact, it was not uncommon for persons desiring police positions to purchase them from local politicians. If someone wanted to become a police captain, for instance, the going rate was $12,000. Because a police captain's annual salary at the time was $3,000, it meant that the person would have to make up the cost of his appointment through various forms of graft.[22]

Police brutality and the use of excessive force were also commonplace among police officers. It was not unusual for police officers to beat up suspects to extract confessions from them. Also, beatings by police were often meted out to low-level offenders as an informal punishment. These were early meanings of what later became known as stationhouse adjustments.

Because police officers were frequently controlled by economic and political interests, those officers were used in various ways to enforce labor laws. If employees of a particular company decided to go on strike and riot for higher wages, for instance, it was not uncommon to summon the police to break up these strikes and subdue rioters. Between 1880 and 1890, for example, there were more than five thousand strikes in New York, nearly two thousand strikes in Chicago, and more than two hundred strikes in Cleveland and St. Louis. Thus, police became known as strikebreakers in these and other cities.[23] At the request of political bosses and wealthy merchants, police officers would frequently break up union meetings and harass labor leaders.

These events should not be interpreted to mean that nothing was being done to control the police. As early as 1853, for instance, New York appointed a Board of Police Commissioners to investigate and remove certain police officers from their positions. But the Board of Police Commissioners was comprised of the mayor, the city recorder, and the city judge. These persons were supposed to be impartial arbiters and objective investigators. But they were not. The board was merely a facade designed to placate the public into thinking that something was being done about corrupt police officers and officials.[24]

During the late 1800s, however, the public was becoming increasingly disenchanted with policing as they were accustomed to it. Religious interests objected strongly to the police protections afforded brothels and gambling establishments. It was only a matter of time before public opinion became galvanized and a Progressive movement was launched, which signaled significant change in the nature and operations of policing.[25] In 1883, the Pendleton Civil Service Act was passed by Congress. This act was significant because it prompted cities to establish civil service mechanisms for selecting police officers and other government functionaries on the basis of merit rather than one's political connections.[26]

The August Vollmer Era

In 1908 August Vollmer, the chief of police of Berkeley, California, established formal professional and educational training for his police officers. Using academic specialists in various forensics areas from a nearby university, Vollmer started an informal academic regimen of police training, including investigative techniques, photography, fingerprinting, and anatomy, among other academic subject areas. By 1917, he persuaded the University of California–Berkeley to establish a criminology and law enforcement curriculum for the purpose of providing his new recruits with formal academic training. These pioneering efforts by Vollmer are regarded as important precedents of what are now known as Peace Officer Standards and Training (POST) programs in most U.S. jurisdictions.

Vollmer's policing innovations were quite influential on modern policing. He pioneered a motorized police force for more effective patrolling for his officers. Vollmer also established the use of two-way radios in police cars. He also created more effective police selection methods, basing officer appointments on emotional, educational, and physical fitness through selection by test. Screening tools for new recruits included extensive interviews with psychologists. Vollmer is considered the founder of police professionalization, and the period during which Vollmer made these changes is considered the beginning of the professionalization movement.

One of Vollmer's students was O. W. Wilson, a former police chief in Wichita, Kansas, and Chicago, Illinois. Wilson eventually became the first dean of the School of Criminology at the University of California–Berkeley in 1950. Furthermore, Wilson was successful in centralizing police administration and creating command decision making, not only in Berkeley, but in many other cities during the 1950s and 1960s.[27]

In 1931, a report was issued of the first nationwide study of the U.S. criminal justice system that was conducted under the auspices of the federal government. President Herbert Hoover in 1929 had appointed a National Commission on Law Observance and Enforcement, known subsequently as the Wickersham Commission. After two years of investigation, the Wickersham Commission issued a fifteen-volume report. One of these volumes examined police lawlessness and concerned police abuse of authority. The report also criticized the apparent inconsistency throughout the United States concerning the selection, training, and administration of police recruits. The obvious implication was that changes in existing recruitment and training practices for subsequent police officers were in order, and the Wickersham Commission recommended the implementation of such changes in the near future. These were ideas for change supported by both Vollmer and Wilson. Over the next several decades, more sophisticated police selection and training methods were established in many jurisdictions and have been reasonably successful in improving the quality of officers in police departments generally.

The military-like organization of contemporary police departments is reflective of the centralization of police organization contemplated by Wilson. World War II veterans entered law enforcement in large numbers in the late 1940s and 1950s, and the interplay of organizational ideas leading to military-style agencies would not be considered unusual. The military model of police organization typifies most contemporary police departments.

Police Misconduct during and after the Vollmer Era

August Vollmer did much to change the professionalism of police officers and police departments. However, he failed to eradicate corruption and misconduct of police, even within his own department. During the 1900s and continuing to the present, police misconduct has continued to be pervasive in U.S. society. It is unlikely that police misconduct will ever be eliminated entirely. Instances of various forms of police misconduct, including both graft and excessive use of force, have continued throughout every decade during the 1900s. Several examples of police misconduct during this period are noted below.

During the 1920s and 1930s, gambling, prostitution, and illegal alcohol manufacture and distribution were enterprises that continued to receive police support. Al Capone and other gangsters in the Chicago area were especially visible in perpetuating police corruption and misconduct. Although many of these gangsters were subsequently convicted and imprisoned for their crimes, the police were largely unaffected by these events. They simply adjusted and adapted to changing times, altering their misconduct to fit whatever was happening in particular jurisdictions.

In the 1940s, for instance, racial violence was widespread. A deadly race riot erupted in Detroit in 1943. Police officers in Detroit were criticized because they neglected to act to protect persons from racial violence. In fact, racial violence has continued to the present. Highlights of racial violence include the Watts riots in Southern California in 1965 and the riots that errupted after the Rodney King incident in Los Angeles in the early 1990s.

Graft and corruption within many police departments has been commonplace over the years, with several departments attracting special attention from the media. These forms of police misconduct were not confined to cities such as New York, Chicago, and Los Angeles. In Philadelphia in 1951, for instance, an investigative committee found that extensive graft and corruption existed among police officers and administrators who were protecting prostitution and gambling interests. In the early 1960s, Denver, Colorado, police officers were involved in an elaborate burglary ring where stores and restaurants were being looted. Police officers were using their cruisers to haul away stolen merchandise from these establishments.

A most critical event of the 1970s occurred in 1972 when New York police officer Frank Serpico came forward to alert public officials about widespread graft and corruption within the New York Police Department (NYPD). A special commission was appointed by Mayor John V. Lindsay to investigate Serpico's allegations. The commission became known as the Knapp Commission, named after its chairman, Whitman Knapp, but its formal name was the Mayor's Commission to Investigate Allegations of Police Corruption.[28] The Knapp Commission held public hearings and issued recommendations and findings. It found essentially that police corruption was widespread. It found corruption among plainclothes officers, detectives, who were supposed to enforce gambling laws, and that gambling payoffs were enormous. Furthermore, the commission found corruption relating to narcotics trafficking. The primary recommendation of the Knapp Commission was that the governor appoint a special deputy attorney general with jurisdiction in various New York counties and authority to investigate and prosecute all crimes involving corruption in the criminal process. Numerous indictments and convictions of police officers occurred on the heels of the Knapp Commission activities and recommendations.

Despite the Knapp Commission's recommendations and subsequent indictments and convictions of numerous police officers involved in the NYPD corruption scandal, corruption did not end in the NYPD. During the 1980s the Buddy Boys were discovered to exist. These Buddy Boys consisted of at least thirty-eight rogue officers of the NYPD 77th Precinct who stole money and drugs from dealers and others and profited from illicit drug resales. The NYPD Internal Affairs Division became aware of these activities and investigated. The results of their investigation led to more indictments, convictions, and resignations of police officers in the 77th Precinct.

Additional investigations of the NYPD continued into the 1990s with the formation of the Mollen Commission in 1994. This commission was charged with investigating drug corruption, robberies, and thefts committed by New York police officers, as well as their excessive use of force. Several officers were subsequently indicted and convicted as the result of this investigation.

Corruption and police misconduct are not exclusively found in large cities such as New York. In 1998, for instance, corruption and misconduct were found and dealt with in numerous smaller cities and towns throughout the United States, as well as in some of the larger cities. In Cicero, Illinois, and West New York, New Jersey, for instance, the entire police command structures were replaced because of systemic corruption. Forty-four police officers in Cleveland, Ohio, were charged in a corruption probe. In Mahoning County, Ohio, the sheriff was indicted and several other officers were charged with felony theft and conspiracy to commit theft. Police officers in Dallas, Texas; Erie County, New York; and Pioneer Village, Kentucky, faced charges in the shooting deaths of innocent civilians.[29]

The Law Enforcement Assistance Administration

In the midst of different incidents involving police misconduct, various vested interest groups and action organizations continued lobbying for more effective monitoring and control of police behaviors. More police reform and change occurred in 1968 when the Law Enforcement Assistance Administration (LEAA) was created. The LEAA was one outgrowth of the President's Crime Commission during 1965–1967, a time of great social unrest and civil disobedience. The LEAA allocated millions of dollars to researchers and police departments over the next decade for various purposes. Many experiments were conducted with these monies, many of which led to innovative patrolling strategies in different communities.

In 1973, the National Advisory Commission on Criminal Justice Standards and Goals promulgated several important goals for police departments in order to clarify their policing functions. These goals are as follows:

1. Maintenance of order
2. Enforcement of the law
3. Prevention of criminal activity
4. Detection of criminal activity
5. Apprehension of criminals
6. Participation in court proceedings
7. Protection of constitutional guarantees
8. Assistance to those who cannot care for themselves or who are in danger of physical harm
9. Control of traffic
10. Resolution of day-to-day conflicts among family, friends, and neighbors

11. Creation and maintenance of a feeling of security in the community
12. Promotion and preservation of civil order.[30]

These goals continue to be incorporated into mission statements of most police departments today.

The Importance of Studying Police Misconduct

Why is it important to study police misconduct? The primary reasons to study police misconduct are as follows:

1. Police officers are expected to adhere to and abide by higher standards than those expected of the general public.
2. Public confidence in police departments is based, in part, upon continued good conduct of police officers who enforce the law.
3. Police misconduct arises when certain conditions are present; it is important that these conditions are understood to the extent that something can be done to change them.
4. Police-community relations can minimize the incidence of certain forms of police misconduct.
5. Community-oriented policing promotes a cooperative atmosphere within which certain forms of police conduct are discouraged.

The Pervasiveness of Police Misconduct

The pervasiveness of police misconduct among police departments throughout the United States cannot be underestimated. For instance, a survey of 1,151 law enforcement agencies was conducted in October 1990.[31] A representative sample of agencies from U.S. cities and counties with populations of ten thousand or more was obtained. Study results showed widespread police misconduct and numerous public allegations of it. Tort actions were filed against police officers, resulting in awards to citizens in excess of $2 million, depending on the jurisdiction and the nature and type of misconduct alleged. The misconduct by police officers that generates such lawsuits is often blamed on police agencies for failure to train their officers properly. In order to minimize lawsuits in which police misconduct is alleged, police agencies can

1. Train law enforcement personnel in the policies and pro-cedures they are expected to observe;
2. Ensure that all officers have copies of these policies;
3. Provide regular training of supervisors; and
4. Create an atmosphere wherein disciplinary action is the norm if policies and procedures are violated.[32]

Establishing policies for police officers, providing them with a chain of command for effective supervision, and creating an at-mosphere in which disciplinary action will ensue if the policies are violated are critical steps toward minimizing police miscon-duct. However, cooperation from police officers themselves is an equally critical requirement. One major factor that perpetuates police misconduct is unwritten rules that are tacitly supported by many police officers. These unwritten rules encourage officers not to betray other officers whenever misconduct is discovered or witnessed.

Unwritten Codes of Conduct

Unwritten rules are similar to the codes of conduct generally en-dorsed by prison inmates—do not inform against friends. Prison inmates insulate themselves from administrators and the correc-tional officers who directly supervise them.[33] A "we" and "they" mentality is adopted. For more than a few police officers, citizens are potential enemies to be tolerated.[34] Citizens initiate lawsuits against police officers for various forms of misconduct. Many po-lice officers believe that citizens do not understand and cannot empathize with officers who put their lives on the line daily. In this antagonistic context, it is easy to see why police develop these attitudes and why misconduct occurs.[35] Civil liability cases against police officers where misconduct is alleged, for instance, account for about 40 percent of all case filings against officers.[36] Police officers are aware of their vulnerability to such litigation and seek to protect themselves from it in various ways.

Police Discretion

There are several different types of police discretion. These in-clude (1) by-the-book traditional discretion and (2) mandatory arrest policies versus complete officer autonomy. Police officers observe numerous law violations daily. Persons jaywalk, that is, they walk across major traffic thoroughfares at points not designated by crosswalks or traffic lights. Persons sleep on park benches or loiter and beg in subway terminals. Automobiles are partially parked in "No Parking" zones. Persons in bars get into fights and commit aggravated assault against one another, sustaining serious physical injuries. Inattentive motorists may run red lights. Police officers may choose to ignore these violations. An infinite number of situations exist daily in which police discretion is required. Much of this discretion is unregulated. Other forms of police discretion are governed closely by specific department policies.

By-the-Book Traditional Police Discretion

Traditional police discretion is the exercise of decision making resulting from the confluence of factors that impinge upon officers from their formal police training, education, common sense, and split-second interpretation and assessment of circumstances of their citizen encounters.[37] The definition is a blend of professional individual and/or collective judgments that preserve and promote community and citizen safety, respect for the law, and citizen rights to due process and equal treatment under the law. It recognizes citizen rights to privacy and equal treatment as set forth by the Fourteenth Amendment as well as the right of communities to ensure that their safety and security are not compromised. Professionalization recognizes the formal training officers receive through law enforcement training academies and other educational experiences.

Mandatory Arrest Policies versus Complete Officer Autonomy

In many police departments, department policies give officers absolutely no latitude to make decisions about whether arrests should be made. In the early 1990s, for instance, many police departments established mandatory arrest policies involving spousal abuse incidents. If police officers were called to investigate a complaint involving domestic violence, the department policy meant that one or the other spouse would be arrested and taken to jail. There was no question about whether the officers should arrest someone. This discretionless situation meant that police behavior was compulsory, not discretionary, regardless of the officers' personal feelings, judgments, or observations about the seriousness of the spousal abuse incident or nature of the complaint.

Another instance of mandated police action leading to arrests is the establishment of sobriety checkpoints in various cities where persons who are drunk or under the influence of drugs or other substances are automatically arrested if caught.[38] In many cities, police departments direct officers to establish checkpoints on major city thoroughfares, usually during late evening hours, as a means of deterring and/or apprehending those driving under the influence of alcohol or drugs. When these checkpoints are operated, officers usually ask to see one's driver's license and registration and to verify that those documents are in order. When drivers respond to such officer requests, the odor of alcohol or slow-moving awkward responses cause officers to suspect drivers of driving under the influence of either drugs or alcohol. This definition of the situation or situationally based discretion often leads to arrests and driving-while-intoxicated (DWI) or driving-under-the-influence (DUI) charges.

Most police-citizen encounters involve on-the-spot decision making and the exercise of discretion, however. If officers observe a crime being committed, they must decide whether the crime is serious enough to make an arrest. But police officers may elect to ignore some law violations because they are relatively harmless or trivial. In many jurisdictions, for instance, jaywalking is a crime, but jaywalking laws are seldom enforced. Thus, police officers often prioritize crimes in terms of their seriousness. Officers exercise their judgment about whether to stop and arrest particular citizens for relatively minor offending behavior. Should speeders on major highways be stopped and given tickets for traveling 67 miles per hour in a 65-mile-per-hour zone? In these traffic situations, informal standards are often established, and different tolerances are created. It may be that in some jurisdictions police officers may stop and ticket speeders only if speeders exceed the speed limit by 10 miles an hour or more. These informal standards vary greatly among jurisdictions. Some police departments have zero-tolerance traffic policies, meaning that any observed speeding behavior must be ticketed. Thus, persons traveling 31 miles per hour in a 30-mile-per-hour zone will be stopped and cited. An obvious benefit for those jurisdictions with zero-tolerance policies relating to speeding is that more revenue is generated for city, county, or state governments. But the adverse effects of such zero-tolerance policies may be poor public relations and negative images of the police by affected citizens.

The American Bar Foundation Survey of Criminal Justice

In the early 1950s, a survey was commenced by the American Bar Foundation (ABF) to examine closely criminal justice decision making from arrests through parole supervision.[39] This survey sought to replicate, in part, a survey of criminal justice and police officer performance conducted in the 1930s and is known as the Wickersham Report. The ambitious and comprehensive project undertaken by the ABF was extended to include examinations of prosecutorial and judicial decision making and discretion as well as police conduct relative to arrests and other police-related matters. Parole board decision making was also examined.

The ABF survey's chief consultant, Lloyd Ohlin, remarked that "field teams of observers were sent into . . . cities and rural areas of three states . . . they rode in police cars on all shifts with all units . . . they observed station house behavior . . . they watched prosecutors review cases and charge defendants . . . they sat in courtrooms, talked to judges, and watched arraignments and sentencing . . . they spent time with probation officers, read presentence investigation reports, and observed supervision; they sat with parole boards and came to understand the release and revocation decisions."[40] One of the survey's field representatives and research associates was Herman Goldstein. Goldstein summarized some of the major survey findings relative to police discretion. Some of his findings are outlined below:

1. The police do many things besides investigate crime and arrest offenders.
2. Even within conduct labeled criminal, the incidents the police are called on to handle are infinite and unpredictable, requiring flexibility in responding to them.
3. The police use their authority to arrest to achieve many objectives other than the initiation of a criminal prosecution.
4. The police—and especially individual police officers—exercise enormous discretion.
5. Although evidence of a crime may be present, the police often decide not to arrest.
6. The police are a part of the criminal justice system; their actions heavily influence other agencies in the system, whose actions, in turn, strongly influence the police.[41]

Goldstein's observations highlight the diffuseness of police officer discretion as well as how exercises of discretion can affect other important criminal justice system components. Police officers' actions described by ABF field observers included taking intoxicated persons into protective custody, clearing the streets of prostitutes, responding to a wide range of disputes, directing traffic and enforcing parking limits, checking alleged trespassers, investigating accidents, censoring movies and books, finding missing persons, checking suspicious circumstances, handling stray animals, providing first aid, and collecting overdue library books and the assessed fines.[42]

The ABF survey highlighted the complexity of police officer discretion during their routine decision making. Subsequent results led to (1) establishing police training programs that stressed decision making and discretion and (2) professionalizing police officers in different ways. More education has been stressed as a part of the police officer selection process, with possession of a bachelor's degree preferred as a minimum educational prerequisite. Computer-simulated crime situations involving prospective police recruits have become commonplace as technological advancements have expanded into law enforcement. Personality and aptitude tests have been added to screen officer applicants more effectively. However, higher amounts of education or IQ do not necessarily mean that better officers will be hired or that those hired will be more effective in performing their jobs.

Situationally Based Discretion and Officer Misconduct

Most of the discretionary action of police officers occurs under diffuse circumstances in which police officer actions are known only to the police officers and the citizens they encounter, and thus it is impossible to monitor all police actions at all times for supervision, evaluation, or accountability. Motorists stopped on highways or pedestrians detained briefly by curious police officers in high-crime areas are usually the only witnesses to police-citizen encounters, other than the police officers themselves. Widely different versions of events may be related, one version by the arresting officer and the other version by the arrestee. In court, greater weight is often given to the testimony of police officers rather than that of defendants. One reason is that many citizens believe that police officers always tell the truth and would never lie under oath. But there is ample evidence to indicate that police officers may commit perjury, for whatever reason, to solidify their cases against criminal defendants.[43] Sometimes, however, situationally based discretion is preserved by means of videotape. But even videotaped incidents do not enable us to determine in any absolute sense whether the officer(s) acted properly or whether the allegations of arrested persons are to be believed. For instance, the well-publicized incident involving Rodney King and Los Angeles police officers in 1990 is a notorious example of the application of situationally based police discretion. In this instance, a motorist, King, was speeding and he was pursued by police officers on a lengthy chase through Los Angeles streets. The subsequent stop of King and his passengers resulted in an apparent assault of King, who was alleged by police officers to resist the arrest. More than twenty officers surrounded King, and he was beaten with night sticks and shot several times with a stun gun before police were able to "subdue" him. An attentive apartment dweller across from the scene recorded several minutes of the incident on videotape, particularly the portion where officers were hitting King with their sticks. Two trials were subsequently held, alleging assorted violations of King's rights as a citizen and certain criminal claims. A California jury acquitted three of four officers charged with criminally assaulting King. However, a federal court tried the officers on a different set of criminal charges and two officers were found guilty by the federal jury. In the meantime, King sued the city of Los Angeles for injuries he sustained when arrested.

Despite that police officers had been videotaped and appeared to be beating King unmercifully, their attorneys convinced the state jury that the officers had acted appropriately and in response to King's resisting arrest. All jurors witnessed the recorded event, and despite the clarity of the beating King received by police, many different interpretations were made of it. It failed to resolve the matter of whether the officers had acted properly. In the aftermath of the King incident, many police cruisers have been equipped with videotaping equipment to bolster their subsequent court cases when drunk drivers and others are stopped for assorted traffic violations or suspicious behavior. The Georgia Highway Patrol, for instance, installed the In-Car Video System in many of its vehicles. The uses of such equipment have been for providing visual evidence of DWI stops and subsequent substantiation of court testimony against defendants.[44] However, the units have also caused officers to become more conscious of their own conduct relative to citizens stopped on Georgia highways.

Some jurisdictions report little, if any, change from previous operating procedures among police officers after the King incident. For instance, Texas enacted a Public Intoxication Law (PIL), which provided for either incarceration, release on one's own recognizance, release to another responsible adult, or release to a voluntary treatment program for chemical dependency.[45] The PIL placed Texas law enforcement officers in positions of determining whether those arrested appeared dangerous to themselves or to others. In some of the smaller Texas communities, police officers used the new PIL to incarcerate large numbers of persons who would not otherwise be incarcerated. Many arrestees were arrested when their behaviors only remotely fell within the "dangerousness to self or others" definition of probable cause for arresting someone for public intoxication. In these instances, police discretion was truly situationally based and, by inference, discriminatory.

It has been suggested that police discretion is influenced by extralegal factors such as race, gender, or socioeconomic status.[46] It has been reported, for instance, that, in a survey of 4,097 officers from three large-city and two small-city police departments in two southern states, race appeared to influence strongly the decision-making process at various stages, commencing with arrests. Interestingly, large-city officers exhibited the greatest arrest disparity compared with that of small-city police officers. In these larger cities, police officers were more consistently discriminatory toward black arrestees than with white arrestees under similar arrest circumstances.[47] However, Samuel Walker indicates that, considering the history of criminal justice during 1960–1990, the record indicates that there has been some success at controlling discretion throughout the criminal justice system. Disparities among those arrested for various offenses on the basis of race, gender, or socioeconomic status have gradually been reduced.[48]

Racial/ethnic, gender, or socioeconomic minorities might not be the only ones subject to discretionary abuses by police. In some cities, such as Chicago, mentally ill offenders are arrested at higher rates than are offenders who do not show signs of any mental illness. However, their own somewhat deviant or peculiar conduct may do much to call attention to themselves compared with the conduct of the population of non–mentally ill persons. A more detailed analysis of Chicago's mentally ill arrestee population suggests that only those who exhibit multiple psychological problems or severe mental illness are taken into custody. And often, the disposition of such arrests is diversion to treatment alternatives throughout the community.[49]

Police mistreatment of people who are mentally ill might be exaggerated, at least according to some reports. The police role in the postdeinstitutionalization community management of those who are mentally ill was investigated and included seventy-nine police encounters with eighty-five people with mental disorders. Although it was clear that those who were mentally ill stood a greater chance of being arrested compared with those not mentally ill, certain bureaucratic and/or legal restrictions were implemented to cause officers to divert many of these persons to hospitals rather than to jail. Linda Teplin, the investigator, concluded her analysis by noting that police should develop the following policies relative to persons suspected of being mentally ill: (1) police officers must be trained to recognize and handle the offender with a mental disorder; (2) police officers should use the least restrictive alternative, and wherever possible, they should consign such persons charged with misdemeanors to a mental health treatment facility; and (3) modes of care other than hospitals should be provided for police referrals of offenders with mental disorders.[50]

Police Officers and the Courts

Decision making by police officers in their daily encounters with citizens frequently involves other components of the criminal justice system. Police officers collect evidence at crime scenes and prepare arrest reports. On the basis of the quality of evidence collected at crime scenes by police, or the accuracy of information from the reports they file against arrestees, prosecutors may or may not be able to follow through with criminal prosecutions. The quality of evidence collected and/or the manner in which arrests were made and rights of suspects were observed often contaminate a prosecution. One important feature of an arrest pertains to the Miranda warning, which is verbal advice to arrestees that anything they say may be used against them later in court; that they have a right to an attorney; that they have a right to have an attorney appointed for them if they are indigent; that they have a right to remain silent, to refrain from self-incrimination, and to halt questioning at any time; and that they have a right to have an attorney present during any interrogation (*Miranda v. Arizona*, 1966). Failure to administer the Miranda warning to arrestees fatally flaws any arrest and any subsequent information obtained from interviewing suspects. Even very incriminating information may be excluded from court testimony if the conditions under which it was obtained vary from approved police procedure and if the Miranda warning is not recited. Even under conditions in which suspects are given the Miranda warning numerous times while being questioned, cases may be lost because of technical violations of interrogation rules by police officers.

Dantzker cites various points within the criminal justice system at which police officer discretion is crucial to successful investigations, prosecutions, and convictions. These include (1) police officer–prosecutor relations and communications; (2) police officer–court relations and communications; and (3) police officer–corrections relations and communications.[51]

Police Officer–Prosecutor Relations

Whenever police officers arrest criminal suspects, there are several procedural activities that are obligatory. Repeated Miranda warnings may be insufficient under certain circumstances. Dantzker says that although the relation between police officers and prosecutors should be one of the closest, it is often the worst. One problem inherent in the police officer–prosecutor relation may be the less-than-adequate training and education that police officers receive concerning the finer points of the law. If police officers do not familiarize themselves with current legal issues relating to their conduct and interactions with citizens, they may unwittingly prejudice an arrest so that a suspect's prosecution is undermined. Case dismissals based on legal technicalities are common, and often the source of these legal technicalities is police officer indiscretion when arresting suspects and collecting evidence.

Dantzker says that "in the world of the prosecutor, crime is represented by facts on a piece of paper that must meet strict written guidelines . . . [whereas] crime to police is applied—a function of the street; the requisite, neat guidelines of the courtroom do not always fit."[52] These problems between police officers and prosecutors regarding how searches and seizures should be handled may jeopardize seriously any criminal investigation and/or prosecution.

Police Officer–Court Relations

Whenever police officers give testimony in court, they are subject to critical cross-examinations by defense counsels. Did they obtain a warrant to conduct a proper search of the defendant's premises? Did they have probable cause to justify obtaining the warrant? Did they collect evidence carefully? Did they limit the scope of their search to the specifications of the warrant? If the search was warrantless, did they have proper grounds to conduct it? Did they properly advise defendants of their rights? Many officers have been accused of finding incriminating evidence first and then constructing a rationale to justify an otherwise illegal search. In more than a few cases, police officers, detectives, and federal agents have perjured themselves in court to enhance the likelihood of a conviction. In any case, procedural irregularities in law enforcement are given little tolerance by the court and the opposing counsel.

Dantzker notes that the educational level of police officers is often that of a high school graduate.[53] Also, police officer understanding of the law is inadequate. Police officers have been known to make up their own law and operate according to some unwritten street code when conducting their patrols. Thus, street justice is often dispensed without formal court action. Dantzker believes that better police-prosecutor relations should be established to generate a larger proportion of successful prosecutions.

Controlling Police Discretion

How can police discretion be regulated or controlled? Controlling police discretion does not mean to stifle or repress it. In this instance, "controlling" means to regulate conduct in ways that mutually benefit police officers and citizens. One important point of community-oriented policing is for police officers to acquire a better understanding of community interests and priorities. This understanding is enhanced by interacting with various community residents more closely and on a fairly regular basis.

Controlling police discretion may also refer to both internal and external strategies, such as internal affairs divisions in police departments and citizen complaint review boards. Internal affairs investigates complaints against police officers made by citizens. It also investigates information or evidence about possible officer corruption or dishonesty. However, many community residents do not believe that police departments are capable of making objective evaluations of their own personnel. This is because police officers in numerous jurisdictions have effectively established a blue wall of silence, sometimes known as the code of silence, by which police officers will not report the wrongdoing of other officers if it is detected or observed.[54] Many communities have established citizen or civilian complaint review boards, consisting of various community leaders and police department representatives.[55] These external mechanisms are intended to suppress police personalities and their affiliations with police departments while they are being investigated for various forms of misconduct. Civilian complaint review boards are considered impartial and objective when investigating allegations of police misconduct.

In view of the current popularity of community-oriented policing and its likelihood of continuing, it makes sense to give more credence to civilian complaint review boards as useful and integrative mediums whereby errant police officers can be sanctioned. Unfortunately, there are more than a few police officers as well as police department administrators who view civilian complaint review boards as unable to get in touch with the police perspective and to resolve disputes and settle allegations fairly.

Conclusion

Police misconduct has existed since the first vestiges of law enforcement in ancient times. Key factors in promoting and perpetuating police misconduct are decentralized decision making, local political control and appointment of police officers, and insufficient accountability systems or mechanisms.

Police misconduct is best understood in the context of the police mission. The police mission varies among police departments, although it articulates general policies of police conduct and values that have many similarities. Not all officers have a thorough understanding of the police mission, however. Police officers learn how to perform their jobs, although they often receive contradictory advice from those who train them. Thus, there are both written and unwritten codes of conduct that police officers internalize. Police officers are charged with enforcing the laws of their jurisdictions and are held to a higher standard of conduct compared with that of citizens. Police officers have broad discretionary powers and are trusted to exercise this discretion effectively. When officers abuse their discretionary powers, misconduct occurs.

There are many forms of police misconduct, although the most common forms include graft, corruption, and the use of excessive force against citizens. Relatively recent forms of police misconduct originated in the shire-reeve system of England and were perpetuated by American colonists. After the Revolutionary War, law enforcement practices in the United States continued to be influenced by models established by English law enforcement, particularly the Metropolitan Police of London, established in 1829. Despite more centralized organizational structure and greater accountability within various police departments, the 1800s and early to mid-1900s were characterized by a high degree of local political control, which led to widespread police corruption in many different forms.

The U.S. Congress passed laws governing the selection of police officers on the basis of merit rather than political connections. Many cities and towns throughout the United States established civil service commissions, which have done much to remove subjectivity from the police selection and recruitment process. In the early 1900s, August Vollmer pioneered many innovations that were useful in contemporary law enforcement practices. He ushered in the era of police professionalism, and his methods are widely used today.

Although there have been substantial changes in police organization and operations in most police departments throughout the United States, police misconduct remains pervasive. Various commissions have been established to investigate police misconduct and police operations over the years. These commissions have usually been effective at providing temporary solutions to local problems when encountered. Nevertheless, there continues to be fairly frequent incidents and allegations of police misconduct. No jurisdiction is exempt from such incidents or allegations.

Notes

1. George L. Kelling, *"Broken Windows" and Police Discretion* (Washington, DC: U.S. National Institute of Justice, 1999).

2. George S. Bridges and Martha A. Myers, eds., *Inequality, Crime, and Social Control* (Boulder, CO: Westview Press, 1994).

3. James F. Doyl, "Police Discretion: Legality and Morality," in *Police Ethics: Hard Choices in Law Enforcement*, eds. William C. Heffernan and Timothy Stroup (New York: John Jay Press, 1985).

4. Howard Cohen, "A Dilemma for Discretion," in *Police Ethics: Hard Choices for Law Enforcement*, eds. William C. Heffernan and Timothy Stroup (New York: John Jay Press, 1985).

5. Larry T. Hoover and Edward T. Mader, "Attitudes of Police Chiefs toward Private Sector Management Principles," *American Journal of Police,* 9:25–37, 1990.

6. Larry S. Miller and Michael C. Braswell, "Police Perceptions of Ethical Decision Making: The Ideal vs. the Real," *American Journal of Police,* 11:27–45, 1992.

7. Velmer S. Burton, Jr., James Frank, Robert H. Langworthy, and Troy A. Barker, "The Prescribed Roles of Police in a Free Society: Analyzing State Legal Codes," *Justice Quarterly,* 10:683–695, 1993.

8. Linda S. Miller and Karen M. Hess, *Community Policing: Theory and Practice* (Minneapolis/St. Paul, MN: West Publishing Company, 1994), 71–72.

9. Herman Goldstein, "Administrative Problems in Controlling the Exercise of Police Authority," *Journal of Criminal Law, Criminology, and Police Science,* 58:160–172, 1967.

10. Louis A. Radelet and David L. Carter, *The Police and the Community,* 5th ed. (New York: Macmillan, 1994).

11. Patrick B. Adamson, "Some Comments on the Origin of the Police," *Police Studies,* 14:1–2, 1991.

12. Patricia A. Kelly, ed., *Police and the Media: Bridging Troubled Waters* (Springfield, IL: Charles C. Thomas, 1987).

13. William G. Bailey, *Police Science, 1964–1984: A Selected, Annotated Bibliography* (New York: Garland Publishing Company, 1986).

14. Mary Jeanette Hageman, *Police-Community Relations* (Beverly Hills, CA: Sage, 1985).

15. Robert Trojanowicz and Bonnie Bucqueroux, *Community Policing: A Contemporary Perspective* (Cincinnati, OH: Anderson Publishing Company, 1990), 46.

16. M. Lee, *A History of Police in England* (London, UK: Methuen and Company, 1901).

17. Pamela D. Mayhall, *Police-Community Relations and the Administration of Justice* (Englewood Cliffs, NJ: Prentice-Hall, 1985).

18. J.L. Lyman, "The Metropolitan Police Act of 1829," *Journal of Criminal Law, Criminology and Police Science,* 55:141–154, 1964.

19. Raymond B. Fosdick, *American Police Systems* (New York: Macmillan, 1920).

20. Ibid., 377.

21. Victor E. Kappeler, "St. Louis Police Department," in *The Encyclopedia of Police Science,* ed. W.G. Bailey (New York: Garland, 1989).

22. J.F. Richardson, *Urban Police in the United States* (Port Washington, NY: National University, Kennikat Press, 1974).

23. S. L. Harring, *Policing a Class Society* (New Brunswick, NJ: Rutgers University Press, 1983).

24. Samuel Walker, *A Critical History of Police Reform* (Lexington, MA: Lexington Books, 1977).

25. C. Uchida, "The Development of the American Police," in *Critical Issues in Policing: Contemporary Readings,* eds. R.G. Dunham and G.P. Alpert (Prospect Heights, IL: Waveland Press, 1997), 18–35.

26. V. G. Strecher, "Revising the Histories and Futures of Policing," in *The Police and Society: Touchstone Readings,* ed. V. Kappeler (Prospect Heights, IL: Waveland Press, 1995), 69–82.

27. O. W. Wilson and Roy C. McLaren, *Police Administration,* 4th ed. (New York: McGraw-Hill, 1977).

28. New York Mayor's Commission, *The Knapp Commission Report on Police Corruption* (New York: George Braziller, 1973).

29. James A. Conser and Gregory D. Russell, *Law Enforcement in the United States* (Gaithersburg, MD: Aspen Publishers, 2000), 508–510.

30. National Advisory Commission on Criminal Justice Standards and Goals, *Report of the National Advisory Commission on Criminal Justice Standards and Goals* (Washington, DC: U.S. Government Printing Office, 1973), 103–105.

31. Charldean Newell, Janay Pollock, and Jerry Tweedy, *Financial Aspects of Police Liability,* Baseline Date Report, Vol. 24, No. 2 (Washington, DC: International City/County Management Association, 1992).

32. Ibid., 4–6.

33. Joy James, ed., *States of Confinement: Policing, Detention, and Prisons* (New York: St. Martin's Press, 2000).

34. Mark Green, *Investigation of the New York City Police Department's Response to Civilian Complaints of Police Misconduct* (New York: Office of the New York City Public Advocate and the Accountability Project, 1999).

35. Ruth Friedman, "Municipal Liability for Police Misconduct: Must Victims Now Prove Intent?" *Yale Law Journal,* 97:448–465, 1988.

36. Victor E. Kappeler, *Critical Issues in Police Civil Liability* (Prospect Heights, IL: Waveland Press, 1993).

37. Gary W. Cordner and Donna C. Hale, eds., *What Works in Policing? Operations and Administration Examined* (Cincinnati, OH: Anderson Publishing Company, 1992).

38. Ronald J. Allen, "Supreme Court Review," *Journal of Criminal Law and Criminology,* 81:727–1001, 1991.

39. American Bar Foundation, *American Bar Foundation Survey of Criminal Justice: Pilot Project Reports,* 7 vols. (Madison, WI: University of Wisconsin, Madison, Law School, 1957).

40. Lloyd E. Ohlin and Frank J. Remington, eds., *Discretion in Criminal Justice: The Tension between Individualization and Uniformity* (Albany, NY: SUNY Press, 1993).

41. Herman Goldstein, "Confronting the Complexity of the Policing Function," in *Discretion in Criminal Justice: The Tension between Individualization and Uniformity,* eds. Lloyd E. Ohlin and Frank J. Remington (Albany, NY: SUNY Press, 1993), 31.

42. Ibid., 31.

43. Michel Girodo, "Undercover Probes of Police Corruption: Risk Factors in Proactive Internal Affairs Investigations," *Behavioral Sciences and the Law,* 16:479–496, 1998; Gerald E. Kelly, *Honor for Sale: The Darkest Chapter in the History of New York's Finest* (New York: Sharon, 1999); Kim Michelle Lersch, "Police Misconduct and Malpractice: A Critical Analysis of Citizens' Complaints," *Policing,* 21:80–96, 1998; Los Angeles Police Department Board of Inquiry into the Rampart Area Corruption Incident, *Public Report* (Los Angeles, CA: Los Angeles Police Department Board of Inquiry, 2000); Samuel Walker and Nanette Graham, "Citizen Complaints in Response to Police Misconduct: The Results of a Victimization Survey," *Police Quarterly* 1:65–89, 1998.

44. John Mark Johnson, *The Georgia State Patrol's In-Car Video System* (Lexington, KY: Council of State Governments, 1992).

45. Michael J. Olivero, Russell Hansen, and Amelia M. Clark, "An Assessment of Police Implementation of the Texas Public Intoxication Law in Small Texas Cities: What Is Dangerous to Self or Others?" *American Journal of Police,* 12:127–148, 1993.

46. Edward J. Escobar, *Race, Police, and the Making of Political Identity: Mexican Americans and the Los Angeles Police Department, 1900–1945* (Berkeley, CA: University of California Press, 1999); Judith A. Greene, "Zero Tolerance: A Case Study of Police Policies and Practices in New York City," *Crime and Delinquency,* 45:171–187, 1999; Yolander G. Hurst, James Frank, and Sandra Lee Browning, "The Attitudes of Juveniles toward the Police: A Comparison of Black and White Youth," *Policing: An International Journal of Police Strategies and Management,* 23:37–53, 2000.

47. Dennis D. Powell, "A Study of Police Discretion in Six Southern Cities," *Journal of Police Science and Administration,* 17:1–7, 1990.

48. Samuel Walker, *Taming the System: The Control of Discretion in Criminal Justice* (New York: Oxford University Press, 1993).

49. David B. Kalinich and Jeffrey D. Senese, "Police Discretion and the Mentally Disordered in Chicago: A Reconsideration," *Police Studies,* 10:185–191, 1987.

50. Linda A. Teplin, *Keeping the Peace: The Parameters of Police Discretion in Relation to the Mentally Disordered* (Washington, DC: U.S. National Institute of Justice, 1986).

51. Mark Dantzker, *Understanding Today's Police* (Englewood Cliffs, NJ: Prentice-Hall, 1995), 39–48.

52. Ibid., 41.

53. Ibid., 43–44.

54. Gabriel J. Chin and Scott C. Wells, "The Blue Wall of Silence As Evidence of Bias and Motive to Lie: A New Approach to Police Perjury," *University of Pittsburgh Law Review*, 59:233–299, 1998.

55. Greene, 171–174.

2

Issues and Controversies

This chapter examines selected constitutional amendments as they pertain to police misconduct. Included is a description of police understanding of the law and how the law is customized by individual officers. These customized interpretations of the law may or may not comport with constitutional guarantees. Different types of police misconduct are described in greater detail. Police misconduct is either violent or nonviolent. Violent police misconduct is police brutality and the excessive use of force. A force continuum is presented to depict various stages of force used to subdue criminal suspects. Nonviolent police misconduct encompasses graft and corruption as well as perjured testimony by police officers in court. The chapter concludes with a discussion of mechanisms both within and without police departments to monitor and sanction police misconduct, including internal affairs bureaus and citizen complaint review boards.

Selected Constitutional Issues and Police Behavior

The U.S. Constitution contains numerous provisions that set forth a variety of citizen rights. Most of these are embodied within the first ten constitutional amendments known as the Bill of Rights. Police officers exercise discretion daily that may or may not violate these rights. Often, these infringements are not clear-cut or a matter of public record. However, lawsuits are sometimes filed involving one or more allegations of law enforcement conduct and certain rights infringements. Featured here are potential rights infringements relating to the First, Second, Fourth, and Fourteenth Amendments.

The First Amendment (1791)

> Congress shall make no law respecting an establishment of
> religion, or prohibiting the free exercise thereof; or abridging
> the freedom of speech, or the press; or the right of the people
> peaceably to assemble, and to petition the government for a
> redress of grievances.

The parts of the First Amendment relevant for police officers are
that Congress shall make no law . . . prohibiting the free exercise
[of religion] . . . or abridging the freedom of speech, or of the
press; or the right of the people peaceably to assemble. . . ." Thus,
freedoms of speech, religion, press, and peaceful assembly are
explicitly outlined. Law enforcement officers must decide whenever citizen conduct goes beyond what is contemplated by the
First Amendment.

For instance, an officer of the Alabama Highway Patrol observed a large truck traversing a major highway. On the truck's
bumper were several stickers, some with profanity. Other stickers
depicted persons defecating and urinating. The officer stopped
the truck and cited the driver for a violation of Alabama's obscenity ordinance, which, among other things, prohibited the dis-
play of such stickers. Subsequently, a U.S. district court in
Alabama determined that Alabama's obscenity statute could not
be upheld (*Baker v. Glover*, 1991).[1] In this particular situation, a
highway patrol officer took offense to the displayed stickers on
the truck. Thus, he exercised discretion to stop the truck and cite
the driver for violating a seldom-enforced ordinance.

In another bumper-sticker incident, a police officer in a California city stopped a female motorist for speeding. However, instead of citing her for speeding, he criticized her political bumper
sticker, which favored a particular legislative bill, and issued her
a citation, claiming that she had waved a political sign at oncom-
ing motorists and continually pressed a "Walk" button at a cross-
walk to hold up traffic. Witnesses to the incident did not support
the officer's version of what she did. Instead, they indicated that
the pattern of the officer's conduct effectively inhibited the
woman's political activity (*Sloman v. Tadlock*, 1994).[2] The court
ruled the officer's conduct to be unwarranted. Further, the court
said the officer's conduct chilled the free speech of the motorist
and was a substantial or motivating factor making the officer liable for violating her rights.

Police officers are often drawn into disputes relating to constitutional rights infringement allegations because many of the laws police officers are sworn to uphold are unconstitutionally vague and overbroad (*Kreimer v. Bureau of Police for Town of Morristown,* 1992;[3] *Pestrack v. Ohio Elections Commission,* 1987;[4] *State v. Jones,* 1993[5]). When any statute is vague or lacks precision as to what conduct is prohibited, police officer discretion becomes increasingly important. But it is not up to police officers to determine what is unconstitutionally vague and what isn't; courts make these types of decisions. Nevertheless, whenever police officers are confronted by incidents or depictions that are subject to various interpretations, their discretionary abilities come into play and decisions to arrest or not to arrest are made.

Most city ordinances are not unconstitutionally vague. A city may pass an ordinance prohibiting homeless persons from sleeping overnight in public parks on benches. In one instance, a homeless person was arrested after he had given publicly televised interviews about his views concerning the mayor's homeless policy that made it a misdemeanor to lodge in any public place without permission of the owner. In this case, the homeless arrestee had spent the evening in a park plaza, sleeping. He claimed that his arrest was in response to his televised "speech" and thus was a violation of the "free speech" provision of the First Amendment. The court declared that police officers were simply enforcing a city ordinance prohibiting lodging overnight in a public park (*Stone v. Agnos,* 1992).[6]

The Second Amendment (1791)

> A well-regulated militia, being necessary to the security of a free State, the right of the people to keep and bear arms, shall not be infringed.

The Second Amendment provides for a "well-regulated Militia, being necessary to the security of a free State . . . [and] the right of the people to keep and bear arms." This particular amendment has generated considerable controversy. Many citizens believe that, because of this amendment, they are entitled to carry concealed firearms whenever they choose. However, the U.S. Supreme Court has declared that the right to bear arms is not absolute; further, the right to bear arms is subject to reasonable regulation by the state under its police powers (*Cody v. United States,* 1972;[7] *State v. Spencer,* 1994[8]).

The Fourth Amendment (1791)

> The right of the people to be secure in their persons, houses, papers, and effects, against unreasonable searches and seizures, shall not be violated, and no warrants shall issue, but upon probable cause, supported by oath or affirmation, and particularly describing the place to be searched, and the persons or things to be seized.

Police officers are almost always in positions of investigating, questioning, and arresting suspicious persons or criminal suspects, and they have legitimate rights to search those to be arrested as well as various places within their control (e.g., automobiles, rooms in homes). Nevertheless, the Fourth Amendment has continually been modified by changing circumstances and exceptions. Even the wording of the Fourth Amendment has been given different interpretations by the U.S. Supreme Court. First, it has been determined that not every search and seizure made without a warrant is necessarily prohibited (*Commonwealth v. Bosurgi*, 1963).[9] Neither does the Fourth Amendment forbid searches without warrants, only unreasonable ones (*Weaver v. Williams*, 1975).[10] Thus, police officers who intend to conduct a search of a citizen or a citizen's vehicle or home must determine whether their search is reasonable or unreasonable. Various circumstances change the reasonableness interpretation made by officers.

Police officers do not always keep up with the latest U.S. Supreme Court rulings relating to Fourth Amendment exceptions that materially affect their work. However, some officers manage to keep pace with U.S. Supreme Court opinions and know a great deal about the law and its applications within the totality-of-circumstances context. Further, many police officers know that, even if they secure a defective search warrant, they may act in good faith, as though the warrant were unflawed, and they will conduct their searches anyway. Thus, the totality of circumstances and good faith exceptions to warrantless searches or defective-warrant searches may be used by officers to justify their conduct relative to searches of persons or their possessions. Courtroom tests of police motives that prompted them to conduct searches and seizures are tests of police discretion and whether it was exercised appropriately. Considerable latitude exists when deciding the legal bases of their conduct in each case.

The Fourteenth Amendment (1868)

All persons born or naturalized in the United States, and subject to the jurisdiction thereof, are citizens of the United States
and of the State wherein they reside. No State shall make or enforce any law which shall abridge the privileges or immunities
of citizens of the United States; nor shall any State deprive any
person of life, liberty, or property, without due process of law;
nor to deny to any person within its jurisdiction the equal protection of the laws

The Fourth Amendment ensures U.S. citizens the right to due
process and to equal protection under the law. The equal protection clause of the Fourteenth Amendment is most often cited by
citizens when complaining about police officer excesses, misconduct, or the exercise of questionable discretion. One of the most
frequent allegations raised by citizens under the Fourteenth
Amendment pertains to questionable stops, detentions, questioning, and arrests because of one's minority status. Thus, if
white police officers stop black or Hispanic citizens for any reason, these encounters are often labeled discriminatory.[11] In the
1970s, the Philadelphia Police Department was the target of numerous suits brought by minority citizens alleging that their
rights had been infringed by police officers in that department.[12]
Other police departments have been targets of similar suits.[13]

There is almost no perfect solution to the problem of requiring law enforcement officers to enforce the law equitably. Although extralegal factors such as race, ethnicity, socioeconomic
status, and gender should not influence police discretion, the fact
is that more than a few police officers discriminate in various
ways against citizens on the basis of these factors. Numerous
homicides of suspects by police associated with the fleeing-felon
rule have been prevalent among the states.[14] Many of the fleeing
felons killed by the police officers were black. One implication is
that a disproportionate number of blacks were being killed by
police to the extent that blacks were not benefiting from the equal
protection clause of the Fourteenth Amendment.

Efforts have been made in recent years by police departments to establish procedures designed to minimize constitutional rights violations against citizens who are criminal
suspects. Currently, the standard applicable to the use of deadly
force by police against suspects is the 1985 ruling in *Tennessee v.
Garner.*[15] This is known as the defense-of-life standard, whereby

police officers may use deadly force against fleeing suspects only if their own lives or the lives of innocent citizens are in danger or jeopardy. Garner was a Memphis, Tennessee, juvenile who was shot and killed by police officers because he ran away and didn't stop when ordered to do so. He and a companion were loitering in a vacant house in the middle of the night. Thus, police applied the death penalty to his offense, burglary, when under other circumstances he may have simply been apprehended and returned to the custody of his parents after a verbal reprimand from a juvenile court judge.

Police Understanding of the Law

Police officers' responsibilities begin when the police officers receive authority from a government to enforce the law. Police officers are theoretically controlled by ethical standards of conduct. Ideally, police officers attempt to balance individual rights with keeping the peace, and loyalty to colleagues versus telling the truth under oath about possible wrongdoing.[16]

Police ethics are often characterized as an objective enterprise, under a theory of political obligation. It has been suggested that the police role, when conceived as that of a public agent, places obligations on police agencies and officials to behave in ways that bring basic democratic values to life. Some degree of citizen participation is required to ensure police officer adherence to these democratic values.[17] Police officers as public agents must accept offenders as clients in a professional-client relation. Morality is an important part of the police officer decision–making process.[18] But over time, police officers develop their own definitions of appropriate conduct with different groups of citizens throughout their communities. These customized interpretations of police-citizen encounters may vary from by-the-book regulations furnished by their own police agencies.

Sherman indicates that communities vary widely in the exercise of police discretion and in the problems requiring policing. In most instances, police patrols are largely unfocused, responding only to calls for service.[19] Each community raises different issues and generates different scenarios for police officers. Through close police officer–citizen contacts, police departments can establish better, more relevant patrolling procedures that will most effectively meet community needs.

Explanations for Individualized Interpretations of the Law

At least five different rationales employed by law enforcement officers as reasons for selective enforcement decisions or discretionary actions that may appear unjust to citizens have been identified and are as follows:

1. The legislature did not intend for some laws to be applied literally; the law was intended to apply only to the situation where wrong occurs.
2. The statute in question is out of date; to apply it to a contemporary situation would be an injustice.
3. The behavior violates the law, but if I arrest the perpetrator, the official system will not handle the matter justly.
4. If an arrest is made, the official system will not treat the offense seriously enough.
5. The community does not support enforcement of the law in some cases.[20]

These different explanations provide us with insight into police misconduct and abuses of discretion. Police officers often decide which laws to enforce on the basis of their relevance to ongoing activities in the community and whether such laws are pertinent. Although we know that updating the law is a legislative function, police officers make such decisions on the street daily. They observe numerous petty infractions that may, indeed, be outdated. Thus, they prioritize their arrests according to offense seriousness and community relevance. One outcome of community-oriented policing is that police officers will have a clearer picture of neighborhood enforcement priorities. These priorities may or may not conflict with officer-defined ones.

Many offenders who are arrested by the police pose serious risks to officer safety. Thus, when these same offenders are released by the courts within a few hours or days of their arrest for serious crimes, police officers feel justified in their cynical attitudes about what will happen to certain persons after their arrests.

However, for both citizens and police officers, customized or individualized interpretations of the law by either party will often lead to both botched cases and/or lawsuits. But police officers in almost every jurisdiction are acquiring greater skills and expertise annually, as departments everywhere are upgrading their selection criteria for new recruits. Accordingly, there is a greater sense of professionalism among police officers today, and they are increasingly relied upon to make good judgments and exercise sound discretion.

Strict adherence to the law by law enforcement officers might seem to be the solution to abuses of discretion, but this is not always the case. In one situation, a Georgia police officer encountered a heavily intoxicated person in an open parking lot. The person could neither walk nor stand without the officer's assistance. Further, he was so intoxicated that he could not talk. Yet, he was some distance from the nearest roadway. Thus, he was not boisterous, loud, or profane. No city ordinance covered this situation so that the intoxicated person could be arrested for public drunkenness. The officer decided to ignore the intoxicated person. Later, the intoxicated person wandered into the street and was accidentally killed by an automobile. The police officer was subsequently sued in civil court in a wrongful death action.[21]

Most police departments find it difficult to enforce consistently high standards of accountability for police to observe in their diverse public encounters.[22] In short, police officers make on-the-spot decisions about whether to move beyond simple verbal warnings or reprimands to more formal actions against those stopped and questioned because of suspicion. Considering the circumstances or situation, law enforcement officers may be more or less aggressive.

Most discretionary actions by police officers are nonviolent. But there are enough instances of officer conduct to attract citizen attention to sometimes questionable discretionary behaviors. Exercising discretion is a part of being a police officer. Not every law is clear-cut. As an officer's experience increases, so does his or her ability as an officer to make on-the-spot decisions in tough situations. It should be noted that a police officer's exercise of discretion is not bad. There are several positive aspects of police discretion. Police officers are trained to uphold the law and to make decisions about social events and persons encountered that are consistent with this general theme. Officer discretion is not intended to harm citizens; rather, it is designed to help them. Accordingly, Pollack-Byrne notes, for instance, that officer discretion is a good thing. However, she says that it is critical that an officer's moral and ethical standards are high and that one's police powers should not be abused to the extent that community security and confidence in the police department are jeopardized.[23]

Types of Violent Police Misconduct

There are various types of police misconduct. Criminologists and others have attempted to establish typologies or classifications that depict varieties of such behavior. For instance, David Carter established a fourfold typology of police misconduct according to the following designations: (1) physical abuse/excessive force, (2) verbal/psychological abuse, (3) legal abuse/violations of civil rights, and (4) police sexual violence toward women.[24]

Physical Abuse/Excessive Force

Physical abuse and/or excessive force includes applying considerably more force than is necessary to effect an arrest. When officers injure suspects they arrest, especially when there is little or no need for the use of such force, citizens label such behavior as physical abuse or excessive force. The ultimate excessive force is deadly force. The intent of this typology is that physical abuse and excessive force is limited to situations where one's life is not taken. Thus, deadly force would be in a class by itself. In the present case, apprehension of criminal suspects by officers using physical abuse/excessive force would include all forms of physical abuse by which bodily injuries may or may not result.

Verbal/Psychological Abuse

Verbal/psychological abuse is taunting or ridicule. When police officers make an arrest, they may utter insulting remarks or taunt the arrestee. When police officers interrogate suspects or transport prisoners from one site to another, they may engage in verbally abusive behaviors. Often, these behaviors occur in settings where the actual events cannot be corroborated. In one-on-one interactions between officers and various citizens, the courts clearly side with the testimony of officers, whether it is true or false.

Legal Abuse/Violations of Civil Rights

Title 42, Section 1983, of the U.S. Code contains provisions protecting one's civil rights. Whenever police officers act in ways that may infringe one's civil rights, affected citizens may file Section 1983 actions. The issues involved in civil rights cases cover various forms of police misconduct and abuses of authority. Civil rights violations and legal abuses are frequently alleged by criminal suspects and others. For instance, more than a few police officers have been accused of creating their own grounds for searches of persons or their property. In the case of *State v. Jones* (1994), two Hackensack, New Jersey, police officers were conducting surveillance of an apartment building.[25] They observed two men, Jones and Collier, drive into the parking lot. The men were not the objects of the surveillance. One of the officers recognized Collier as a person for whom an arrest warrant had been prepared, although the officer did not know the nature of the warrant. In fact, the warrant had been issued for failure to pay parking fines. The officers approached Jones and Collier, who fled into a nearby apartment and locked the door. Officers kicked in the door and placed Jones and Collier under arrest. At about the same time, the officers found some drugs and drug paraphernalia and a stolen wallet in dresser drawers in the apartment. Both were charged with burglary of an automobile from which the wallet had been taken a day earlier. The drug materials and wallet were introduced as evidence against these men and they were convicted. They appealed, alleging the search of their apartment without warrant to be illegal. Ultimately, the appellate court declared the search of their apartment unlawful because the officers could not forcibly enter a home without a warrant to arrest a suspect for a minor offense. Although the officers contended that their arrest was based upon "hot pursuit," this did not, by itself, justify the forced entry of the apartment. Also, the officers did not know that there was contraband or evidence of a crime that could be easily destroyed. The convictions were overturned.

In any civil rights case involving law enforcement officers, allegations of officer misconduct are based on the unreasonableness of the conduct. The intent of lawsuits against police aims both to compensate victims and to deter future police wrongdoing. It is often difficult to assess the actual impact of such civil litigation upon police misconduct. Indirect gauges are available, however, such as higher insurance rates, larger compensation settlements, and increased media coverage of police misconduct issues. Police misconduct cases are becoming increasingly important to police administrators. Further, administrative actions are likely to be taken within police departments in a stronger effort to deter police misconduct.[26]

Police Sexual Violence toward Women

One of the more undesirable types of police misconduct is sexual violence toward women. Female motorists are targets of certain police officers in various jurisdictions. It is unknown how much sexual violence toward women is perpetrated by the police. Police sexual violence (PSV) toward women includes those situations in which a female citizen experiences a sexually degrading, humiliating, violating, damaging, or threatening act committed by a police officer through the use of force or police authority.[27]

In one incident, two female motorists were made to strip and allow themselves to be searched in the back seat of a police cruiser. They were ordered to place themselves in the cruiser back seat on their hands and knees, with their legs spread. In this position and in plain view of onlooking male officers, female officers searched these women's vaginas with their fingers, probing for drug contraband. Their justification for this body-cavity search was that one of their relatives was suspected of dealing in drugs. Thus, to get to their relative, the police resorted to PSV in their case. These two women were threatened with future "searches" if they did not give police incriminating evidence about their relative (*Timberlake v. Benton*, 1992).[28]

In another case, a woman suspected to be a drug courier was roused from her sleep one evening while in bed with her husband. She was taken to a hospital, where she was given a body-cavity search by a several police women, who probed her vagina with both gloved and ungloved hands and fingers (*Rodriguez v. Fuetado*, 1991).[29] In North Little Rock, Arkansas, another case involved an officer, Lukie, who regularly picked up female motorists accused of driving while intoxicated. Lukie would drive these women to remote locations, where he offered to forget about the DWI charges in exchange for their performing oral sex on him (*Parrish v. Lukie*, 1992).[30] In most of these cases, juries were generally supportive of police officers and believed their version of events despite overwhelming evidence to the contrary.

Much of this police misconduct is attributed to the extreme power differential between policemen and female citizens. Because there is often a code of silence or secrecy among police officers in jurisdictions where such behavior occurs, victims of PSV are relatively powerless to cause such behaviors to be discovered and terminated. A critical element throughout the vast PSV behavioral continuum is the sexist nature of conventional police culture.[31]

Types of Nonviolent Misconduct

Nonviolent misconduct by police officers is most often associated with varying degrees of graft or corruption. Officers who accept gratuities in exchange for special favors to citizens exhibit one type of misconduct. They profit through illicit social exchanges. Some officers give false testimony in court against suspects to enhance the case against them and heighten the chances of a conviction. Thus, officers may receive unofficial perks or graft in the course of their performing the police role, or they may offer incriminating but false information against citizens charged with crimes.

Unofficial Perks

Examples of corruption among police officers range from minor favors, such as courtesies to waive tickets for speeding or DWI for other officers, to bribery and extortion.[32] Barker says that police work is ideal for engaging in patterns of deviance and corruption because many officers are socialized to engage in corruption and these same officers condone it over time. Barker studied police corruption in one department and identified ten types of corrupt behavior. He asked officers the extent to which each would not report to other police officers the actions listed. The corrupt patterns included the following:

1. Corruption of authority (acceptance of discounts or free meals, services, or liquor)
2. Kickbacks (money, goods, and services)
3. The spoils from unlocked buildings
4. Extortion
5. Protection of illegal activities (of vice operators or businessmen)
6. Traffic fixes
7. Misdemeanor fixes
8. Felony fixes
9. Direct criminal activities (burglary, robbery)
10. Internal payoffs (off-days, better work assignments).[33]

In every case, a substantial number of officers questioned said that they would rarely or never report these types of conduct to other officers. Based on this and other studies, Barker has concluded that police deviance is not a peculiar form of deviant conduct. Further, the police peer group indoctrinates and socializes rookies into patterns of acceptable corrupt activities, sanctions deviations outside these boundaries, and sanctions officers who do not engage in any corrupt acts.[34]

Graft and the Knapp Commission in New York City

Police corruption is a serious problem extending far beyond corrupt rank-and-file uniformed officers. Police corruption exists at all levels within the power hierarchies of police departments largely because of a police culture that promotes loyalty over integrity. Honest officers are often silent because they fear reprisals from other officers for informing on them. Supervisors are often at fault because they tacitly condone such behaviors and function as role models to many of their subordinates.[35]

In the late 1960s, Frank Serpico and another detective from the New York City Police Department (NYPD) brought widespread police corruption to the attention of the mayor. The mayor appointed a commission, later known as the Knapp Commission, to investigate Serpico's allegations, which were later verified. The commission made various recommendations to isolate and eliminate existing corruption. The commission reported that corrupt officers were divided into two categories: "grass eaters" and "meat eaters." Grass eaters are those officers who accept simple gratuities and payoffs that come their way. By comparison, meat eaters aggressively misuse their powers for personal gain. The commission said that, although the grass eaters may not engage in the large-scale corruption of meat eaters, they pose a most serious problem. Basically, they are rookies who come into the NYPD and are faced with a situation in which it is easier to be corrupt than it is to remain honest. Because of the large number of corrupt police officers, they make corruption respectable. Further, they perpetuate a code of silence (sometimes referred to as a blue wall of silence) relative to officer wrongdoing. It is difficult for outsiders to detect graft and corruption and to suppress it once it has been detected.

Some of the factors defined by the Commission as fostering and perpetuating this form of police misconduct include the distinction made by officers between dirty money and clean money. Thus, officers found it easier to accept money from gamblers compared with money from drug pushers because police officers considered drug trafficking a more serious crime. The branch of the NYPD to which one is assigned is a second factor. Plainclothes or undercover work increases one's opportunities for corruption. The third factor is where the officers are assigned. Certain parts of New York are more conducive to corruption than others. A fourth factor is the officer's assignment. Patrol car assignments created opportunities for officers in these units to profit from local graft. The fifth factor is rank. The higher one's rank, the greater the monetary rewards from graft.[36]

Perjury and Dropsy Testimony

Many criminal convictions are obtained by prosecutors as the result of perjured testimony from police officers who seize contraband illegally and contrary to Fourth Amendment search-and-seizure standards. Perjury by police officers is especially serious because officers are committed to abiding by a higher moral standard than that of the general public. Under what circumstances do police officers and other law enforcement officers (e.g., Drug Enforcment Administration agents, Federal Bureau of Investigation agents) commit perjury? What does perjured testimony accomplish? In the general case, perjury by police officers is designed to (1) justify illegal conduct and/or (2) strengthen weak cases against criminal defendants. In some instances, perjury by police officers occurs because of the pressures of police agency policies to make more arrests for vice offenses (drugs, prostitution, and gambling) and the greater need to get convictions. This pressure encourages officers to engage in shortcuts that involve illegal practices.[37] Occasional perjury is one way of accomplishing several ends, including securing convictions against criminal defendants and protecting informants. Line police officers are not the only law enforcement officers who engage in perjury, however. All law enforcement agencies are tainted by perjury disclosures.

In the case of police officers who testify against criminal suspects, perjured testimony on their part has intensified subsequent to the holding in *Mapp v. Ohio* (1961).[38]

In short, the *Mapp* case defined the exclusionary rule prohibiting the admission of evidence in court that had been obtained illegally. The exclusionary rule itself was specifically designed to deter and prevent police misconduct relative to searches of persons, their automobiles, and homes. After the *Mapp* decision, police testimony was subjected to more intensive scrutiny to determine whether the police officers acted in ways that would exclude any evidence they may have obtained through illegal means.

Dropsy Testimony

The *Columbia Journal of Law and Social Problems* reported research in 1968 about an investigation of the New York Police Department and police officers' allegations regarding their discovery of narcotics evidence.[39] The period covered by this research involved the immediate previous six months before the *Mapp* decision and the immediate six months after the *Mapp* decision. The Narcotics Bureau, uniformed officers, and plainclothes detectives were questioned about how they discovered illegal drugs in the possession of different drug suspects. It is fairly commonplace for suspects carrying illegal contraband to throw it away if running from police. Many of these suspects also have illegal drugs concealed on their person. Thus, police officers can discover these drugs either from observing contraband thrown away or dropped on the ground and from frisks of the suspect's clothing. Before the *Mapp* decision, two-thirds of all evidence was obtained by searches of suspect's clothing. After *Mapp*, between 80 and 90 percent of all contraband was discovered because suspects had dropped the contraband. Thus, dropsy testimony became prevalent in various courts, where police officers increasingly alleged that their suspects had dropped incriminating evidence. It is both unusual and unlikely that suspects would suddenly begin to drop incriminating evidence for police to discover, in New York or any other jurisdiction.

Police perjury is only one example of the wide gap between the formal rules and the actual operation of police agencies.[40] Many attorneys believe that police perjury, especially in drug and victimless crime cases, is particularly widespread. The U.S. Supreme Court notes that ideally police officers will conform their conduct to the dictates of the Court relative to searches of drug suspects. However, it is strongly indicated that in cases in which they testify that their suspects dropped the narcotics in their presence, police officers by committing perjury have been able to avoid the requirements of the Fourth Amendment prohibiting unreasonable searches and seizures. Thus, courts have found it necessary to establish safeguards to minimize such perjury. These include closely scrutinizing dropsy testimony and requiring the government to prove the legality of warrantless arrests and searches and seizures by a preponderance of the evidence.[41]

Violent Misconduct and Deadly Force

The Spirit and Letter of the Law

The spirit and the letter of the law are quite different. Police agencies are continually attempting to establish and implement policies seeking to clarify what officers may or may not do under different circumstances. Citizen reactions to police behaviors that relate to excessive force suggest that certain socioeconomic variables are influential. For instance, a study was conducted to investigate public attitudes toward police use of excessive force.[42] A random sample of citizens was asked whether they approved of police officers striking adult male citizens under some circumstances. About 70 percent of the white respondents and 43 percent of the black respondents approved of officer use of force. It was subsequently found that those persons with greater power, status, and advantages (particularly white, more educated men and more wealthy) were more likely to favor the police use of force than less privileged groups (especially ethnic minorities who are more frequently subjected to excessive force by police). It is generally accepted, however, that a workable framework for the development of police ethics is found in the theory of political obligation. The police role obligates officers to behave so as to bring basic democratic values to life. It requires the development of representative/democratic forms of organization to encourage citizen participation in democratic processes.

Police Brutality and Excessive Force

No clear-cut standards exist that guide police officers regarding when to apply excessive force in subduing suspects. No consensus exists regarding which variables are important in excessive-force situations or how these variables might interact.[43] An examination of officers who have been cited for use of excessive force suggests that in an actuarial sense they tend to have personality disorders, previous job-related experiences such as justifiable shootings, a heavy-handed patrol style and sensitivity to challenge, and other personal problems. Attempts to involve psychiatrists and psychologists in the training and monitoring of police behaviors have been only partially successful. In most instances, psychologists and other professionals are more likely to involve themselves in post–excessive force counseling situations. Such after-the-fact remedies do little to prevent the occurrence of excessive force applied by officers generally.[44]

Even in departments and under conditions where excessive force has been highlighted through media reports, such as the Rodney King incident in Los Angeles, little evidence exists that suggests that police departments aggressively move to deter misconduct within their own ranks. One reason for continuing laxity of police departments to act aggressively to curtail excessive force by its officers is that excessive force charges are difficult to sustain. Three factors have been identified that operate against citizens who often make complaints of excessive force against police officers:

1. Citizens making excessive force charges are often perceived as marginal individuals with little credibility.
2. Complainants have often been arrested for a legitimate offense or on a cover charge, again undermining their credibility.
3. Nonnegotiable uses of force represent the core of the police role, and high evidentiary requirements are necessary to sustain citizen complaints.[45]

Hot Pursuit

Most police departments have hot pursuit policies that govern conditions under which the hot pursuit of suspects may be undertaken. Some of these policies are broader than others. There is no question that police department hot-pursuit policies influence the actual behaviors of patrol officers. One study of 614 officers in eleven different police agencies found that in jurisdictions with liberal pursuit policies the numbers of pursuits were twice as large as found in jurisdictions with more restrictive pursuit policies.[46] However, policy guidelines regulating pursuit situations may not always be clear-cut. Further, officers may make their own interpretations of department pursuit policies.

The Force Continuum

A force continuum has been described.[47] This force continuum is depicted in Table 2.1.

The Federal Law Enforcement Training Center model depicted in Table 2.1 depicts gradated or escalating amounts of force, applied in accordance with the nature of suspect coopera-

Table 2.1
The Federal Law Enforcement Training Center (FLETC) Force Continuum

Level of Resistance	Level of Enforcement	Response
Assaultive (serious bodily injury)	5	Deadly force
Assaultive (bodily injury)	4	Defensive tactics
Resistance (active)	3	Compliance techniques
Resistant (passive)	2	Contact controls
Compliant (cooperative)	1	Verbal commands

Source: F.R. Graves and G. Connor, "The FLETC Use-of-Force Model," *The Police Chief* 59 (1992):56-58.

tion or resistance. Suspects who are cooperative are given verbal orders by officers. Those who are designated as "resistant" might not hear the officer's verbal orders and might need some contact control. Suspects who are actively resistant might need to be physically restrained through arm grips. If suspects elevate their resistance to assaultive levels and cause bodily injury to officers, officers use more aggressive defensive tactics, including disabling moves with their batons. When the level of bodily injury rises to serious, deadly force is a consideration to minimize the threat posed by dangerous suspects.

Force continuums such as FLETC are useful to the extent that they enable new police officers to adjust their level of force to effect arrests to the appropriate level fitting particular suspects. These continuums serve as "force guidelines" rather than clear-cut indications of what officers should do under each circumstance they encounter. It is impossible to dictate precisely what each officer should do under any condition. But developing such continuums is a good indication that police departments recognize the need to provide their officers with the best training so that they can anticipate in general ways what force might be needed.

Deadly Force

Deadly force is any effort to apprehend or subdue suspects that results in their death. Before 1985, police officers in virtually every police department in the United States followed what was known as the fleeing felon rule. The fleeing felon rule is a legislatively sanctioned provision that permits police officers to prevent the escape of any fleeing felon by means of any force, including deadly force. Thus, pre-1985 fleeing felons, such as burglars, rapists, robbers, car thieves, and drug dealers, could be prevented from escaping from police by means of potentially deadly force. In short, police officers were entitled to shoot at, and possibly kill, fleeing felons attempting to avoid arrest.

In 1985, the U.S. Supreme Court heard the case of *Tennessee v. Garner*.[48] This case originated in Memphis, Tennessee, in the late 1970s. Police were originally advised that someone was in a vacant house in a Memphis suburb about 2:00 A.M. one morning. Police officers arrived at the scene in time to see some boys running away. They shouted at the boys to stop, but their warnings were to no avail. Subsequently, one of the officers drew his revolver and fired at the fleeing boys, striking one in the back of the head, killing him instantly. The dead boy, Garner, was fifteen years old. He and a friend had been exploring a vacant house at the time. If he had been apprehended, Garner's crime would have been simple trespassing, possibly burglary, although there was nothing in the home to steal. His punishment would have been a possible fine and probation. Instead, an officer imposed the death penalty on Garner by shooting him in the act of fleeing.

The U.S. Supreme Court concluded in Garner that a much greater penalty had been exacted than would have been imposed under other circumstances. Accordingly, the Court set forth new "deadly force" provisions. These provisions destroyed the fleeing felon rule, causing it to be unconstitutional. The new provisions guiding the application of deadly force by police are that deadly force will be used only when the lives of officers or innocent bystanders are jeopardized by fleeing suspects. Thus, a new "defense-of-life" standard was created for all deadly force applications. Police officers must now justify their application of deadly force to show that their own lives or the lives of innocent citizens were definitely in jeopardy by the actions of certain suspects who were subsequently killed by police.

The U.S. Supreme Court continued to clarify the defense-of-life standard set forth in Garner in 1989 in the case of *Graham v. Connor*.[49] Actually, the case did not pertain to deadly force; rather, it was relevant for excessive force, regardless of whether it was lethal or nonlethal. The facts of the case are that Graham was a diabetic and was taking insulin on a regular basis. Graham asked his daughter to drive him to a convenience store in Charlotte, North Carolina. Graham wanted to buy some orange juice to avoid a negative insulin reaction. The line in the store was too long and so Graham left the store and asked his daughter to drive him to another market. At another store, Graham purchased the juice and exited hurriedly. He had his daughter drive him to a friend's house. A police officer observed Graham's allegedly furtive movements when leaving the second store and followed the automobile Graham's daughter was driving. They drove to a friend's house, and when Graham exited the vehicle, he passed out. The officer observed Graham falling down and assumed he was drunk. The officer propped Graham up against the hood of his car. Graham pleaded with officers to examine his diabetic identification card in his wallet, but he was told to "shut up" by one of the officers. Subsequently, he was wrestled into a police car, where he suffered assorted injuries, including a broken foot, wrist cuts, bruised shoulders, and ear damage. Graham was subsequently released without charge. Graham brought suit against the arresting officers. Lower courts affirmed the officers' conduct, but the U.S. Supreme Court ruled in favor of Graham. They declared that "objective reasonableness" under the Fourth Amendment should be used to assess the appropriateness of officer conduct. The U.S. Supreme Court declared that the following standards should govern excessive force cases:

1. Any claim of excessive force against police officers should be analyzed in relation to Fourth Amendment standards.
2. The proper legal standard in such matters is the objective reasonableness standard.
3. Four factors or circumstances should be considered when applying force of any kind:
   a. Is there an immediate threat to officers posed by the suspect?
   b. How severe is the crime(s) alleged?
   c. Is the suspect actively resisting arrest?
   d. Is the suspect attempting to escape custody?

It is in the *Graham* context that excessive force standards are currently applied by police officers. The FLETC model examined in the previous section is a derivative of *Graham* and includes guidelines fitting different levels of resistance by suspects.

Rationalizing Misconduct

Police officers who engage in misconduct of different kinds have devised various explanations or rationales for their misconduct. These rationales have become routinized and generally accepted, despite the absence of a legal basis for them.[50] Generally, police officers tend to deny responsibility for potential or real citizen injuries. Thus, officers attempt to neutralize deviance they may exhibit. For instance, officers may use excessive force on citizens who attempt to resist or who otherwise challenge police authority. When police officers overreact in these situations, they may say later, "I didn't mean it." Or they may deny injury. They may say, "We didn't hurt anybody" when they commit perjury to justify illegal searches. Another neutralization technique is the denial of a victim, which means that whenever a suspected criminal is physically injured by police, it is justified because the suspect has committed other crimes for which he or she has not been apprehended. Therefore, police do not consider the suspect a victim in the sense that he or she is innocent of any wrongdoing. In these cases, police officers may fail to find illegal contraband when searching the premises of a known drug dealer. In the process, they may physically abuse and seriously injure the suspect. Later, they say, "He had it coming. He just didn't have drugs this time."

A fourth neutralization technique is to condemn the condemners. Police department administrative orders and policies may seek to control officer misconduct. Nevertheless, those engaging in misconduct persist. They claim that, "Everybody is picking on me." A fifth type of neutralization is an appeal to higher loyalties. Sometimes police officers commit perjury to protect other officers or to justify destruction of evidence. They claim, "I didn't do it for myself. I did it for the good of the department and for justice." Whether we agree or disagree with these rationales, the fact is that many police officers use them, and frequently. This is because these techniques of neutralization have become internalized. Internalization is a psychological process of adopting and incorporating various behavioral standards and attitudes into one's personality system and regarding such standards and attitudes as fundamental and valid. If more than a few officers in any given police agency internalize these techniques of neutralization, peer justification for misconduct is established and intensified.[51]

Detecting and Controlling Police Misconduct

Two major types of systems, internal and external, are used to control or regulate the incidence of police misconduct.[52] Internal mechanisms for controlling police misconduct are largely the domain of internal affairs divisions. External mechanisms are civilian complaint review boards or their equivalent.

Internal Affairs Divisions

Police accountability has as its goal to attain a balance between competing publics, interests, and mechanisms, on the one hand, and responsiveness and legality on the other.[53] Internal affairs divisions of police departments are investigative mechanisms staffed by senior police officials and whose function it is to determine whether officers are guilty of any type of misconduct. Every large police agency has an internal affairs division. These divisions are viewed with some disdain by most line officers. Investigations by internal affairs personnel are often clandestine, and frequently police officer informers are used for obtaining evidence against other officers. One common complaint with internal affairs divisions is that they are suspected of subjectivity when it comes to investigating their own officers. Some persons believe that it is impossible to be objective if some police officers, acting as internal affairs officers, are required to investigate other officers. But there are different opinions, depending upon whether one is a civilian or a police officer. Police officers who are investigated by internal affairs personnel view them as the enemy. Any sanctions that issue from internal affairs investigations are viewed as betrayals of officers. One way of correcting this problem is to create an independent investigative body unrelated to police officers. Here civilian complaint review boards become relevant and useful.

Civilian Complaint Review Boards

Civilian complaint review boards consist largely of citizens independent of police agencies. Such boards investigate allegations of police misconduct and exert considerable control over police agency policies, disciplinary practices, and other internal matters related to police misconduct.[54] Civilian review boards became popular during the 1960s but were not received well by police officers. One reason was that these early boards lacked the sanctioning power to punish officers found guilty of misconduct. Verbal warnings and reprimands seemed to be the limits of civilian complaint review board sanctions. Subsequently, civilian complaint review boards have been given greater sanctioning powers when investigating allegations of police misconduct. A survey conducted between 1990 and 1992, for instance, found that nineteen of thirty-four police departments developed civilian review boards with substantial sanctioning powers.[55] This trend seemed indicative of national patterns, with no discernable geographical effect.

Proponents of civilian complaint review boards offer the following arguments in support of them.

1. Police agencies cannot be objective when investigating and sanctioning their own officers in response to allegations of misconduct; police agencies are biased in favor of their own officers whenever allegations of misconduct are raised.
2. Independent citizen boards are objective in this regard and can impose necessary sanctions, if warranted and needed.
3. Public trust in police generally is enhanced through establishing independent civilian boards without police agency vested interests.
4. Citizens are more responsive to community-oriented policing when police officers are subject to independent accountability mechanisms.
5. Civilian boards can clear officers of excessive force or misconduct charges just as easily as they can find compelling evidence against them.

Opponents of civilian complaint review boards offer the following arguments against them.

1. Civilians cannot empathize with police officers and the high level of risk associated with their work.
2. Civilians do not understand the necessity for police to use force in subduing suspects.
3. The authority of police agencies to sanction their own officers is terribly undermined by a parallel civilian sanctioning mechanism.
4. Civilians are biased against police officers whenever police misconduct is alleged.
5. Civilians are simply not qualified to judge the performance and behaviors of police officers; thus, civilian review boards are meaningless.

There is some truth to support all of these views about civilian complaint review boards, regardless of whether they are favorable and supportive or unfavorable and unsupportive. Civilian review boards are not perfect. Nevertheless, they offer an objective alternative to police agencies that are internally impaired from being able to investigate their own officers. Some boards have attempted to bridge the civilian-officer gap by including police administrators as board members. These situations seem productive in view of the member exchanges and discussions that occur.

Decertification

A major sanction against police misconduct is decertification. Decertification is the process of revoking the certificates or licenses of police officers by their departments or certifying authorities. In at least thirty-one states, Peace Officer Standards and Training boards implement decertification proceedings against officers who have been found guilty of misconduct, including unconstitutionally obtaining evidence against citizen/suspects or performing abusive conduct. Officers who have been decertified by these boards cannot work as police officers again until such time as they are recertified.[56]

Screening Methods for Recruitment

It has been suggested that devising better screening mechanisms during the process of recruiting new police officers can do much to prevent those inclined toward misconduct from becoming sworn officers. Some of the more common methods used by police departments today to minimize or prevent the hiring of officers who are unfit for police work and who will likely engage in misconduct are:

1. Administering psychological tests to identify those who are sadistic, depressive, or otherwise unqualified police applicants
2. Instituting training programs that go well beyond state-mandated levels
3. Offering better firearms training and awareness
4. Hiring police legal advisors.[57]

Conclusion

Several constitutional amendments are directly relevant to the issue of police misconduct. The First and Second Amendments to the Constitution pertain to freedoms of speech, religion, the press, and peaceful assembly, as well as to the right to bear arms. Some police misconduct has occurred in relation to these amendments and their breach by police. The Fourth Amendment is perhaps the most visible and frequently contested because police officers are always in contact with citizens and conducting searches of their persons, personal effects, automobiles, and homes. The Fourteenth Amendment is critical because of its guarantee of equal protection to all citizens. Whenever the rights of citizens are infringed by police officers in whatever context, it is likely that the Fourteenth Amendment will be cited as one of several infringements.

Police actions against citizens arise from the positions of police officers as law enforcement officers. However, there are differences between what police officers believe the law is and how it should be applied and how citizens interpret the laws. When citizens disagree with police officers about how the law should be enforced, both nonviolent and violent encounters can follow. Nonviolent forms of police misconduct include verbal and psychological abuses and assorted violations of civil rights. Other types of nonviolent police misconduct include perjury, dropsy testimony, and graft. Violent forms of police misconduct include police brutality and the excessive use of force relating to arrests and subduing criminal suspects. The most serious form of violent police misconduct is deadly force when it is unwarranted. Most police departments have policies relating to various types of force that officers may use. When either violent or nonviolent misconduct occurs, investigations ensue. These investigations can be conducted internally, within police departments, by internal affairs divisions or they may occur externally through civilian complaint review boards.

Notes

1. *Baker v. Glover,* 646 F.Supp. 1511 (1991).
2. *Sloman v. Tadlock,* 21 F.3rd 1462 (1994).
3. *Kreimer v. Bureau of Police for Town of Morristown,* 958 F.2d 1242 (1992).

4. *Pestrack v. Ohio Elections Commission,* 926 F.2d 573 (1987).

5. *State v. Jones,* 865 P.2d 138 (1993).

6. *Stone v. Agnos,* 960 F.2d 893 (1992).

7. *Cody v. United States,* 460 F.2d 34 (1972).

8. *State v. Spencer,* 876 P.2d 939 (1994).

9. *Commonwealth v. Bosurgi,* 375 U.S. 910 (1963).

10. *Weaver v. Williams,* 509 F.2d 884 (1975).

11. Ellis Cashmore and Eugene McLaughlin, eds., *Out of Order? Policing Black People* (New York: Routledge, 1991).

12. Frank Anechiarico, "Suing the Philadelphia Police: The Case for an Institutional Approach," *Law and Policy,* 6:231–250, 1984.

13. Brenda D. Crocker, "When Cops Are Robbers: Municipal Liability for Police Misconduct under Section 1983 and Bivens," *University of Richmond Law Review,* 15:295–317, 1981.

14. Lawrence W. Sherman, "Execution without Trial: Police Homicide and the Constitution," *Vanderbilt Law Review,* 33:71–100, 1980.

15. *Tennessee v. Garner,* 471 U.S. 1 (1985).

16. Howard S. Cohen and Michael Feldberg, *Power and Restraint: The Moral Dimension of Police Work* (New York: Praeger, 1991).

17. Philip W. Rhoades, "Political Obligation: Connecting Police Ethics and Democratic Values," *American Journal of Police,* 10:1–22, 1991.

18. Frank Fair and Wayland D. Pilcher, "Morality on the Line: The Role of Ethics in Police Decision Making," *American Journal of Police,* 10:23–38, 1991.

19. Lawrence W. Sherman, "Policing Communities: What Works?" in *Communities and Crime,* eds. Albert J. Reiss and Michael Tonry (Chicago, IL: University of Chicago Press, 1986).

20. Pamela D. Mayhall, Thomas Barker, and Ronald D. Hunter, *Police-Community Relations and the Administration of Justice* (Upper Saddle River, NJ: Prentice-Hall, 1995).

21. Ibid., 155.

22. Carl B. Klockars, "The Dirty Harry Problem," in *Moral Issues in Police Work,* eds. Frederick A. Elliston and Michael Feldberg (Totowa, NJ: Rowman and Allanheld, 1985).

23. Joycelyn M. Pollock-Byrne, *Ethics in Crime and Justice: Dilemmas and Decisions* (Pacific Grove, CA: Brooks/Cole Publishing Company, 1989) 83.

24. David L. Carter, "A Taxonomy of Prejudice and Discrimination by Police Officers." in *Police Deviance,* eds. Thomas Barker and David L. Carter (Cincinnati, OH: Pilgrimage, 1986) 150–152.

25. *State v. Jones*, 649 A.2d 89 (1994).

26. Candace McCoy, "Lawsuits against Police: What Impact Do They Have?" *Criminal Law Bulletin*, 20:49–56, 1984.

27. Peter B. Kraska and Victor E. Kappeler, "To Serve and Pursue: Exploring Police Sexual Violence against Women," *Justice Quarterly*, 12:85–111, 1995.

28. *Timberlake v. Benton*, 786 F.Supp. 676, M.D. Tenn. (1992).

29. *Rodriguez v. Fuetado*, 575 F.Supp. 1439 Mass. (1991).

30. *Parrish v. Lukie*, 963 F.2d 8th Cir. (1992).

31. Kraska and Kappeler, 106–107.

32. John Dombrink, "The Touchables: Vice and Police Corruption in the 1980s," in *Police Deviance*, 2nd ed., eds. Thomas Barker and David L. Carter (Cincinnati, OH: Anderson Publishing Company, 1991); John Kleinig and Albert J. Gorman, "Professional Courtesies: To Ticket or Not to Ticket," *American Journal of Police* 11 (1992):97–113.

33. Thomas Barker, "Peer Group Support," in *Police Deviance*, eds. Thomas Barker and David L. Carter (Cincinnati, OH: Pilgrimage Press, 1986) 12–13.

34. Ibid., 19.

35. New York Commission to Investigate Allegations of Police Corruption, *Commission Report* (New York: New York Commission to Investigate Allegations of Police Corruption, 1994).

36. Ibid., 24–28.

37. Martin A. Greenberg, "The Control of Police Conduct: A Key Issue for Security Executives," *Journal of Security Administration*, 13:63–72, 1990.

38. *Mapp v. Ohio*, 367 U.S. 643 (1961).

39. Commentary, "Effect of *Mapp v. Ohio* on Police Search and Seizure Practices in Narcotics Cases," *Columbia Journal of Law and Social Problems*, 4:94, 1968.

40. Fred Cohen, "Police Perjury: An Interview with Martin Garbess," *Criminal Law Bulletin*, 8:365–375, 1972.

41. *Georgetown Law Journal*, "Police Perjury in Narcotics 'Dropsy' Cases: A New Credibility Gap," *Georgetown Law Journal*, 60:507–523, 1971.

42. John Arthur and Charles E. Case, "Race, Class, and Support for Police Use of Force," *Crime, Law and Social Change*, 2:167–182, 1994.

43. John Kavanagh, "The Occurrence of Violence in Police-Citizen Arrest Encounters," *Criminal Justice Abstracts*, 26:319–330, 1994.

44. Ellen M. Scrivner, *The Role of Police Psychology in Controlling Excessive Force* (Washington, DC: U.S. National Institute of Justice, 1994).

45. David B. Griswold, "Complaints against the Police: Predicting Dispositions," *Journal of Criminal Justice*, 22:215–221, 1994.

46. Robert J. Homant and Daniel B. Kennedy, "The Effect of High Speed Pursuit Policies on Officers' Tendency to Pursue," *American Journal of Police*, 13:91–111, 1994.

47. F.R. Graves and G. Connor, "The FLETCH Use-of-Force Model," *The Police Chief*, 59:56–58, 1992.

48. *Tennessee v. Garner*, 471 U.S. 1 (1985).

49. *Graham v. Connor*, 108 S.Ct. 1865 (1989).

50. Gary W. Sykes, "Street Justice: A Moral Defense of Order Maintenance Policing," *Justice Quarterly*, 3:497–512, 1986.

51. Victor E. Kappeler, Richard D. Sluder, and Geoffrey P. Alpert, *Forces of Deviance: Understanding the Dark Side of Policing* (Prospect Heights, IL: Waveland Press, 1994), 127–130.

52. Douglas W. Perez, *Common Sense about Police Review*. Philadelphia, PA: Temple University Press, 1994.

53. Erella Shadmi, "Controlling the Police: A Public and Integrative Approach," *Policing and Society*, 4:119–129, 1994.

54. Edward J. Littlejohn, "The Civilian Police Commission: A Deterrent to Police Misconduct," *University of Detroit Journal of Urban Law*, 59:6–62, 1981.

55. Samuel Walker and Victor W. Bumphus, *Civilian Review of the Police: A National Survey of the 50 Largest Cities, 1991* (Omaha, NE: Department of Criminal Justice, University of Nebraska, 1991).

56. Steven Puro and Roger Goldman, "Police Decertification: A Remedy for Police Misconduct," in *Police and Law Enforcement*, eds. Daniel B. Kennedy and Robert J. Homant (New York: AMS Press, 1987).

57. Wayne W. Schmidt, "Section 1983 and the Changing Face of Police Management," in *Police Leadership in America*, ed. William A. Geller (New York: Praeger, 1985).

3

Chronology

This chapter provides a timeline of the origination of the police in different societies, from the ancient era to the present. First, several significant eras are described in which political, economic, and social factors combined to create a role for persons to perform law enforcement tasks. Second, a timeline is presented that details important events, such as the advent of training programs, particularly policing styles; historical acts; and critical incidents that have shaped the nature of policing, the roles of law enforcement officers, and how police misconduct is defined.

Significant Eras

Ancient Era (3000 B.C.–400 A.D.)

The ancient era is characterized by kin policing, which relied heavily on traditional familial systems for establishing rules and enforcing them. This meant that the family unit was responsible for justice relating to acts committed against the family (e.g., theft, trespass, assault). Family members were expected to capture and punish offenders. Thus, punishment was highly individualized and varied in severity among families. In early Mesopotamia, there was constant warfare between cities. Nubian slaves who were captured were forced into service as the first police force for the victorious cities. The Mesopotamians dressed these Nubian slaves in different colored clothing to distinguish their rank and function regarding law enforcement tasks. These slaves became mercenary-like units, and they patrolled marketplaces and communities.

The first organized police force was established in Rome under Gaius Octavius in 27 B.C. Its members were known as the Roman Vigiles. Subsequently, the Praetorian Guard became the first nonmilitary and nonmercenary police. The original Praetorian Guard consisted of nine thousand men who were hand-picked and grouped into nine cohorts of one thousand men each.

Middle Ages (400–1600)

During the Middle Ages, policing evolved into a watch system. There was a great deal of lawlessness. England had the highest rate of prostitution and more robbers and thieves than any other country. The watch system emerged after the Norman Conquest in 1066. Before the watch system, English villages relied on a tithing system by which adults were responsible for their village members' behaviors. Tithings were all men in a community over the age of twelve who were required to look after other community members. After 1066 a frankpledge system was established. The frankpledge system existed from 1066 to 1300, and it continued in various forms until the colonial era. Under this system, tithings were grouped into ten each, and ten tithings were organized into a hundred. Hundreds were supervised by constables who were appointed by the king. Ten hundreds were overseen by shire-reeves. Shires were English counties and reeves were chief law enforcement officers of these counties. Sheriffs in U.S. jurisdictions derive their name from shire-reeves.

Colonial Era (1600–1800)

The colonial era perpetuated the shire-reeve system developed in England. During this period, England was establishing more sophisticated and specialized law enforcement organizations. One of these was the Bow Street Runners, who became the first detectives. But in the American colonies, communities continued to rely on the watch system. Law enforcement personnel were largely volunteers. This work was often so tedious that watch duty was assigned as a punishment to persons who had been found guilty of committing minor offenses.

Spoils Era (1800–1900)

England created the Metropolitan Police of London in 1829 largely because of the lobbying efforts of Sir Robert Peel. His organizational skills yielded an agency of highly specialized operatives known as "bobbies," named after him. Meanwhile in the United States, various cities established semiorganized police departments patterned after the Metropolitan Police of London. New York City is credited with establishing the first police department with a professional, paid police force. Police officers became known as "coppers," because of the copper badges they wore on their uniforms to distinguish themselves from other citizens and to highlight their policing functions. Police departments in other cities were quickly established. The Texas Rangers were created in 1845 and were recognized as the first state police organization. Early federal law enforcement agencies were established during this period as well, including the Secret Service, Border Patrol, and postal inspectors. This was also a time when private policing agencies, such as Pinkerton's and Brink's, were founded.

A dark mark on the Spoils Era was widespread corruption among police agencies, however. There were few, if any, internal controls governing police conduct. The major reason the Spoils Era received that particular name was because of the strong degree of political control over police forces exerted by local politicians. Police departments and officers were used by wealthy politicians to protect their interests. Therefore, police officers were often ordered to break up strikes of laborers who protested low wages and unfair labor practices. These police were like private armed forces operating at the whim of influential political interests.

Progressive Era (1900–1920)

The Progressive Era sought to change how police agencies were operated. Between 1900 and 1920, many changes in police organizations occurred concerning police operations and professionalism. One general change was the establishment of civil service commissions, which depoliticized police recruitment and took the control over police officers from politicians. Civil service commissions operated to equalize opportunity; police officer selection more strongly emphasized one's expertise and skills rather than one's political connections. Police professionalism was honed to a high level by August Vollmer, the first police chief in Berkeley, California. Vollmer is known as the founder of police professionalism, largely because of his innovations and attempts to change the nature of selection, recruitment, and training of prospective police officers. Vollmer introduced the scientific method, fingerprint repositories, and uniform crime reporting, and he was instrumental in integrating academics with police operations through the establishment of crime laboratories.

Two major organizations were established during this period. The International Association of Chiefs of Police was created in 1902. The Fraternal Order of Police was established in 1915. Both of these organizations promoted police professionalism and helped to unify and solidify police officers nationally.

Gangster Era (1920–1950)

The Gangster Era occurred largely because of Prohibition and the passage of the Volstead Act and the Eighteenth Amendment in 1919. Making alcohol consumption illegal in a nation where alcohol was very popular created optimum conditions for gangs to flourish. Organized crime developed into a large-scale enterprise during this period. Infamous names such as Al Capone and John Dillinger were associated with crimes that capitalized on the nation's problems. The stock market crash of 1929 and the Great Depression that followed contributed greatly to lawlessness. The Federal Bureau of Investigation was officially established in 1935 to combat organized crime and violations of federal laws.

In 1931 the Wickersham Commission convened and concluded that there were numerous faults with U.S. policing. The commission advocated significant reforms in order for policing operations to improve. One particular recommendation was to professionalize policing by requiring police officers to increase their education. Thus, in many large-city police departments, a college education became a prerequisite for employment. August Vollmer was again at the forefront of the movement to educate the nation's police forces. At his strong suggestion, many police agencies incorporated intelligence, personality, and abilities testing as a part of their selection and recruitment processes. However, educational requirements for new police recruits were softened with the end of World War II and returning GIs who sought police work were given special consideration despite their lack of educational training.

One of Vollmer's former students was O. W. Wilson, who became chief of police in Wichita, Kansas, from 1928 to 1939. He also was chief of police in Chicago, Illinois, from 1960 to 1971. Wilson authored the Police Code of Ethics and did much to modernize police organization and operations.

Revolutionary Era (1950–1970)

Civil rights, especially rights pertaining to people of color and other minorities, were at issue during the revolutionary era, which was characterized by widespread civil disobedience and unrest. Several significant U.S. Supreme Court decisions prohibiting segregation in schools and other places were handed down during this period. The Ku Klux Klan was especially strong in the South and fomented a great deal of rioting. Crime rates tripled between 1950 and 1970, causing the establishment of several national commissions to investigate the roots and causes of crime. One of these commissions was the National Advisory Commission on Civil Disorders, established in 1968 after major civil rights rioting in various cities. This commission blamed the police for starting several riots that resulted in numerous deaths. The U.S. Supreme Court also decided several landmark cases that were aimed at preventing or minimizing police misconduct. Most important were the cases of *Mapp v. Ohio* (1961) and *Miranda v. Arizona* (1966). The *Mapp* case modified the exclusionary rule and required that all police officers must preface their searches of persons or their automobiles or premises with the serving of a valid search warrant based upon probable cause. The *Miranda* case established the Miranda warning, which obligated police officers to advise arrestees that they were entitled to counsel before being interrogated. Before *Mapp* and *Miranda,* police officers and agencies took many liberties regarding searches and seizures of one's person, automobile, or premises, and interrogations of criminal suspects were quite brutal under particular circumstances. Until these cases, police officers were unfettered and could operate freely to conduct their searches, seizures, and interrogations as they saw fit.

In 1965 President Lyndon B. Johnson established the President's Commission on Law Enforcement and Administration of Justice. This commission was extremely critical of the police and their tactics for enforcing the law. In 1968 the Omnibus Crime Control and Safe Streets Act was passed. This act infused large sums of money into the criminal justice system for the purpose of professionalizing the police. This act also led to the creation of the Law Enforcement Assistance Administration (LEAA), which existed until 1982. During its operation, the LEAA provided $7 billion to police departments throughout the nation for research, development, and evaluation of programs. A critical part of the LEAA was the contribution made to subsidizing police officers who enrolled in college classes to improve their educational skills. Many departments of criminal justice and most universities throughout the United States today owe their origins to the LEAA and its emphasis on academic training.

Current Era (1970 to Present)

During the 1970s, several important foundations were established, including the Police Foundation and RAND Institute. Various commissions were created as well, largely to investigate police corruption and graft at all levels of police organization. Gambling, drug trafficking, and prostitution were targeted because police involvement in these illegal activities was most visible and pervasive.

A major reform in policing was the establishment of community-based policing and police-community relations. These innovations sought to bring police officers closer to the public and neighborhoods where they patrolled. It was believed that community policing could do much to control crime and decrease it in affected cities and towns. Community policing is the concept of decentralizing policing operations and encouraging citizens and police officers to work together to solve crime problems in various communities. Today, community policing thrives because it is a popular method for reducing crime and the fear of crime. It has successfully been used to improve police-community relations.

Despite these different innovations to promote better police-community relations, there are always police department scandals that cause certain citizens to distrust the police. The New York Police Department, the Los Angeles Police Department, and the New Orleans Police Department (NOPD) are three of several large-city police departments that have been saddled with major corruption problems in the recent past. At one point, the National Guard was almost used for police functions in New Orleans, because it was believed that most of the NOPD was corrupt. However, administrative changes, resignations, and reassignments were made and the need for the National Guard diminished over time. It is likely that police misconduct in various forms will always persist, despite our best efforts to remedy it.

Policing Timeline

28 B.C.–   Praetorian Guards established by Augustus in
A.D. 14   Rome. Praetorian Guards were the personal body-
           guards of Augustus and protectors of the peace

throughout Rome. Augustus also established the Urban Cohorts, a general law enforcement unit to maintain the peace in Rome.

14 B.C.   Vigiles, or night watchers, created. First established as a fire-fighting unit, the Vigiles were later assigned policing duties of making arrests for theft, burglary, and assault; capturing runaway slaves; and serving as guards at public bathhouses. Vigiles were the first units to be used in Roman communities for law enforcement and social control functions. Augustus has been proclaimed by some historians as the founder of policing because of his establishment of the Vigiles.

400s   England established tything, or tithing, system, consisting of ten families living in close proximity to serve self-protection and crime prevention purposes. Ten tithings comprised a hundred, and several hundreds made up shires, or English counties. These were presided over by reeves, or chief law enforcement officers and magistrates. Shire-reeves, or chief law enforcement officers of English counties, held court frequently to adjudicate both criminal and civil cases.

1066   Norman Conquest. Modified shire-reeves (the term "sheriff" is a composite of shire-reeve and it today is the name for the chief law enforcement officer of most U.S. counties) by establishing Courts of Leet, or local police courts, as a substitute for courts conducted by shire-reeves.

1090s   Establishment of peace guilds in England to serve as social control mechanisms. Peace guilds were private, voluntary associations arranged in ten groups with ten headmen. These guilds contributed financially to a general fund for the purpose of apprehending criminals.

1215   *Magna Carta* signed by England's King John; obligated men to take part in the observance of peace through the frankpledge system.

1285   Statute of Winchester enacted by Edward I. Created a police system lasting for almost 500 years; provided for watch-and-ward system of protection, or night watch system, in which all male adults participated); a duty to render a hue and a cry whenever offenses were observed or detected; the arming of all males ages 15 to 60 to defend the country and maintain order; and the removal of brush and most trees 200 feet from the king's highways to protect against ambush by highwaymen, or robbers.

1634   Night watchmen and constables were appointed in villages and cities in both England and the American colonies.

1634   Plymouth, Massachusetts, appointed Joshua Pratt as a constable to be the sealer of weights and measures, surveyor of land, jailer, and announcer of marriages.

1658   New Amsterdam (later New York City) authorized a group of citizens known as the rattlewatch. These consisted of eight paid watchmen to maintain the peace and alert citizens if they observed crimes in progress.

1666   France established national police force under Louis XIV. A council was appointed by Louis XIV that established police powers and procedures, regulated possession of firearms, and created the lieutenant of police for Paris. The lieutenant of police had jurisdiction over Paris security; repression of civil disorders; cleaning and lighting streets; regulating moral behavior of citizens; regulating social affairs pertaining to hospitals, prisons, and jails; and policing the marketplace.

1693   First uniformed police officer appointed by the mayor of New Amsterdam.

1700s   Heavy reliance by American colonies on watchmen style of policing in most communities.

1715   Riots Act passed by British Parliament, permitting London to raise monies for all police purposes; empowered constables to make arrests.

1740s   Creation of slave patrols, especially in Southern

colonies. Slave patrols had quasi–police authority to protect citizens from runaway slaves, inhibit insurrection, and apprehend runaway slaves. Some historians maintain that the slave patrols of the South were America's first modern-style police forces.

1749   City of Philadelphia permitted by British to appoint police wardens with the authority to hire watchmen.

1751   Creation of Bow Street Runners, established by Sir Henry Fielding. The Bow Street Runners were the first detectives created in any existing police department.

1767   Regulators created in South Carolina. The Regulators were a vigilante group established to enforce the law.

1782   Creation of foot patrol officers in London, largely because of Henry Fielding's brother, John Fielding, who was a magistrate of Bow Street court.

1789   Judiciary Act authorized by President George Washington. Act created first federal district courts as well as first federal marshals to enforce federal laws.

1794   Whiskey Rebellion occurred in western Pennsylvania. U.S. Marshals and thirteen thousand state militiamen were involved in the enforcement of tax collection on the manufacture of whiskey by Pennsylvania distillers.

1799   Napoleon established police system in France with Joseph Fouche named as the first minister of general police.

1805   Establishment of police horse patrol in London. The horse patrol enabled police officers to increase their response time in answering calls for service from citizens who reported crimes.

1821   Establishment of dismounted horse patrol in London. One of the first foot-patrol operations of any organized police agency.

1829   Metropolitan Police of London (established under An

Act for Improving the Police in and Near the Metropolis). Established standardized guidelines for police officers in London, including there should be around the clock patrolling; and officers should wear distinctive uniforms and a top hat, carry no weapons other than a truncheon, and carry a small staff with a crown on one end to symbolize royal authority. First commissioner of Metropolitan Police of London was Sir Robert Peel. His co-commissioners were Richard Mayne, an attorney, and Charles Rowan, a former military colonel. Considered the "new police," officers became known as "bobbies" after Robert "Bobby" Peel, the commissioner. Followed Peel's Principles, which included statements about the police mission and police conduct. Such principles specified priorities such as crime prevention, respect from the citizenry, respect for the law, minimizing the use of force in order to improve public cooperation, and use of physical force as a last resort in subduing suspects; police efficiency is measured by the absence of crime and disorder; police organization is established along military lines; police are under governmental control; distribution of crime information is essential to preventing crime; good police qualities include even temperament and well-groomed appearance; all officers should be assigned a number; police recruits are hired on a probationary basis; and police records should be maintained to correct distribution of police strength.

1819   Act banning slave trade. U.S. Marshals required to enforce the law banning the African slave trade.

1835   Texas Rangers formed in Texas. Considered the first state police agency in the United States.

1837   Broad Street Riot. Occurred in Boston, Massachusetts, and prompted city to establish broad police reforms. Marshal Francis Tukey was hired to establish a competent and efficient police force.

1844   New York Police Department patterned after Metropolitan Police of London.

1850   Fugitive Slave Trade Law. U.S. Marshals involved in tracking down runaway slaves and returning them to their lawful owners.

1851   San Francisco Committee on Vigilance. Establishes vigilante forces to maintain peace and deal with criminals.

1855   German tavern keepers revolt in Chicago; also known as the Large Beer Riots. Tavern owners protested 500 percent increase in liquor licensing fees and prohibition of Sunday liquor sales. Leads to rioting in which many are killed and injured. Police officers are accused of using excessive force in dealing with rioters.

1866   Civil Rights Act. Federal legislation specifying rights to citizens regardless of race.

1871   Anti-Chinese riot in Los Angeles, where twenty-three Chinese are killed. Police officers are accused of using excessive force in dealing with rioters.

1877   Labor strikes in West Virginia, Pittsburgh, and Chicago. In two days, sixteen soldiers and fifty strikers are killed. More than 125 locomotives, two thousand freight cars, and depot burned and destroyed in Chicago. Police officers are accused of using deadly or excessive force.

1886   Haymarket Riots in Chicago. Labor disputes trigger violence against police during which bombs explode, killing one police officer and injuring five others. Police officers accused of using excessive force against demonstrators.

1891   City Vigilance League created in New York City. Short-lived citizen's group (two years) formed to conduct investigations into allegations of New York Police Department officer and administrative corruption.

1893   National Chiefs of Police Union. Unionization contributed to police professionalization.

1894   Lexow Commission. Named after Senator Charles Lexow, commission investigated Tammany Hall machine politics and exposed New York City Police Department corruption. Uncovered a pervasive pattern of brutality, election fraud, police involvement in various types of fraud, and administrative corruption.

1902   International Association of Chiefs of Police (IACP) (formerly National Chiefs of Police Union). Richard Sylvester served as president of the IACP from 1901 to 1915.

1913   Police Judiciaire, which replaced the Surete, established in France.

1913   Curran Commission. Investigated gambling, prostitution, and corruption in New York City. Discovered veil of secrecy legislatively imposed on the investigative, disciplinary, and prosecutorial processes of law enforcement agencies regarding the excessive use of force. Recommended public access to personnel records of police officers who were the subjects of criminal investigations and brutality against civilians.

1915   Fraternal Order of Police established.

1915   International Association of Women Police (formerly International Association of Policewomen).

1919   Boston police strike.

1921   Tulsa, Oklahoma, race riot. Thirty are killed, and seven hundred are injured. Police officers are accused of using deadly and/or excessive force in dealing with rioters.

1929   Eliot Ness selected to head new federal law enforcement group known as the Untouchables. Group was known for using unorthodox methods for law enforcement purposes to apprehend federal criminals.

The Wickersham Commission (National Commission on Law Observance and Enforcement). Chaired by George W. Wickersham, attorney general of the United States under President Herbert Hoover, the Wickersham Commission investigated police corruption and recommended that politics should be removed from police organizations. A 1931 report issued by the commission recommended that certain bureaucratic guidelines be followed including selecting police administrators on the basis of competence and experience; requiring patrolmen to be of good moral character and physical strength; initiating guidelines for minimum and maximum age, weight, and height requirements; offering adequate salaries and attractive fringe benefits for all levels; providing adequate training for police recruits and those on active duty; improving communications among officers and between officers and the general public; establishing a crime prevention unit; hiring qualified women police to supervise juvenile delinquents and female criminals; and establishing state bureaus of criminal investigation.

1932   Seabury Commission. Chaired by Samuel Seabury. Commission investigated illegal alcohol distribution and police corruption in New York City. Results of investigation led to resignation of Mayor James J. Walker and led to the reform administration of Mayor Fiorello H. LaGuardia (1933–1945).

1934   Union violence in Chicago at the Republic Street Plant. Police officers used deadly force and shot and killed ten picketers in what later became known as the Memorial Day Massacre.

1943   Detroit race riots. Police officers accused of using excessive force in dealing with demonstrators.

1943   Zoot suit riots in Los Angeles. Police officers accused of using excessive force in dealing with demonstrators.

1949   Brooklyn grand jury. Convened to investigate gambling, payoffs.

1955   Rosa Parks, a black woman, refuses to give up her seat to a white passenger on a bus in Montgomery, Alabama. Incident leads to police intervention and rioting, including a boycott of the bus system of Montgomery. Police officers accused of racism and of using excessive force in dealing with demonstrators.

1956   Racial violence in Clinton, Tennessee. Police officers accused of using excessive force in dealing with black demonstrators.

1957   President Dwight D. Eisenhower orders integration of Central High School in Little Rock, Arkansas, and sends federal troops to enforce his order. Police officers are accused of using excessive force.

1960   Racial violence in New Orleans, Louisiana. Police blamed for using excessive force.

1962   President John F. Kennedy sends troops to the University of Mississippi at Oxford to protect first black student admitted to the school. Police accused of using excessive force in dealing with protesters.

1964   Race rioting in Chicago; New York City; Rochester; Philadelphia; Jersey City; and Patterson and Elizabeth, New Jersey, resulting in 952 injured and six killed.

1965   President's Commission on Law Enforcement and Administration of Justice. Commission was broadly charged with investigating the causes of crime.

1965   Los Angeles (Watts) race riots, resulting in thirty-six killed, 895 injured. Violence spreads to San Francisco, where another two hundred are injured and six are killed. Police are blamed for misconduct and excessive use of force in these riots.

1968   Omnibus Crime Control and Safe Streets Act. Also known as the Safe Streets Act and the Crime Control Act, this act established the Law Enforcement Assistance Administration, which provided billions of dollars of assistance to criminal justice development.

1968   Law Enforcement Assistance Administration. Provided more than $7 billion in aid to police departments and universities for evaluation research on different and innovative methods of policing and police training. Criminal justice programs were established and local funding was provided for police departments for improvements in training, communications technology, and weapons. Disbanded in 1982.

1968   National Advisory Commission on Civil Disorders. Known as the Kerner Commission, examined racism in the United States and the contributions of police in fomenting racism. Called attention to poverty and lack of opportunity for advancement among blacks in ghettos of larger cities. Noted that police symbolize white racism and white repression in an atmosphere of hostility and cynicism. Highlighted double standard existing among some police officers to discriminate against blacks.

1968   Democratic National Convention held in Chicago. Police riot ensues, involving 192 officers injured, 49 citizens hospitalized, 425 civilians treated in hospitals and released, 200 treated on the scene, 400 given treatment for effects of tear gas or mace, 81 police vehicles damaged or destroyed, and 668 arrested. Police officers accused of using excessive force in dealing with protesters.

1969   Commission on Causes and Prevention of Violence.

1970   Kent State University protest involving the burning of Reserve Officers Training Corps's (ROTC) buildings and the shooting and killing of several students by members of the National Guard. Excessive force is alleged on the part of police and the National Guard who were summoned to control rioters.

1970   Commission on Campus Unrest.

1970   Commission on Civil Rights.

1970   Commission on Obscenity and Pornography.

1970   The establishment of the Police Foundation. This foundation, funded by the Ford Foundation with an initial $30 million, is created to help the police be more effective in doing their job, whether it be deterring robberies, intervening in potentially injurious family disputes, or working to improve relationships between the police and the communities they serve. The general mission of the Police Foundation is to foster improvement and innovation in U.S. policing.

1971   Antiwar march in Washington, DC; twelve thousand arrested by police. Police officers accused of using excessive force.

1972   Commission on Marijuana and Drug Abuse.

1972   Knapp Commission. Established to investigate drugs and corruption in the New York Police Department.

1973   National Advisory Commission on Criminal Justice Standards and Goals.

1974   Deadliest year in law enforcement history, with 268 officers killed in the line of duty.

1976   Commission on Gambling.

1976   Commission on Disorders and Terrorism.

1976   Commission on Private Security.

1976   Commission on Organized Crime.

1976   Establishment of the Police Executive Institute by the Police Foundation. Goals of the institute are to provide executive development training for top police managers.

1976   National Advisory Commission on Higher Education for Police Officers. Assembled by the Police Foundation.

1979   National Information and Research Center on Women in Policing. Established by the Police Foundation in response to a growing need for information directly affecting women in law enforcement.

1980   Racial disturbances in Miami, Florida. Police officers accused of excessive force.

1982   "Broken-window" theory advanced by James Q. Wilson and George L. Kelling after a study of the Newark Foot Patrol conducted by the Police Foundation. The fact that officers are checking to see if there are any "broken windows" seems to reduce citizen fear of crime and disorder. Thus, the "broken windows" theory is that the mere presence of police officers in neighborhoods makes citizens feel more secure.

1985   Police officers storm and firebomb a home believed to be the site of the radical group, MOVE. Fires from police actions spread, killing eleven and causing two hundred persons to become homeless.

1986   Police Liability Program launched by the Police Foundation to reduce the exposure of local governments to the costs of defending inadequate and wrongful conduct suits stemming from police actions at the operational and administrative levels. The program has conducted seminars and workshops for police administrators, legal officers, mayors and city managers, state and county executives, and other government officials.

1987   Training division established by the Police Foundation to assist police agencies to improve accountability, performance, service quality, and community satisfaction with police services.

1991   Rodney King beating in Los Angeles. More than twenty police officers converge on Rodney King, a motorist who is driving erratically, and several of his companions. Subsequently four officers beat King severely and are criminally charged.

1991   Christopher Commission. Established and chaired by Warren Christopher who investigated charges of police brutality in connection with fifteen police officers and the beating of Rodney King, a Los Angeles motorist.

1992   Detroit police chief William Hart was sentenced to a maximum of ten years in federal prison for embezzling $2.6 million from a secret police department fund and for income tax evasion. The fund was used for under-cover officer drug buys and to pay out to informants.

1992   Four officers charged with beating Rodney King placed on trial in Simi Valley, California, acquitted. On April 29, riots erupt throughout Los Angeles, lasting for five days. Losses include 40 deaths, 2,382 injuries, more than 5,000 buildings burned or destroyed, 40,000 jobs lost, and more than $1 billion in property damage. Police arrest 5,633 people. Rioting spreads to other U.S. cities.

1992   National Center for the Study of Police and Civil Disorder. Established by the Police Foundation, the center assists law enforcement officers to acquire knowledge and tools to improve their operational and administrative practices.

1993   Two officers tried in federal district court in relation to Rodney King beating and convicted.

1993   Third Decade Fund for Improving Public Safety. Established by the Ford Foundation with a $10 million grant and operated by the Police Foundation.

1993   The Mollen Commission, headed by former judge and deputy mayor Milton Mollen, established to investigate charges of corruption in New York City. Discovered the Buddy Boys, a whole police precinct where the officers involved were actually buying (busting) and selling drugs. Instances of corruption, even among senior police officials, were found. One convicted police officer, Michael Dowd, gave extensive information about other police officers involved in a ring of drug-dealing police officers.

1997   Office of Community Oriented Policing Services conducted a national survey to reveal the attitudes of police about sensitive questions of police abuse of authority.

1997   Establishment of Crime Mapping Laboratory by the Police Foundation.

1997   Chicago police superintendent Matt Rodriguez resigned after a report in a local newspaper that he maintained close ties with convicted criminals, including ex-convict Frank Milito.

2000   *Survey of Police Attitudes Toward Abuse of Authority: Findings from a National Study,* published by the Police Foundation. Survey assesses police attitudes about the use of force; the code of silence; the role of extralegal factors; methods of controlling abuse of authority; the impact of community policing; and the importance of race, rank, and gender.

2000   National Center for the Study of Police and Civil Disorder. Established by the Police Foundation, assists police agencies and communities in developing effective policies and procedures to deal with some of the most historically complex and difficult issues confronting law enforcement and the communities they serve.

2000   Institute for Integrity, Leadership, and Professionalism in Policing (IILPP). Established by the Police Foundation to improve accountability, leadership, and professional development, and to provide the tools to police to more effectively manage their resources. Four program areas are featured to provide technical assistance, technology, and training to the nation's law enforcement agencies, municipalities, and communities: assessment, technology, professional development, and the National Center for the Study of Police and Civil Disorder.

4

Biographical Sketches

Warren Minor Christopher (1925–)

Warren Minor Christopher was born in Scranton, North Dakota. He was a lawyer and held several government posts, including that of deputy attorney general under President Lyndon B. Johnson (1967–1971). From 1977 to 1981, Christopher served as deputy of state under President Jimmy Carter. He was appointed by President Bill Clinton as secretary of state in 1993. Christopher also chaired the Christopher Commission to investigate the reasons for the rioting that followed the Rodney King beating incident in 1991.

Patrick Colquhoun (1745–1820)

Patrick Colquhoun was a wealthy Scottish merchant who migrated to London in 1789. He had been a former magistrate in Glasgow and was subsequently appointed a justice of the peace in 1792. Colquhoun was influenced by the work of Henry Fielding and his brother, John Fielding, particularly with their ideas that magistrates and constables should be provided salaries instead of fees, an ancient practice. Colquhoun also was concerned about the working class and sought to alleviate poverty and hunger, which he believed was a primary cause of crime. Colquhoun published several influential works, two of which were *A Treatise on the Police of the Metropolis* and *A Treatise on the Commerce and Police of the River Thames*. He was also interested in reforming police administration in London. He wanted to improve police performance, and he believed that effective police leadership could help to accomplish this objective. He proposed a police force to contend specifically with major problems of pilfering and piracy that were occurring on the Thames River. Subsequently, his ideas led to the creation of the marine police, who patrolled the Thames River on a regular basis to prevent crime. Under Colquhoun's supervision, the amount of piracy on the river declined substantially and Colquhoun's crime prevention methods were widely adopted in other areas with vast waterways.

Henry "Feilding" Fielding (1707–1754)

Henry Fielding was born at Wedmore, England, on April 22, 1707. The family name of "Feilding" was used by his father, Edmund, because it was aristocratic. Henry Fielding changed his last name to the more conventional spelling when he was older. He attended the University of Leiden in Holland and became a playwright and author of farces and comedies. Among his more notable writings was the work, *Tom Jones*, published in 1749. In 1740 Fielding became a lawyer after attendance at Middle Temple. He became a circuit judge on the large Western Circuit near London. Subsequently he served as a judge at Middlesex. In 1751, he wrote a pamphlet entitled *An Inquiry into the Causes of the Late Increase of Robbers, etc.*, which promoted sweeping changes in the law and how the law was enforced. By 1754, Fielding had established the Bow Street Runners, a small organization of police officers who were considered "fleet of foot" and who attempted to apprehend common thieves. Fielding was most influential in laying the foundation for the first modern police force and was a guiding force in the work and efforts of Sir Robert Peel who subsequently formed the Metropolitan Police of London.

Raymond B. Fosdick (1883–1972)

Raymond B. Fosdick was born in Buffalo, New York, on June 9, 1883. He graduated from Princeton University in 1905 and obtained a law degree from New York Law School in 1908. From 1910 to 1913, Fosdick was the appointed commissioner of accounts for New York City. He investigated city and county government in an effort to rid New York of corrupt politicians and corporations participating in illegal activities. He studied numerous police problems, including political police control, inadequate police leadership, limited tenure of police administrators, inadequate police investigative techniques, organizational inflexibility, and a lack of effective supervision in investigative work. Fosdick in 1915 completed a study of seventy-two U.S. large-city police departments. He believed that police chiefs and administrators should be well-educated, well-paid, and given tenure to ensure their loyalty and commitment to their departments.

One of the administrative problems Fosdick addressed concerned the monotonic administration of police departments throughout different cities. He found that most of these organizations consisted of two major branches: a uniformed police officers' division and a detective division. The uniformed police officers' division was further subdivided into beats for patrolling purposes. In many departments, control over these different beats was relegated to different administrators who had contrasting philosophies about how best to perform police work. Such administrative diversity was untenable, according to Fosdick, because it led to poor communication among officers and relatively primitive patrolling methods and styles.

Fosdick promoted the primary idea of dividing all police departments into three basic divisions, with single administrators over each division: patrol, investigation, and crime prevention. These, he said, were primary policing functions. But for these three divisions to be implemented effectively, three major problems had to be overcome. The first of these problems was poor police organization, which in turn fostered poor interpersonal relations between supervisors and their respective patrol forces. A second major problem was that legislatures of various states had created for police extraneous and unrelated jobs such as issuing licenses for saloons and other businesses, supervising dog pounds, and collecting taxes. The third problem was that many unskilled, unfit, and uneducated police executives were in place in many departments, and their presence significantly hindered progressive reform efforts to improve departmental efficiency and effectiveness.

Among Fosdick's other accomplishments are that (1) during World War I, he was a special representative of the War Department in France and a civilian aide to General John Pershing during the Paris Peace Conference; (2) he served as undersecretary general for the League of Nations during 1919–1920; and (3) he wrote the book, *Toward Liquor Control*, published in 1933.

Leonhard Felix Fuld (1883–1965)

Leonhard Felix Fuld was born in New York City and attended Columbia University, where he received his Ph.D. He published *Police Administration* (New York: G.P. Putnam) in 1909. This book was a critical study of police organizations in the United States.

Fuld covered topics ranging from the selection of police officers to police organization and stressed that, in all problems of administration, efficiency and humanity must be emphasized. Fuld was critical of the system employed in U.S. jurisdictions whereby police chiefs and superintendents were chosen from the rank and file. In fact, Fuld's European experience had been that police chiefs and other police administrators were selected from university graduates and former army officers with executive backgrounds.

Fuld considered police administration a demanding task requiring a broad education and experience not ordinarily found among rank-and-file police officers. Fuld believed that police administrators should be strong professionals who would command considerable respect from their subordinates and administer with integrity and objectivity. His criticisms of U.S. police administrator selection methods focused upon the political nature of these administrative appointments. Furthermore, he noted that good physical condition was required, together with the ability to pass a civil service examination, seniority, and sufficient money to live on, so that they would not be susceptible to bribes or dependent upon monetary incentives from those seeking favors.

Fuld wrote that police officers should be expected to adhere to a much higher code of ethical conduct and morality compared with that of ordinary citizens. He advised that the patrol officers required close supervision because of their demonstrable performance of shirking their responsibilities and routine duties. Thus, selection and training requirements were, in Fuld's view, fundamental to selecting the highest quality officers who would interact favorably with the public to be served. Fuld believed that the process of officer selection should be totally devoid of politicalization. Education was considered as the major means whereby officers could be promoted. Fuld believed that police sergeants should be able to write and prepare detailed and complex reports and have a thorough knowledge of police business. They should be discreet, intelligent, and have a general knowledge of criminal law. Fuld also believed that the most important rank in police departments was captain. This was because of two fundamental duties performed by captains: administration and policing. Administrative duties articulated by Fuld included clerical, janitorial, and supervisory functions, whereas policing duties included maintaining the peace and protecting life and property.

Daryl Gates (1926–)

Daryl Gates became chief of police of the Los Angeles Police Department (LAPD) in 1978. Earlier, in 1972, Gates had pioneered special weapons and tactics (SWAT) teams to react to acts of terrorism or encounters with felons committing armed robbery and other violent crimes. These SWAT teams have been emulated in many other police departments throughout the United States. While Gates was chief, he established a highly sophisticated Emergency Command and Control Communications System (ECCCS), which greatly accelerated police response time to civilian calls for service. This system consisted of computers installed in police vehicles for more rapid communications and response. Because narcotics were a continuing problem in the Los Angeles area, Gates also established the Drug Abuse Resistance Education (D.A.R.E.) program. D.A.R.E. was based on Gates's contention that the present generation had already surrendered to drug dependency and that the country's future lies with the readiness of our children to resist drug involvement. D.A.R.E. usually involves police officers who visit schools to share drug information with students in an effort to deter them from using drugs. Chief Gates oversaw a police department of 7,200 sworn officers and 2,500 civilian personnel. The LAPD was only about a fourth the size of the New York Police Department (NYPD), although the populations of both cities were comparable. Thus, Gates was obligated to do much more with considerably fewer resources than his NYPD counterpart. Another contribution was that Gates made extensive use of volunteers from the community as an aid to law enforcement officers. Gates established ninety-four different groups of 55,305 members for several Neighborhood Watch programs. This program was established during the mid-1980s. Gates resigned in 1992 after the Rodney King incident, in which several LAPD officers were charged with police brutality in the beating of a black motorist.

J. Edgar Hoover (1895–1972)

J. Edgar Hoover was born in Washington, D.C., and was educated there. During World War I, he worked as a special assistant on counterespionage activities under the U.S. attorney general. In 1924, Hoover became the first director of the Bureau of Investigation, which was renamed the Federal Bureau of Investigation (FBI) in 1935. He established the first training academy for FBI agents and was primarily responsible for requiring FBI agents to be attorneys or certified public accountants to qualify as agents. Among his other accomplishments was the establishment of a modern crime laboratory and accompanying technology, including latent fingerprinting, detailed compilations of criminal records, statistical data about crimes and criminals, and computerization through the National Crime Information Center. He served as FBI director until his death in 1972.

William Travers Jerome (1859–1934)

William Travers Jerome was born in New York City in 1859. He became a lawyer and was prominent in reform. He served on the Lexow Commission in 1894 to investigate New York City Police Department corruption and managed the successful mayoral campaign of William L. Strong that same year. Jerome helped to frame the legislation that created the court of special sessions in 1894, and he became a justice of that court in 1895. Between 1901 and 1909, Jerome was a district attorney in New York. He continually pursued cases of corruption and fraud perpetrated by dishonest police officers and administrators. He led a crusade against illegal gambling and political corruption. Often, he would lead surprise raids on illegal gambling establishments in person. He died in 1934.

Vivian Anderson Leonard (1898–1984)

Vivian Anderson Leonard earned his bachelor's and master's degrees in Texas and a Ph.D. from Ohio State University. He joined the Berkeley, California, Police Department in 1925. Subsequently, he served as the superintendent of the records and identification division of the Ft. Worth, Texas, Police Department from 1934 to 1939. Between 1941 and 1963, he became a member of the faculty at Washington State University in Pullman, where he became a professor of police science and administration. He was active in several professional organizations and authored seven texts, including *Police Organization and Management* (1950), *Police Personnel Administration* (1970), and *Police Crime Prevention* (1972). Subsequently, Leonard founded the Academy of Criminal Justice Sciences and Alpha Phi Sigma, the national criminal justice honor society.

Richard Mayne (1796–1868)

Richard Mayne, a lawyer, was one of London's first two police commissioners. He assisted Robert Peel in establishing the Metropolitan Police of London in 1829.

William H. Parker (1902–1966)

William H. Parker began his policing career in 1927 as a member of the Los Angeles Police Department (LAPD). During World War II, he served in the U.S. Army with distinction and was highly decorated, winning the Purple Heart, the French Croix de Guerre with Silver Star, and the Italian Star of Solidarity. Interestingly, he served under Orlando W. Wilson, a colonel who was assisting in the reorganization of European police departments. Subsequently, Parker returned to Los Angeles to resume his duties with the LAPD. In 1950, he became chief of police of the LAPD and served in that position until 1966. His contributions to police professionalism, especially within the LAPD, were that he demanded excellence and outstanding behavior from his officers. He was much concerned about projecting a positive public image through his officer corps, and subsequently, the LAPD rose to prominence and excellence under his direction. While Chief of the LAPD, he demanded that only highly qualified personnel should be recruited and that they should receive the best training. Thus, he was credited with modernizing the LAPD in terms of its buildings, equipment, and procedures.

Sir Robert Peel (1788–1850)

British home secretary in 1829, Robert Peel founded the Metropolitan Police of London, one of the first organized police forces in the world. Robert Peel was born in Bury, Lancashire, England, in 1788. He attended Harrow School and Oxford, where he excelled in classics and mathematics. In 1809, Peel won a Parliamentary seat from Tipperary and entered the House of Commons. In 1810, Peel became undersecretary for war and the colonies in the Tory government of Sir Spencer Perceval. After holding several government posts, Peel became a cabinet minister and home secretary in 1822. From 1822 to 1825, Peel reformed the jails and reduced the number of offenses punishable by death. He made further reforms in the criminal laws of England from 1826 to 1827. In 1829, Peel influenced the passage of the

Metropolitan Police Act, which established the Metropolitan Police of London. This organization eventually became known as Scotland Yard. Those working for Peel in the new Metropolitan Police were known as "Peelers," named after him. His work in later years involved various social and political reforms. He supported free trade and lobbied for greater free trade laws. He died in a horse-riding accident in July 1850.

Theodore Roosevelt (1858–1919)

Theodore "Teddy" Roosevelt was born in New York City on October 27, 1858. He attended Harvard University from 1876 to 1880. He became one of the youngest members of the New York State Assembly at age twenty-three. He served as U.S. civil service commissioner from 1889 to 1895. In 1895, Roosevelt became president of the Board of Police Commissioners in New York City in an effort to detect and ferret out corruption. He promoted the use of call boxes, or a system of telephones, that allowed citizens to report crimes rapidly and greatly increased the response time of police. From 1897 to 1898, he was assistant secretary of the navy. In 1898, Roosevelt gained fame as a Rough Rider as the result of serving with the First U.S. Volunteer Cavalry Regiment during the Spanish-American War. He became a hero of the Spanish-American War when he led a charge up San Juan Hill, Cuba, in July 1898. Roosevelt was elected governor of New York in 1898 and vice president of the United States in 1900. He became president of the United States after the assassination of William McKinley in 1901. During his term as president, Roosevelt was instrumental in passing the Department of Justice Appropriations Act of 1908, which created the Bureau of Investigation (renamed the Federal Bureau of Investigation in the 1930s). During his lifetime, Roosevelt authored thirty-eight books and numerous articles on diverse subjects.

Charles Rowan (1782–1850)

Colonel Charles Rowan was one of London's first two police commissioners and a career military officer. Rowan believed in mutual respect between the police and citizens and this would be crucial to the success of the Metropolitan Police founded by Sir Robert Peel. Together with Richard Mayne, Charles Rowan substantially assisted Robert Peel in formulating Peel's principles governing police conduct.

Bruce Smith (1892–1955)

Bruce Smith wrote *Police Systems in the United States* in 1940 (New York: Harper and Brothers). His book outlined various administrative problems of police departments that had previously been neglected. He recommended that the principles of organization found in private industry and the military should be applied to police departments as a general model.

Smith was critical of many police departments because they often operated according to outmoded authoritative patterns that subsequent scientific developments had proved unsound and ineffective. Police departmental growth and specialization had occurred and was widespread throughout the United States. In short, many police departments had failed to keep pace with such change. Thus, there were inadequate controls to foster a synthesis of control functions in a way that would promote unity of action. Smith believed strongly in particular organizational principles applied to the span of control in any organization, whereby administrators would have a certain amount of control over particular numbers of officers. He believed that no supervisor should have any more than five or six subordinates to supervise at any given time. Smith's work indicated the need for greater authoritative specialization by differentiating between varied police tasks. These tasks included patrol, traffic control and regulation, criminal investigation, communication and records control, property management, personnel management, crime prevention, and morals regulation.

Smith proposed that organizational effectiveness could be enhanced or improved through reorganizing police departments through centralization, whereby fewer administrators would assume the responsibility for departmental activities. Although Smith believed in specialization of functions and tasks, he also cautioned that too much task specialization might be detrimental to effective police operations. Thus, he encouraged a department-by-department analysis to tailor particular administrative forms to fit particular departments, thus promoting and maintaining managerial flexibility.

During his career, Smith was director and member of the Institute of Public Administration. Smith believed that during the early 1900s, there had been a substantial decline in the quality of U.S. cities. He linked this decline to a general reduction in the number of beat patrol officers in major U.S. cities. He believed that traditional beat patrol officers were at the center of a network of social controls such as family, church, and neighborhood associations in the neighborhoods that they patrolled. Further, beat patrol officers related well with the people in whose neighborhoods they patrolled because they were recruited largely from these same immigrant communities.

The most troubling aspects of the criminal justice system, according to Smith, were political payoffs of local police officials, appointments or promotions made on the basis of political sponsorship, the crude nature and composition of the police force, and a generally inefficient police staff. Smith believed that in order to reestablish the integrity of U.S. communities, beat patrolling should be reinitiated and embodied with professional values of merit, integrity, and efficiency. Interestingly, the community policing or "back-to-the-people" movement, which embraced many of the ideals espoused by Smith, became immensely popular during the 1980s and continues to be a dominant theme in U.S. law enforcement.

Richard Sylvester (no dates)

Richard Sylvester was the former police chief of Washington, D.C., and founder of the International Association of Chiefs of Police. He called for professional standards for police officers, and he stressed the need for higher education, extensive training, professional integrity, and a clearly defined organizational structure to regulate police officers' activities.

August Vollmer (1876–1955)

August Vollmer was born in New Orleans, Louisiana. He became a Berkeley, California, town marshal in 1905. At the outset, he commanded only three deputies. As Berkeley grew in size and importance, Vollmer subsequently became the chief of police of Berkeley. Vollmer was perhaps the most progressive police administrator of his time. He immediately expanded the size of his police force to include both day and night patrols. Furthermore, he formed the first bicycle patrol in 1911, thus permitting foot patrol officers to have greater mobility and respond more quickly to calls for service. He was keen on maintaining police presence in Berkeley, and during his first few years in office, he installed red lights at major intersections, which served as emergency notification systems for police officers.

Vollmer relied heavily on academic specialists in various areas of forensics. He pioneered a formal academic regimen of police training, including the practice of various investigative techniques, such as photography and fingerprinting, and the study of anatomy and other academic subjects. Vollmer also interrogated various arrestees and determined that almost all of them engaged in particular criminal practices that differentiated them from each other. Thus, he was among the first to identify and separate criminals according to their *modus operandi*, or method of operation. This system became known as the Modus Operandi (MO) System, the first of its kind in the United States. Vollmer networked with police chiefs throughout the United States on a regular basis, seeking new and different information about police investigative techniques and crime-solving strategies. In 1906 Vollmer established a basic records system in the police department. In 1907 he involved a professor of biology at the University of California–Berkeley to assist his detectives in a criminal investigation. Because of the contributions of this professor, Vollmer became convinced that scientific knowledge could be most valuable in solving crimes and detecting criminals. The work by the biologist was used to analyze blood, fibers, and soil to solve the Kelinschmidt murder case that same year.

One of Vollmer's most significant contributions was the creation of a police school in 1907 that many law enforcement training academies are fashioned after today. In his version of a police school, Vollmer had instructors teach prospective officers a wide variety of subjects. He blended both academic professors with seasoned police professionals as instructors at his police school in order to groom a more sophisticated type of trained police officer. Eventually, the police school boasted a three-year curriculum, including courses on fingerprinting, first aid, criminal law, anthropometry, photography, public health, sanitation, and police methods and procedures. Vollmer believed strongly that a liberal education was essential for anyone performing the role of police officer.

In 1913, Vollmer converted his entire patrol officer division to a mobile unit with automobiles. Thus, the Berkeley, California, police department became the first major police department to become fully mobilized. By 1916, Vollmer had hired professors of pharmacology and bacteriology to become full-time criminalists in his police school to assist in improving the quality of his police recruits. Also in 1916, Vollmer established the first School of Criminology at the University of California–Berkeley. In 1918, Vollmer began to involve college students and hired many of them as part-time police officers to administer various psychological, intelligence, and neurological tests to all police officer applicants. By 1921, Vollmer was experimenting with the polygraph, or lie detector, as an interrogation device. Also that same year, he began to use psychiatric screening as a part of the police officer recruitment process. Contemporaneous with this development, Vollmer equipped each of his mobile police units with crystal sets and earphones (radios) in his Model-T touring cars. These were the first radio cars used in the United States. In 1923, Vollmer established the first Junior Traffic Police Program. In 1924, he established one of the first single fingerprint systems. He created the first Crime Prevention Division in 1925.

Earlier in 1923, Los Angeles, California, hired Vollmer as its police chief on a one-year appointment. The Los Angeles Police Department (LAPD) had experienced an unusually high level of police corruption, gambling, and illegal liquor sales. Vollmer hired ex-convicts from the Los Angeles area to gather information about police corruption. On the basis of his investigations, Vollmer promoted numerous honest officers and required more than three thousand officers to take an intelligence test. These test scores were used to demote, reassign, and promote particular officers, depending upon their scores. Corrupt politicians in Los Angeles rejected Vollmer and his ideas, which were not well-received by the LAPD generally. After one year of administrative reform in Los Angeles, Vollmer returned to Berkeley. After Vollmer's departure from Los Angeles, police department operations there returned to their original condition, complete with corruption, gambling, and illegal liquor sales.

Vollmer's work with the LAPD was not without merit, however. Many other police departments throughout the United States began to emulate the work of Vollmer and his recommendations for police reorganization and administration. Vollmer was adamant that one of the most important factors in contributing to a successful police department was high morale and tenure associated with the job of chief police administrator. Vollmer was variously known as the founder of modern police science, the dean of U.S. law enforcement, and "America's greatest cop." Plagued with ill health in his older years, he ended his own life in November 1955.

Alice Stebbins Wells (1882–1957)

Alice Stebbins Wells was the first sworn policewoman in the United States. In 1909, Wells went to work for Los Angeles County as a social worker. At that time, almost every large city employing women in government assigned them as matrons or workers rather than as full-fledged police officers. The following year, Wells petitioned the City Council to provide for a Los Angeles police woman, and the ordinance passed. She joined the Los Angeles Police Department (LAPD) in 1910. She received a book of rules, a first aid book, and a man's police badge. Subsequently she was issued a policewoman's badge, Badge #1. Wells designed and made her own tailored blue uniform to be worn on the job and at special occasions. She was originally assigned to juvenile probation and to its first probation officer, Leo W. Marden, by Mayor George Alexander and the Los Angeles City Council. By 1913, Los Angeles had hired three policewomen and three police matrons in the LAPD. The number of policewomen grew to thirty-nine by 1937.

Wells's initial assignments were to dance halls, skating rinks, penny arcades, movies, and other recreational places attended by women and children. She also was assigned to search for missing persons. She was instrumental in furthering principles dealing with delinquency prevention, and certain juvenile units in police departments can be traced directly to Wells's influence. Wells believed that more women should become involved in police work, and she is remembered especially for her work in enabling well-qualified women to perform protective and preventive work among juveniles and female criminals. Later in her career, she toured more than one hundred cities in an effort to recruit more women into police officer roles. New York and Massachusetts were among the first outside of Los Angeles to enact statutes authorizing the hiring of women as police officers. In 1915, Wells founded the International Association of Women Police (formerly known as the International Policewomen's Association), which was a forum for exchanging ideas and encouraging the use of women in policing roles. Wells established the first class dealing with the work of female police officers; the class was offered by the University of California, Los Angeles, Criminology Department in 1918. She also cofounded the Women's Peace Officers Association of California and was its first president in 1928. Wells was appointed as the LAPD historian in 1934 and held that post until 1940.

George Woodward Wickersham (1858–1936)

George Woodward Wickersham was born in Pittsburgh, Pennsylvania, in 1858. He attended Lehigh University and became a lawyer and from 1909 to 1913 he served as attorney general under President William Howard Taft. Interested in constitutional reform and international arbitration, Wickersham in 1931 chaired the National Commission on Law Observance and Enforcement, which was created in 1929 by President Herbert Hoover to study the problem of enforcing national prohibition laws. The commission became known later as the Wickersham Commission because of George Wickersham's influence and chairmanship. The commission was created largely because of Chicago gang wars, which evolved around prohibition.

Although previous commissions had been convened to study prohibition and its effects, the Wickersham Commission was vested with broad powers. Wickersham engaged in the first general assessment of law enforcement in the United States. He directed the creation of committees to study an assortment of law enforcement–related problems, including the causes and costs of crime, the operation of federal courts, and the problem of official lawlessness and police corruption. Interestingly, the most important product stemming from the Wickersham Commission was a stinging indictment of widespread police misconduct. Wickersham's report concluded that the willful infliction of pain on criminal suspects by police was widespread. He also reported that official lawlessness by the police, judges, magistrates, and others in the criminal justice system in many major cities was prevalent. Illegal arrests, bribery, entrapment, witness coercion, fabrication of evidence, third-degree interrogation tactics, police brutality, and illegal wiretapping were some of the many instances of police misconduct his commission uncovered. The commission recommended numerous police reforms. Although police misconduct continues, there is little question that the Wickersham Commission did much to draw public attention to it and decrease its prevalence to some degree for several decades.

Orlando Winfield Wilson (1900–1972)

O. W. Wilson was a former police chief in Wichita, Kansas, and Chicago, Illinois. In 1950, he became the first dean of the School of Criminology at the University of California, Berkeley. Before becoming dean of the School of Criminology, Wilson served during World War II in the military where he worked to reorganize the police forces in Europe. He was successful in centralizing police administration and created command decision making, not only in Berkeley, but in many other cities during the 1950s and 1960s. In 1950, Wilson published *Police Administration* (New York:

McGraw-Hill). The book was a comprehensive compendium of diverse topics, including organization, control, public relations, and leadership. Wilson saw the primary objectives of police departments to be preventing crime and discouraging antisocial tendencies in individuals. The book also delved into ways of repressing criminal activities, effecting criminal arrests, recovering stolen property, and preparing cases for presentation in court. Wilson believed that police administration ought to be centralized and he promulgated various canons surrounding this theme: (1) grouping tasks similar or related in purpose, process, or method in one or more units under the control of a single individual; (2) delineating lines of authority among individual units so that responsibility could clearly be placed; (3) establishing channels of communication through which information can flow upward and downward and which is patterned after the established hierarchy of authority; (4) placing each person and unit within the organization under the immediate control of a central individual to avoid friction resulting from duplication of function and supervision; (5) giving each person no more units than he or she is capable of managing; (6) assigning specific tasks to particular individuals in order to fix responsibility for any subsequent action taken; (7) providing supervision for each person regardless of time or place; (8) having each assignment of responsibility carry with it the requisite authority to fulfill the responsibility; and (9) holding specific persons accountable for the exercise of their authority. Later in his career, Wilson became superintendent of the Chicago Police Department and served in that position from 1960 to 1967.

5

U.S. Supreme Court Cases

Powell v. Alabama, 287 U.S. 45 (1932)

During a train trip in Alabama, two white women were allegedly raped by several young black men. At an unscheduled stop, the train was searched by police, who arrested nine black young men and charged them with rape. Not until the trial date did the judge assign an attorney to represent each man. In one-day trials, each young man was convicted and sentenced to death. They appealed. The U.S. Supreme Court overturned their convictions, citing several violations of constitutional rights. Among other things, the men had not been permitted the assistance of counsel in their own defense until the trial date. Additionally, unreliable and incompetent evidence had been admitted against the men, evidence that would not have been admitted in other courts. The charges had not been properly formulated or delivered to the men, so that they did not understand fully what it was they were supposed to have done and when. Considering the time of the incident, the early 1930s, and race relations in the state of Alabama, the defendants' treatment by authorities was consistent with inequities against blacks in the South generally at that time.

Brown v. Mississippi, 287 U.S. 278 (1936)

Brown was a suspect in a murder. He was visited at his home by a deputy sheriff and brought to the murder scene. He denied committing the murder. The deputy and others hanged him from a tree, let him down, and then hanged him again. Later they tied him to a tree and beat him. A few days later, the deputy came to his home again and arrested him. Brown was taken to jail, where he was beaten repeatedly and told that the beatings would continue until he confessed. He confessed to the murder and was subsequently convicted and sentenced to death. He filed an appeal on the grounds that he had been denied due process under the Fourteenth Amendment. The U.S. Supreme Court agreed. It argued further that the brutality of police officers had rendered his confession and other statements inadmissible in court against him. Coerced confessions to crimes are unconstitutional. His conviction was overturned.

Malinski v. New York, 324 U.S. 401 (1944)

Through informants close to him (his girlfriend and an old friend), Malinski was implicated in the murder of a police officer. He was later arrested and interrogated by police. He made a confession to police after being confronted by witness statements. Malinski was also humiliated by police, who kept him in a state of undress. His arraignment was delayed for four days. He was held without being permitted to speak to anyone other than police, who, he alleged, beat him during the interrogation sessions. He was convicted. He appealed. The U.S. Supreme Court overturned his conviction, noting evident coercion and that other due process rights had been violated during Malinski's processing.

Haley v. Ohio, 332 U.S. 596 (1948)

A fifteen-year-old youth suspected of being involved in a store robbery, Haley was taken into custody one night for interrogation. The police questioned Haley for five hours, rotating their interrogator teams in shifts. They showed Haley confessions from some of his friends implicating him. Eventually, he confessed. At no time was he advised of his right to counsel; an attorney who tried to see him was rebuffed by police. Even his mother was unable to see him. Haley was subsequently convicted of murder and sentenced to life imprisonment. He appealed. Although this case was before the *Miranda* case and defendant's rights were not police priorities when conducting interrogations, the U.S. Supreme Court detected a high degree of coercion in Haley's case. The conviction was overturned, and the U.S. Supreme Court concluded that juvenile suspects may not be coerced into confessing to crimes. Involuntary confessions cannot be used in court.

McDonald v. United States, 335 U.S. 451 (1948)

McDonald and others were suspected of operating a lottery from their home. Police conducted surveillance of them and then, without a warrant, entered McDonald's home through a window after hearing what they thought to be an "adding machine," a device often used in illegal lottery operations. Incriminating evidence was seized and McDonald was subsequently convicted because of it. Because the police had no arrest or search warrants when they entered McDonald's residence and seized the illegal material and equipment, McDonald appealed, alleging that his Fourth Amendment right against unreasonable searches and seizures had been violated. The U.S. Supreme Court summarily overturned McDonald's conviction, holding the evidence inadmissible because it had been illegally seized without probable cause or an arrest or search warrant.

Rochin v. California, 342 U.S. 165 (1952)

Rochin, a suspect allegedly trafficking in narcotics, was visited by sheriff's deputies one evening. Officers found him sitting on his bed partially dressed. Several white capsules were on a nearby nightstand in plain view. When officers attempted to seize them, Rochin grabbed the capsules and swallowed them. Officers immediately brought Rochin to a nearby hospital and ordered physicians to give him an emetic solution to cause him to vomit. The capsules were obtained through a stomach pump and turned out to be morphine. These capsules were used against him later in court and he was convicted. He appealed. His conviction was overturned because of the unreasonableness of the manner of the officer's search and seizure of the capsules. In a written opinion, the U.S. Supreme Court labeled the police tactics offensive and "conduct that shocks the conscience."

Beck v. Ohio, 379 U.S. 89 (1964)

Beck, having a record of criminal activity, was driving down a street in Cleveland, Ohio, when police officers stopped him without probable cause. They did not have a warrant, nor was Beck doing anything to arouse suspicions of criminal activity. They took him to the police station, where they searched him and his car. Some betting slips were found in his socks. He was charged with possessing "clearing house" (betting) slips in violation of state law and convicted. Beck appealed, contending that the clearing house slips had been illegally seized because no lawful search warrant had been obtained and the officers had no probable cause to stop him initially. The U.S. Supreme Court agreed with Beck and overturned his conviction, saying that the officers had no probable cause to stop him, search him or his car, or detain him for any length of time at the police station. That something illegal was discovered as the result of this warrantless search lacking probable cause did not justify the search. Police must have probable cause before stopping anyone and conducting any sort of search of the person or the automobile.

Culombe v. Connecticut, 367 U.S. 568 (1961)

Culombe was suspected of committing several burglaries and homicides. He was taken into custody on unrelated charges of disturbing the peace and held for four days, during which he was extensively interrogated about the burglaries and homicides. His detention for disturbing the peace was admitted by police to be a ruse to keep him in custody to interrogate him. Eventually, he confessed to the crimes and was convicted. He appealed. The U.S. Supreme Court ruled that his confession had been involuntarily given. It said that when an interrogation is so lengthy and protracted, the process becomes the equivalent of extortion to obtain a confession; thus, such an exploitation of questioning, whatever its usefulness, is not permitted. Culombe's conviction was reversed.

Mapp v. Ohio, 367 U.S. 1081 (1961)

Police in Cleveland suspected someone of bomb making or possessing bomb materials. The suspect was believed to be at the home of Mapp, a woman friend. Officers went to Mapp's home and asked to come in. Mapp refused, suggesting that officers get a warrant. The officers left and Mapp called her attorney. The officers returned later, waving a piece of paper and saying that they had a warrant to conduct their search of her premises. Mapp's attorney arrived at the same time. Neither he nor Mapp was permitted to see the warrant. Mapp grabbed the piece of paper and shoved it down her bosom. A police officer quickly retrieved it and handcuffed her. A thorough search of her home disclosed no bomb materials. However, a trunk in Mapp's basement yielded pencil sketches and drawings depicting what officers believed to be pornography. Mapp was subsequently convicted of possessing pornographic material. She appealed to the U.S. Supreme Court, claiming that the officers had no right to search her home. The U.S. Supreme Court agreed with Mapp and overturned her conviction. No warrant had ever been issued and it was unknown what the piece of paper was that police waved in front of Mapp and her attorney preceding their unlawful search of her premises. This is a landmark U.S. Supreme Court case because it established the exclusionary rule to deter police misconduct in search-and-seizure cases. It made the rule applicable to both state and federal law-enforcement officers. Thus, any evidence seized illegally is inadmissible later in court against criminal suspects. The Fourth Amendment protects citizens from unreasonable searches and seizures by the states; this decision by the U.S. Supreme Court overturned the *Wolf* decision and made the Fourth Amendment applicable to states through the due process clause of the Fourteenth Amendment.

Monroe v. Pape, 365 U.S. 167 (1961)

Monroe was a suspect in a Chicago murder. Thirteen Chicago police officers broke into his home one evening and made him and several others stand naked in a room while the police ransacked his residence searching for incriminating information. During the search, officers tore up mattresses, furniture, and emptied drawers. Monroe was taken to the police station, where he was held for several days on "open charges." Eventually, he was released without any charges being brought against him. He filed suit against the police department under Title 42, U.S.C. Section 1983, alleging that his civil rights had been violated. An Illinois court dismissed Monroe's complaint and Monroe appealed. The U.S. Supreme Court declared that the Illinois police had acted improperly and violated Monroe's rights under the Federal Civil Rights Act.

Escobedo v. Illinois, 378 U.S. 478 (1963)

An informant told police that Escobedo had murdered someone. Without an arrest warrant, the police arrested Escobedo and commenced to interrogate him, without benefit of counsel, on his way to the police station. Escobedo asked to speak with an attorney on several occasions during a subsequent long interrogation period. At certain points, he was escorted about the station to various rooms, and at these times, he would see his attorney at a distance down the hall. The attorney was denied access to his client, who was told that his attorney "did not wish to see him" or was "unavailable." After many hours of intensive interrogation, Escobedo eventually confessed to murder and was convicted. He appealed. The U.S. Supreme Court overturned the conviction on the grounds that Escobedo had been denied counsel and that interrogation had proceeded despite his plea to have counsel present. Thus, the denial of counsel to Escobedo when he requested it had violated his right to due process. The case is also significant because the U.S. Supreme Court stressed that initially police officers were merely investigating a murder. At some early point, their mode shifted to accusation and they accused Escobedo of murder. Thus, whenever police officers shift their questioning from investigatory to accusatory, defendants are entitled to counsel and to refrain from conversing with officers unless counsel is present.

Haynes v. Washington, 373 U.S. 503 (1963)

In December 1957, Haynes was arrested by Spokane police shortly after a gasoline station had been robbed. On the way to the police station, Haynes admitted the robbery orally. He was subsequently interrogated by a Spokane detective and was placed in a lineup for identification by gas station attendants and other witnesses later that evening. The following morning, Haynes was again questioned by detectives for about nine and a half hours. He gave two confession statements, signing one but not the other. The next day he was taken before a magistrate for a preliminary hearing. Police continued to insist that Haynes should sign the second confession because he had already signed the first one. He persistently refused to sign the second confession. He was later convicted, with the first signed confession used against him as evidence. He appealed. The U.S. Supreme Court overturned Haynes's conviction, holding that the police interrogation methods had been improper and that Haynes had been subjected to coercive methods in signing the first confession. Thus, such evidence would be inadmissible in a retrial of the case.

Townsend v. Sain, 372 U.S. 293 (1963)

Townsend was suspected of murder in Cook County, Illinois. After his arrest, he was subjected to intensive questioning by police. A doctor from the police department administered Townsend an injection of phenobarbital, known as "truth serum." Under this drug, Townsend gave a confession. He was convicted. He appealed, recanting his confession and saying it had been given involuntarily. He asked to have his confession testimony excluded. His request was rejected, and the doctor who administered the truth serum was not required to testify, although Townsend's attorney had made such a request. Townsend appealed to the U.S. Supreme Court, which overturned his conviction and remanded the case for retrial, not intending to question the factual evidence but rather, to allow the originating trial court the opportunity of hearing the evidence concerning the concealment of testimony by the doctor about the phenobarbital and other matters. Factual discrepancies would be resolved through further court action.

Aguilar v. Texas, 378 U.S. 108 (1964)

On the basis of an informant's information, police in Texas obtained a search warrant to search the home of Aguilar for possible heroin, marijuana, and other narcotics. The police searched Aguilar's home, finding large quantities of narcotics. After Aguilar was convicted, he appealed, contending that there was no probable cause upon which a valid search warrant could be issued. The U.S. Supreme Court overturned Aguilar's conviction, saying that whenever information supplied by informants is used as the basis for search warrants, some information must be provided to the issuing magistrate that supports the credibility and reliability of the informant. That is, in what capacity do officers know the informant, and has the informant provided reliable information in the past? This, in short, is the two-pronged test of informant reliability. Thus, the U.S. Supreme Court established that the standard for obtaining a search warrant by state officers is the same as that which applies under the Fourth and Fourteenth Amendments; a search warrant may be defective when it does not specify any factual basis for the magistrate to form a decision regarding issuance; and officers need to outline the factual basis for the search.

Preston v. United States, 376 U.S. 364 (1964)

Preston was arrested for vagrancy. His car was towed from the arrest scene and searched. Police found two loaded revolvers in the glove compartment. Unable to open the trunk of the car, they entered it by removing the back seat, and they found additional incriminating evidence leading to Preston's conviction for various offenses. He appealed, alleging a violation of his Fourth Amendment right against an unreasonable search and seizure of contraband or illegal items. The government said that the warrantless search of his vehicle was incident to an arrest and therefore valid. Preston appealed again. The U.S. Supreme Court overturned Preston's conviction, saying that the warrantless search of Preston's vehicle had been too remote in time to be considered a search incident to an arrest. Therefore, the incriminating evidence should be suppressed.

Linkletter v. Walker, 381 U.S. 618 (1965)

Linkletter was arrested without a warrant in Louisiana. Police took him to the police station, where they searched him. Then the police went to his home and seized certain property and papers. Subsequently, they searched his place of business, finding incriminating information. All of these searches were conducted without a warrant. The searches were subsequently upheld as valid, based upon probable cause, and incident to an arrest. Linkletter was convicted of burglary. Some time later, in June 1961, *Mapp v. Ohio* was decided, thereby extending the exclusionary rule to all states to deter police misconduct in conducting warrantless searches of a defendant's premises similar to the searches of Linkletter's business and dwelling. Linkletter filed a *habeas corpus* petition, claiming that the evidence police seized in his case ought to have been suppressed, given the decision in the *Mapp* case. The U.S. Supreme Court heard his appeal and upheld his conviction, saying that the exclusionary rule cannot be applied retroactively because his conviction occurred before the *Mapp* decision. The significance of this case is that it demonstrates that subsequent U.S. Supreme Court decisions are not retroactively applied to prior cases. The exclusionary rule does not apply to cases decided before *Mapp.* The U.S. Supreme Court was careful to note, however, that such retrospective applications of rules may be made in future cases, depending upon the issue and law.

Miranda v. Arizona, 384 U.S. 436 (1966)

Miranda was arrested on suspicion of rape and kidnapping. He was not permitted to talk to an attorney, nor was he advised of his right to one. He was interrogated by police for several hours, eventually confessing and signing a written confession. He was convicted. Miranda appealed, contending that his right to due process had been violated because he had not first been advised of his right to remain silent and to have an attorney present during a custodial interrogation. The U.S. Supreme Court agreed and set forth the *Miranda* warning. This monumental decision provided that confessions made by suspects who were not notified of their due process rights cannot be admitted as evidence. Suspects must be advised of certain rights before they are questioned by police; these rights include the right to remain silent, the right to counsel, the right to free counsel if suspects cannot afford one, and the right to terminate questioning at any time.

Pierson v. Ray, 386 U.S. 547 (1967)

Fifteen white and black clergy attempted to use white facilities at an interstate bus terminal in Jackson, Mississippi. Police officers arrested them for disturbing the peace. They waived a jury trial and were convicted, being sentenced to four months. Subsequently, they appealed the case and filed a civil rights suit against the police officers who arrested them, alleging false imprisonment and civil rights violations. Early appellate decisions resulted in favorable verdicts for the officers, so the clergymen appealed to the U.S. Supreme Court, which decided that the clergymen did indeed have standing to seek damages against the Jackson police officers. Their claim under Title 42, U.S.C. Section 1983 was thus upheld and sent back to a civil trial court for further proceedings.

Bumper v. North Carolina, 391 U.S. 543 (1968)

Bumper was a suspect in a rape case. Police went to his home and advised his grandmother that they had a search warrant and wanted to come in and look around. The police did not have a warrant. Nevertheless, the grandmother gave her consent, and police entered the home and found evidence later incriminating Bumper in the rape. He was convicted. He appealed, arguing that the evidence, a rifle, should have been suppressed because the police did not have a warrant. The prosecutor countered by saying that the police were conducting a valid search of Bumper's premises consistent with the consent to search given by the grandmother. The U.S. Supreme Court disagreed with the prosecutor, holding that misrepresentation by police that they have a valid search warrant and the giving of consent as the result of that misrepresentation do not justify a subsequent warrantless search. The incriminating evidence was suppressed and Bumper's conviction was overturned.

Sibron v. New York, 392 U.S. 40 (1968)

Sibron, a convicted drug user and ex-convict, was observed by a police officer in a New York diner conversing with other persons, also known to be involved with drugs. Sibron was sitting at a table while as many as six or eight persons approached him and conversed over a period of a few hours. Nothing was observed exchanged between them, according to the observing officer. However, when Sibron left the diner, the officer approached and said, "Sibron, you know what I want." Sibron began to place his hand in his pocket, but the officer moved quickly and thrust his hand in it instead. The search yielded several glassine envelopes containing heroin. Sibron was subsequently convicted of heroin possession. However, he appealed to the U.S. Supreme Court, and his conviction was overturned. The Court reasoned that officers should be able to protect themselves against possibly armed suspects. Thus, a "pat-down" and frisk are warranted under certain suspicious conditions. However, Sibron had not been observed doing anything illegal, and therefore his pocket search by the observing officer was unreasonable according to the Fourth Amendment. In short, the officer was entitled to pat down Sibron to detect a possible weapon; the officer would not have detected small glassine envelopes of heroin in such a pat-down, however, so the heroin evidence illegally obtained by the officer was excluded. This landmark case limited the scope of a police officer's search of suspicious persons to pat-downs and frisks, unless other special circumstances apply. Sibron's case did not involve special circumstances.

Terry v. Ohio, 392 U.S. 1 (1968)

A thirty-five–year veteran police officer observed Terry and two companions standing on a Cleveland street corner. They moved up and down the street, looking in store windows, returning frequently to the corner and conversing. The officer was suspicious of this behavior and confronted them about their identities and business. He patted down Terry and discovered a revolver. Terry was charged with carrying a concealed weapon and convicted. Terry appealed and the U.S. Supreme Court eventually heard the case. The argument was whether police officers may "pat down and frisk" suspicious persons if the officers have reasonable suspicion that a crime is being contemplated. The U.S. Supreme Court upheld Terry's conviction, determining that police officers may pat down suspects as a means of protecting themselves and determining whether suspicious persons may be armed and pose a danger to them.

Chimel v. California, 395 U.S. 752 (1969)

Chimel was suspected of being involved in the burglary of a coin company in California. Police officers obtained a valid arrest warrant and went to his home to arrest him. When Chimel returned from work, police were waiting for him. They placed him under arrest and then proceeded to search his entire house, as a "search incident to an arrest." In Chimel's attic, they found some of the stolen coins, which were used against him in court. He was convicted of burglary. Chimel appealed. The U.S. Supreme Court overturned his conviction, arguing that the police search of Chimel's residence was well beyond the scope of the arrest warrant. The police should have obtained a search warrant, but they had not. The U.S. Supreme Court said that, in a search incident to an arrest under the circumstances in *Chimel*, police are permitted to search only the defendant's person and the area within the immediate vicinity. Thus, they may search the room where the suspect is arrested but cannot extend their search to other areas of his or her residence without a valid search warrant.

Davis v. Mississippi, 394 U.S. 721 (1969)

Davis was one of twenty-five black youths who were picked up for questioning about a rape in December 1965 in Meridian, Mississippi. The rapist had been described as black. Without arrest warrants or probable cause, police began a systematic process of picking up black men, taking them to police headquarters, interrogating and fingerprinting them, and then releasing them. Davis became a suspect when his fingerprints matched those of the rapist that had been left on the victim's home window. Davis was convicted on the testimony of the rape victim and the fingerprint evidence. He appealed, seeking to suppress the fingerprint evidence. The U.S. Supreme Court overturned his conviction, holding that, when fingerprints are obtained without a warrant or probable cause, they are invalid as evidence against criminal suspects. Thus, the U.S. Supreme Court determined that Davis's Fourth Amendment right against unreasonable searches and seizures had been violated.

Foster v. California, 394 U.S. 440 (1969)

Foster confessed to police the day after a robbery and gave information about the other two robbers who had participated. He was placed in a subsequent lineup with other men, all of whom were shorter. Foster was wearing a jacket similar to the one he had worn in the robbery. The eyewitness could not be sure that Foster was the robber and asked police if he could speak with Foster. After conversing with him in a private room, the witness still could not positively identify him as one of the robbers. A week later, the witness viewed another lineup, this time with Foster and four persons different from those in the first lineup. This time the witness positively identified Foster. Foster was convicted of the robbery. He appealed. The U.S. Supreme Court overturned Foster's conviction (despite his admission) and said that the police methods used were improper because such lineups biased witness identifications of suspects. In this case, the police had violated Foster's right to due process by biasing the lineup for an eyewitness.

Vale v. Louisiana, 399 U.S. 30 (1970)

Vale, a suspected drug user, was under police surveillance. One evening while police were observing his home, a known drug addict spoke with Vale on his front porch and some object was exchanged between them. The police intercepted the drug addict as he left Vale, and they arrested Vale outside his front door. Without a warrant, police proceeded to enter Vale's home and search it incident to the arrest. While searching, they discovered heroin and other narcotics in Vale's bedroom. Vale was convicted. He appealed, contending that police had needed a valid search warrant to search his premises and that a search incident to his arrest had violated his Fourth Amendment right against an unreasonable search and seizure. The U.S. Supreme Court agreed with Vale and overturned his conviction. No exigent circumstances existed in this case because Vale didn't know that his activities were being observed or that he would have time to dispose of his illegal drugs. Arrests of suspects must occur in their homes, not outside of them, and even in this instance, police should have limited their search to areas immediately under the suspect's control, such as the room he was arrested in, not other rooms, such as bedrooms, kitchens, garages, and attics.

Adams v. Williams, 407 U.S. 143 (1972)

An informant known to a police officer told the officer that Adams, who was seated in his car, was carrying narcotics and, further, had a gun in his waistband. The officer approached the car and asked Adams to roll down his window. After Adams complied, the officer saw the gun in plain view, where the informant had said it would be. The officer therefore made an arrest, which then led to a "search incident to an arrest," in which the officer discovered heroin and other weapons in Adams's possession. Adams was convicted. He appealed on the grounds that the officer had not seen him do anything wrong and so should not have arrested him. Police officers may not have sufficient probable cause to arrest a defendant but they must have reasonable cause to stop and frisk suspects for an officer's safety. Stop-and-frisk procedures need not be based on an officer's personal observation but on information supplied by another person. Because the officer was acting on information given by someone known to him, the U.S. Supreme Court upheld the conviction. The significance of the case is that officers do not always have to observe illegal conduct before making an arrest. Rather, informants who have been reliable in the past may justify an officer's investigation of suspicious suspect.

Brown v. Illinois, 422 U.S. 590 (1975)

Brown was arrested in Illinois without probable cause or a warrant and taken to a police station, where he was told his Miranda rights. While at the police station, Brown gave at least two incriminating statements, linking him with a murder. At his trial, he sought to suppress these statements. However, they were ruled admissible and Brown was convicted. He appealed, and the U.S. Supreme Court overturned his conviction, concluding that because his arrest was warrantless and lacking probable cause, the Miranda warning and Brown's statements were inadmissible. It cited the fruits-of-the-poisonous-tree doctrine, which says that, if the arrest was illegal, its illegality taints the "fruits" of the arrest, or confessions given later.

Brewer v. Williams, 430 U.S. 387 (1977)

Williams was a suspect in the disappearance of a ten-year-old girl from a Young Men's Christian Association (YMCA) building on Christmas Eve in Des Moines, Iowa. He was seen leaving the building with something wrapped in a blanket, with skinny legs sticking out. Williams's car was spotted later about 150 miles from Des Moines, and he was apprehended in Davenport. Des Moines police went to Davenport to bring Williams back to Des Moines, and during their return trip they asked him various questions. As it was beginning to snow heavily, they speculated out loud that a small girl's body would be difficult to find out in the snow and that the girl should at least have a proper "Christian burial." Williams broke down, admitted to the crime of murder, and led police to the girl's body. He was subsequently convicted of murder, but he appealed and his conviction was overturned because police had interrogated him without an attorney present during their trip back to Des Moines. A subsequent retrial resulted in Williams's conviction on other grounds, as there was additional incriminating evidence in his automobile. But the Christian burial case, as it is known, clearly illustrates that police officers may not conduct interrogations of suspects without first advising them of their right to counsel.

Franks v. Delaware, 438 U.S. 154 (1978)

Franks was suspected of first-degree rape, second-degree kidnapping, and first-degree burglary. Authorities obtained a search warrant for Franks's premises. When police officers gave a sworn affidavit supporting the warrant, they gave misstatements and untruths. Franks's defense counsel sought to introduce evidence that the search warrant was illegally obtained on the basis of deliberate lies by police, but the judge denied his request. Franks was convicted. He appealed, contending that the search leading to the incriminating evidence against him had been prefaced by an illegal search warrant containing deliberate untruths from police officers under oath. The U.S. Supreme Court overturned his convictions on these grounds. The U.S. Supreme Court said if, after a hearing, Franks established by a preponderance of evidence that false statements led to the issuance of a search warrant and were intentionally made, and if the false statements were necessary to establish probable cause to justify the search warrant's issuance, then the search warrant had to be voided and the fruits of the search excluded from the trial to the same extent as if probable cause had been lacking on the face of the affidavit.

Mincey v. Arizona, 437 U.S. 385 (1978)

Mincey was involved in a raid on his apartment by undercover police officers. One police officer was shot and killed, and Mincey was seriously wounded and taken to a hospital. During the next four days, his apartment was searched extensively by police, who tore it apart. They also interrogated Mincey while he was in the hospital, drugged, and in great pain. Mincey continually asked the police to discontinue their questioning, but they persisted. He eventually gave incriminating statements to police under this debilitating condition in the hospital. These incriminating statements, as well as newly discovered evidence from his apartment, were used against him. He was convicted of murder, assault, and various narcotics offenses. He appealed. The U.S. Supreme Court held that Mincey's Fourth Amendment right against an unreasonable search and seizure had been violated when police searched his apartment for four days without a warrant. Further, statements he gave while hospitalized had been given under coercive circumstances and were therefore inadmissible. Because his due process rights had been violated, his conviction was overturned.

Arkansas v. Sanders, 442 U.S. 753 (1979)

Sanders was stopped in a cab after leaving an airport. An informant had provided a tip to police to watch out for a person carrying a green suitcase containing marijuana. A description of Sanders was also provided. When Sanders arrived at the airport, he was carrying a green suitcase. He entered a cab and the suitcase was placed in the trunk. When police stopped the cab, they opened the suitcase and discovered marijuana. This evidence was used to convict Sanders of marijuana possession. Sanders appealed his conviction, contending that police should have obtained a warrant before opening his luggage. The U.S. Supreme Court agreed, overturned Sanders conviction, and said that, absent exigent circumstances, police are required to obtain a search warrant before searching luggage taken from an automobile properly stopped and searched for contraband. The U.S. Supreme Court said that one's luggage is a repository for one's personal effects, and thus some expectation of privacy exists.

Therefore, a search warrant is required for such luggage searches. Thus, the significance of this case is that there were no compelling circumstances for police officers to act quickly. They had time to obtain a warrant and had failed to do so.

Baker v. McCollan, 443 U.S. 137 (1979)

McCollan was stopped in Dallas, Texas, for running a red light. A cursory check of records revealed that he was wanted in another county on separate charges. He was transported to the other county, where he was jailed for several days. Initially, he protested that this arrest and detention was a case of mistaken identity. Eventually, photographs of the wanted man and McCollan were compared, and it was obvious that police had arrested the wrong person. They released McCollan and he sued for false imprisonment under a civil rights statute. Initially, the court gave him a summary judgment against the county sheriff, and the government appealed. The U.S. Supreme Court heard the case and reversed the lower court. In sum, the Court ruled against McCollan, declaring that the Constitution does not guarantee that only the guilty will be arrested. McCollan had failed to state a claim upon which relief could be granted. As long as police were acting in good faith and provided the accused with due process rights, then the arrest and detention were lawful. As soon as the police recognized their mistake, they had corrected it immediately.

Brown v. Texas, 443 U.S. 47 (1979)

Brown was stopped by two Texas police officers, who asked him to identify himself and explain his presence to them. The officers had no suspicion that Brown was involved in anything illegal. He refused their request and was charged with refusing to cooperate with police and was convicted. He appealed. The U.S. Supreme Court overturned his conviction, because persons may not be punished for refusing to identify themselves if police have no suspicion of their being involved in any type of criminal or suspicious activity.

Dunaway v. New York, 442 U.S. 200 (1979)

Dunaway was involved in a murder, according to a reliable informant; however, sufficient evidence could not be presented to obtain an arrest warrant. Police officers picked up Dunaway anyway (not formally arresting him) and took him to police head-quarters, where he was interrogated for several hours. Subsequently, he made several incriminating statements that led to his being charged with and convicted of murder. Dunaway appealed, contending that police had lacked probable cause to arrest him initially. The U.S. Supreme Court agreed and overturned his conviction. The significance of *Dunaway* is that police officers cannot take persons into custody and interrogate them for purposes of criminal prosecution without showing probable cause. The U.S. Supreme Court declared that Dunaway's detention and interrogation at the station house by police were both illegal, and thus his subsequent confession was inadmissible in court.

Ybarra v. Illinois, 444 U.S. 85 (1979)

A reliable informant advised police officers that a bartender in a certain bar was selling heroin in small tinfoil packets to customers. Further, the informant said that the bartender had told him that heroin would be available for purchase on a given date. With this information, police obtained a search warrant authorizing a "search of the tavern for evidence of the offense of possession of a controlled substance." They entered the bar and advised all present, including customers, that they would be searched. A pat-down of Ybarra, a customer, disclosed a cigarette package, which the searching officer said contained "objects." He retrieved the cigarette package and found heroin in six tinfoil packets. Ybarra was convicted. He appealed, contending that the search had been unreasonable and violative of the Fourth Amendment and the equal protection clause of the Fourteenth Amendment. The U.S. Supreme Court agreed with Ybarra and overturned his conviction, noting that police officers had no reason to suspect him individually in possession of controlled substances. Their warrant was confined to a tavern search, not specific persons in the tavern who were unknown to the police and their informant.

Owen v. City of Independence, Mo., 445 U.S. 622 (1980)

Owen, the chief of police in Independence, Missouri, was fired without explanation by the city manager after citizen complaints about police misconduct. Owen sued the city under a Title 42, U.S.C. Section 1983 civil rights claim. He alleged that he had not been permitted a hearing or given a statement of charges against him; thus his constitutional rights had been violated. Attorneys for the city manager claimed that the city manager was acting in good faith and properly, according to existing city charter provisions. The U.S. Supreme Court declared that Independence did not have immunity from liability under the Section 1983 claim and might not assert the good-faith defense in response to such a Section 1983 complaint.

Payton v. New York, 445 U.S. 573 (1980)

Payton was suspected of the death of a gas station manager. Police went to Payton's apartment to arrest him without a warrant, although they had plenty of time to obtain one. No one was home, and police forced their way in with a crowbar. They found a .30-caliber rifle shell casing on the floor "in plain view." This shell casing was incriminating evidence, and Payton was subsequently convicted of the murder. He appealed. The U.S. Supreme Court overturned Payton's conviction because police had not obtained a valid arrest warrant in a routine felony arrest situation. There were no exigent circumstances compelling police to act quickly. What evidence they later discovered as the result of their illegal entry into Payton's dwelling was inadmissible. The U.S. Supreme Court stressed that the governing factor here was whether there was reason for police to act quickly or whether the arrest of Payton was otherwise routine. The U.S. Supreme Court said the arrest was routine; thus, a lawful arrest warrant for Payton was required.

United States v. Crews, 445 U.S. 463 (1980)

A woman was assaulted and robbed at gunpoint. She notified police and described the assailant. Crews was seen later in the vicinity by police, who stopped him, took him to the police station briefly, photographed him, and released him. Later, the woman was shown Crews's photograph and she identified him as the man who had attacked her. Crews was later arrested and placed in a lineup. The victim again identified him as her attacker. Crews was later charged and tried for armed robbery. During the trial, the victim again identified Crews. He was convicted. He appealed, contending that his initial detention by police and photographing had been unwarranted and not supported by probable cause. Further, he argued that the lineup identification evidence should have been considered inadmissible for the same reason. The U.S. Supreme Court ruled that the actions by police officers in detaining and arresting Crews constituted police misconduct. This misconduct also applied to the photograph and lineup identification of Crews by the victim. However, his conviction was upheld, because the victim also made an in-court identification of Crews independent of the police photograph and lineup under an exception called the independent-untainted-source doctrine. The U.S. Supreme Court said that the illegality of Crew's detention could not deprive the government of the opportunity to prove his guilt through the introduction of evidence wholly untainted by the police misconduct.

California v. Prysock, 453 U.S. 355 (1981)

In January 1978, Prysock and another man murdered a woman, Erickson. Prysock and his companion were arrested shortly thereafter and taken to a police station for questioning. The questioning was preceded by an extemporaneous Miranda warning, in which the officers covered the general points. Prysock indicated a desire to talk with police but without a tape recorder. He also asked if he could have an attorney present later, after talking with police. They said he could have one. Prysock gave incriminating statements to police without the attorney present, at his own insistence, and he was subsequently convicted. He appealed, arguing that the Miranda warning had not been recited precisely and thus his confession ought to have been excluded and his conviction overturned. An appellate court agreed, and the government appealed. The U.S. Supreme Court reinstated his murder conviction, holding that the Miranda warning need not be a virtual incantation of the precise language contained in the *Miranda* opinion; such a rigid rule is not mandated by *Miranda* or any other decision of the Supreme Court. Essentially, Prysock's constitutional rights had not been violated when police gave him the Miranda warning in a general way.

Steagald v. United States, 451 U.S. 204 (1981)

Police agents had been advised by a confidential informant that a wanted fugitive would be at a particular house in Atlanta. They obtained an arrest warrant and proceeded to the house, which belonged to Gaultney. Police saw Gaultney and Steagald standing in front of the house, conversing. Mistaking one of them for the fugitive, the agents drew their weapons, approached Steagald and

Gaultney, and frisked them, determining that neither was the fugitive they sought. Then they proceeded to the house, where Gaultney's wife met them. They ordered her to place her hands against the wall and they proceeded to search the premises thoroughly for their wanted fugitive, who was not there. Instead, they discovered a small quantity of cocaine. They obtained a search warrant for a subsequent search, which uncovered forty-three pounds of cocaine. Steagald was charged with and convicted of possession of cocaine. He appealed, contending that a search warrant should have been obtained before officers entered the house initially and that their subsequent search of the premises had been unreasonable and unlawful. The police contended that their arrest warrant had "entitled" them to search the premises to hunt for their fugitive and that, as the result of their search, the illegal contraband was discovered lawfully. The U.S. Supreme Court strongly disagreed, saying that neither exigent circumstances nor consent existed to entitle these officers to search the premises. Steagald's conviction was overturned because a valid search warrant was required, based upon probable cause, and the officers conducting the search had possessed no such warrant. Thus, all evidence subsequently seized was inadmissible in court against Steagald. The U.S. Supreme Court specifically noted that arrest warrants do not authorize searches of premises in any absolute sense. Search warrants are necessary for the types of searches conducted in this Atlanta residence. Otherwise, such searches are unlawful and violative of the Fourth Amendment provision against unreasonable searches and seizures.

Briscoe v. LaHue, 460 U.S. 325 (1983)

Briscoe was convicted of burglary. He later sued a police officer who had given perjured testimony against him, according to Title 42, U.S.C. Section 1983, a civil rights section. The U.S. Supreme Court held that police officers enjoy absolute immunity from civil prosecutions when they have given testimony, even perjured testimony, against criminal defendants. Officers who allegedly commit perjury are not immune from possible criminal penalties against them if their testimony is determined to be perjured.

Florida v. Royer, 460 U.S. 491 (1983)

Royer was an airline passenger in the Miami airport. Drug Enforcement Administration agents thought he fit a "drug courier profile," inasmuch as he bought a one-way ticket for cash and under an assumed name; he also was young, nervous, and casually dressed and with heavy luggage. He gave police his driver's license with his correct name when requested. He also followed them to a room, again at their request, where they asked him if they could look through his luggage. He consented. They found marijuana, and Royer was eventually found guilty. He appealed, alleging that his Fourth Amendment rights had been violated because of the unreasonableness of his original stop and detention and the subsequent search. The U.S. Supreme Court agreed and overturned his conviction, saying that it is insufficient for police merely to have consent, without probable cause, to make a warrantless search of personal effects, such as luggage. The U.S. Supreme Court stressed Royer's lengthy detention and noted it was a serious intrusion into his privacy, especially as police had no probable cause to engage him in further searches. Consent given after an illegal act by police is tainted by the illegal act.

Los Angeles v. Lyons, 461 U.S. 95 (1983)

Lyons was stopped by Los Angeles police officers for a traffic violation. During the stop, police seized him and placed him in a chokehold. He offered no resistance, and the chokehold was applied without provocation or justification. It damaged Lyons's larynx. Lyons sued Los Angeles, but the city denied him relief. The U.S. Supreme Court heard the case and ruled that Lyons had failed to satisfy the case-or-controversy requirement to show that he had sustained immediate danger from the challenged official conduct (the chokehold). The case significance is that the federal court cannot entertain claims by any or all citizens who do no more than assert that certain practices of law enforcement officers are unconstitutional.

Nix v. Williams, 467 U.S. 431 (1984)

On Christmas Eve, a ten-year-old girl was missing from a YMCA building in Des Moines, Iowa. Eyewitnesses reported later observing Williams leaving the YMCA building carrying a large bundle wrapped in a blanket, with two skinny legs protruding. Officers found Williams's car the next day 160 miles east of Des Moines. At a rest stop between where the car was found and the YMCA building, they discovered items of clothing and other articles. They assumed that the girl's body was probably somewhere between Des Moines and where Williams's car was found. Williams was subsequently found in a nearby town and arrested. While he was being driven back to Des Moines in a police vehicle, police officers engaged him in conversation relating to the girl's whereabouts. Because it had recently snowed, finding her body would be difficult. Officers suggested to Williams that he ought to tell them where her body was so that they could give her a "Christian burial." (This became known as the Christian burial case.) Williams confessed and directed officers to the girl's body. Williams was charged with and convicted of first-degree murder. He appealed, and his conviction was overturned inasmuch as police officers had not advised him of his Miranda rights. He was subjected to a second trial, in which his original confession was excluded. He was convicted again, but this time because the prosecutor showed that the girl's body would have been discovered eventually, thus providing the conclusive evidence against Williams. The significance of this case is that it introduced the inevitable-discovery exception to the exclusionary rule, whereby prosecutors may argue that inculpatory evidence may be introduced against criminal suspects if it can be shown that police would have eventually discovered the incriminating evidence anyway.

Smith v. Illinois, 469 U.S. 91 (1984)

Smith was suspected of armed robbery. Shortly after his arrest, he was taken to police headquarters for interrogation. He was told his Miranda rights but was ambivalent about whether he wanted an attorney to be present during questioning. Specifically, Smith said, "I wanna get a lawyer" before his questioning by police. However, he said, "Yeah and no" when asked whether he wanted to talk with police at that time. In any event, Smith admitted to the crime. During his trial, his attorney attempted to have the incriminating statements against him suppressed but was unsuccessful. Smith was convicted. He appealed to the U.S. Supreme Court, which overturned his conviction. The Supreme Court holding was a narrow one, not necessarily exploring the meticulous circumstances of Smith's confession or the conditions under which it was given. Rather, the Court reasoned that, on several occasions during police questioning, Smith had indicated his intent to have an attorney present. Police were to cease their questioning at that point and obtain an attorney for Smith. They had failed to do so.

Suspects who are in custody but invoke their right to counsel must be provided counsel before further interrogation is conducted.

Thompson v. Louisiana, 469 U.S. 17 (1984)

In May 1982, Jefferson Parish, Louisiana, police officers responded to a report by the daughter of Thompson of a homicide. They went to the house and found Thompson's husband dead of a gunshot wound and Thompson lying unconscious nearby, apparently having recently ingested a drug overdose in a suicide attempt. The daughter reported that her mother had shot her father and then ingested a quantity of pills to attempt suicide. The officers transported Thompson to the hospital, where she was treated for a drug overdose, and they also secured the crime scene. Homicide investigators, without a warrant, arrived a few hours later and conducted a thorough search of every room in the house, discovering a pistol and other evidence. Because the search had been warrantless, Thompson sought to suppress the evidence (e.g., the gun and a suicide note, among other things) from the trial proceedings. Nevertheless, all evidence was subsequently admitted against her in a trial, and she was convicted of second-degree murder. She appealed. The U.S. Supreme Court said that a nonconsensual and warrantless search of the premises had been conducted by police who had had time to get a valid search warrant but had not done so. Therefore, the evidence against Thompson they had seized was inadmissible. The conviction was overturned.

United States v. Leon, 468 U.S. 897 (1984)

Leon, a suspected drug trafficker, was placed under surveillance by Burbank, California, police. Subsequently, police obtained search warrants for three residences and several automobiles under Leon's control. Acting on the search warrants, they seized large quantities of inculpatory drug evidence, which was used against Leon at a trial later, where he was convicted. He appealed to the U.S. Supreme Court, which upheld his conviction. Although the U.S. Supreme Court declared the search warrants invalid, they noted in a rambling and extensive opinion that the officers who abided by the directives outlined by the invalid warrants had been acting in good faith, presuming that the issued warrants were valid. The U.S. Supreme Court also noted that this decision was not to be interpreted as a blanket generalization authorizing officers to act in all instances where defective warrants are issued. The U.S. Supreme Court simply weighed the benefits of suppressing the evidence obtained in Leon's case against the costs of exclusion. The significance of this case is that it creates a good-faith exception to the exclusionary rule. The U.S. Supreme Court's message is that evidence may be admissible if the fault for defective warrants rests with judges, not police officers. The target of the exclusionary rule is police misconduct, not judicial misconduct.

Hayes v. Florida, 470 U.S. 811 (1985)

Hayes was a suspect in a criminal case. He was visited by police, who asked him if they could take his fingerprints. Hayes refused, at which time the police advised him that if he didn't go to the police station voluntarily, he would be arrested. He reluctantly agreed to go, and his fingerprints were taken. They matched those at the crime scene and Hayes was subsequently convicted of the crime. He appealed. The U.S. Supreme Court overturned his conviction, however, holding that there had been no probable cause to arrest Hayes, he had given no consent to go to the police station, and there had been no prior judicial authorization for such fingerprinting. The subsequent investigative detention at the police station had violated Hayes's Fourth Amendment rights against unreasonable searches and seizures. Police must have probable cause to take persons into custody for purposes of taking their fingerprints and subjecting them to interrogations.

Oklahoma City v. Tuttle, 471 U.S. 808 (1985)

The widow of Tuttle sued Oklahoma City officials because a police officer had shot and killed her husband outside a bar where he had been participating in a robbery. Her civil rights action, under Title 42, U.S.C. Section 1983, alleged negligence on the part of Oklahoma City officials in training their officers in the use of firearms. The U.S. Supreme Court ruled that Oklahoma City was not liable for the death of Tuttle and that this shooting showed no sign of gross negligence or negligent training or deliberate indifference.

Tennessee v. Garner, 471 U.S. 1 (1985)

A fifteen-year-old boy, Garner, and a friend were in an empty home in Memphis late at night when neighbors reported the "breaking and entering" to police. Police officers approached the home and saw someone fleeing. They shouted warnings to the fleeing suspects and finally shot at them. One bullet struck Garner in the back of the head, killing him instantly. The standard governing the use of deadly force was that any force could be employed, even deadly force, to prevent the escape of fleeing felons. Because burglary is a felony, those fleeing from the empty home were felony suspects and police believed they were entitled to shoot at them. Many years later, in 1985, the U.S. Supreme Court declared that deadly force had not been warranted in this case, as burglary is punishable with a few years in prison, not the death penalty. This landmark case was significant because it effectively nullified the fleeing-felon standard for using deadly force. Since then, deadly force may be applied to fleeing suspects only (1) if they pose a threat to the lives of officers or (2) if they pose a threat to the lives of others.

Arizona v. Mauro, 481 U.S. 520 (1986)

Mauro went into a store and said he had killed his son. When the police arrived, Mauro admitted the killing and led officers to his son's body. The police arrested Mauro and took him to the police station for questioning. They advised him of his Miranda rights twice, and he told them that he did not wish to answer further questions without an attorney present. His wife arrived and asked to speak with him. The police agreed, saying that they would tape-record the conversation with an officer present in the room. Despite a plea of temporary insanity, nullified by a number of statements in the conversation with his wife, Mauro was subsequently convicted of murder. He appealed, contending that his conversation with his wife should have been suppressed as evidence against him. The U.S. Supreme Court disagreed, saying that the conversation had not been an interrogation, despite the officer's presence and the taping of the conversation by police, because it had not been initiated by the police. Thus, the evidence was constitutionally proper and admissible. The significance of this case was that it further delineated what is or is not a custodial interrogation.

Michigan v. Jackson, 475 U.S. 625 (1986)

A woman planned the murder of her husband and spoke to Jackson and several other men about their possibly carrying out this crime. Jackson was arrested and made various incriminating statements about the conspiratorial nature of the planned murder. At his arraignment, Jackson requested that counsel be appointed for him. A lawyer was provided. The following day, police initiated another interrogation of Jackson, without his attorney present, in which he admitted that he had murdered the woman's husband. Jackson was charged with murder and convicted. He appealed. The U.S. Supreme Court overturned his conviction because his due process right had been violated when he was interrogated without the counsel that had been provided for him. The prosecution argued that Jackson's statement was voluntary and that he had waived his right to have counsel present when giving his murder confession. The U.S. Supreme Court disagreed and said that custodial interrogations that are police-initiated require the presence of an attorney. Without an attorney present, the accused cannot effectively waive his right to be interrogated further. Thus, defendants cannot be interrogated by police once they have invoked their right to silence and have an attorney. However, interrogations and confessions initiated by the suspect are permissible. Thus, if Jackson had requested to speak with officers and had admitted the murder, the confession would have been valid. This case established the Jackson rule, which says that, once a defendant invokes the Sixth Amendment right to counsel, any waiver of that right—even if voluntary, knowing, and intelligent under traditional standards—is presumed invalid if given in a police-initiated discussion and that evidence obtained pursuant to that waiver is inadmissible in the prosecution's case-in-chief. However, suspect-initiated statements can be used to impeach testimony given by defendants on cross-examination.

Pembaur v. Cincinnati, 475 U.S. 469 (1986)

A physician, Pembaur, filed suit against the city of Cincinnati, whose police officers allegedly violated his Fourth and Fourteenth Amendment rights by forcing their way into his clinic to serve a capias on two of his employees. Pembaur was subsequently charged with obstruction of justice and convicted. Pembaur continued his suit against county officials, a suit in which the officials alleged that they were immune from such suits. Pembaur's claim was rejected and he appealed the case to the U.S. Supreme Court. The U.S. Supreme Court reinstated his claim against county officials, saying that the county is liable under Title 42, U.S.C. Section 1983.

Arizona v. Hicks, 480 U.S. 321 (1987)

One evening, persons in an apartment reported that someone from an above apartment had fired a bullet through their ceiling, injuring one of the lower apartment's occupants. Police investigated the upstairs apartment, rented by Hicks. While investigating, they discovered weapons and a stocking cap mask. Also, they noted that the apartment was run down but new stereo equipment stood in plain view. They wrote down serial numbers on the stereo equipment. To see the serial numbers, however, they had to move the equipment. Later, when compared with another crime report, these stereo items were found to have been stolen. A search warrant was obtained for Hicks's apartment. Hicks was arrested, charged with robbery, and convicted. He sought to suppress the evidence against him, alleging that his Fourth Amendment rights had been violated. The U.S. Supreme Court overturned Hicks's conviction, saying that for police officers to invoke the plain-view rule regarding the stereo equipment, they required probable cause to believe the equipment was stolen. Because the police used reasonable suspicion when moving the equipment, their act became a search requiring a proper warrant based upon probable cause. Reasonable suspicion does not, however, rise to the level of probable cause.

Springfield v. Kibbe, 480 U.S. 257 (1987)

In September 1981, Springfield, Massachusetts, police received a telephone call that Thurston was assaulting a woman with a knife in an apartment. Later, police discovered that Thurston had fled in an automobile. His automobile was seen on a highway and followed by police, who attempted to stop it. Thurston would not stop, even after police had erected roadblocks along the highway. At some point, an officer, Perry, gave chase and fired his weapon at Thurston, who was allegedly attempting to run Perry off the road. One bullet struck Thurston in the head, and he died shortly thereafter in a hospital. His relatives filed suit against Springfield police for negligent training, alleging that it had led an officer wrongfully to shoot and kill Thurston. The U.S. Supreme Court heard the case and decided the question of whether a city can be held liable for the inadequate training of its employees. The U.S. Supreme Court held that there was no evidence on the record of deliberate indifference or recklessness in the apprehension of Thurston's fleeing vehicle. Thus, Thurston's relatives failed to prove essential elements of their claim and, therefore, the suit was dismissed as being improvidently granted.

Arizona v. Roberson, 486 U.S. 675 (1988)

Roberson was arrested for a burglary and advised of his Miranda rights. He said he wanted to remain silent until he could speak to an attorney. A few days later, another officer approached Roberson in jail and asked to speak with him about another unrelated crime. The officer gave Roberson his Miranda warning before beginning that interrogation. Roberson made a full confession and was subsequently convicted. On appeal, he requested that his confession be suppressed. The prosecution countered by saying that he had confessed to another separate crime after being given his Miranda warning by another officer. However, the U.S. Supreme Court set aside Roberson's conviction, saying that police may not interrogate a suspect following his invocation of the right to silence and without his attorney present. The fact that the confession involved another crime did not matter. This second interrogation constituted a police-initiated custodial interrogation after an initial right invoked by the defendant to remain silent. The decision did not, however, bar defendants from initiating further conversation with police on their own, whereupon their confessions and incriminating statements would be admissible in court.

Murray v. United States, 487 U.S. 533 (1988)

Drug Enforcement Administration (DEA) agents suspected Murray of dealing in illicit drugs. Placing him under surveillance, they observed him drive a camper into a warehouse. When Murray and an associate emerged from the warehouse twenty minutes later, other DEA agents observed a large tractor trailer with a long, dark container. When the truck departed, it was followed by DEA agents. They stopped the drivers, searched the truck, and discovered marijuana. When the DEA agents watching the warehouse heard about the marijuana, they quickly, without a warrant, forced their way into Murray's warehouse, where they found several large burlap bags of marijuana "in plain view." They left the warehouse, obtained a valid search warrant from a judge, and reentered the warehouse, where they seized the previously viewed marijuana bales. They also confiscated notebooks detailing Murray's drug trafficking and other illicit dealings.

Murray was ultimately arrested, tried, and convicted of trafficking in illegal drugs. He appealed. The U.S. Supreme Court rejected Murray's idea that the evidence should have been suppressed because officers had acted in an illegal manner when they first forced entry into the warehouse. Although the U.S. Supreme Court declared this initial action by police to be misconduct, it concluded that the subsequent search in the context of a valid warrant was a valid search.

City of Canton v. Harris, 489 U.S. 378 (1989)

Harris was arrested in Canton, Ohio, and taken to a police station in a patrol wagon. During the trip, she apparently fell to the floor and was observed sitting on the floor when the police arrived at the station. While at the station, Harris fell several times, was incoherent, and eventually was left on the floor unattended. Police officials never gave her aid or medical attention. Her family later arrived and transported her to a hospital, where she was diagnosed with several emotional ailments and hospitalized. The Harris family later sued police officials and the municipality under Title 42, U.S.C. Section 1983, alleging that Harris's civil rights had been violated because of deliberate indifference by police to Harris's emotional and physical condition. The municipality claimed immunity from such a suit and alleged inadequate police training, for which the municipality denied responsibility. The U.S. Supreme Court disagreed, saying that the municipality was liable to such suits. However, the U.S. Supreme Court said that for plaintiffs to prevail they must show that (1) the city had deliberately failed to train its officers, (2) such training was municipality policy, and (3) the identified deficiency in officer training was directly related to injuries sustained by victims.

Graham v. Connor, 490 U.S. 396 (1989)

Graham was a diabetic who asked his daughter to drive him to a store to buy orange juice for his condition. When he entered the store, there were long lines, and Graham hurried back out and told his daughter to drive him to another store. A police officer observed Graham's quick entry and exit at the store, became suspicious, and stopped Graham's daughter as an "investigative stop" while he determined to find out "what happened" back at the store. In the meantime, Graham became belligerent and was handcuffed by police. He sustained further "injuries" while handcuffed. When police found that nothing had happened at the store, they released Graham, who filed a Title 42, U.S.C. Section 1983 civil rights suit against the officers for using excessive force unnecessarily against him. The U.S. Supreme Court declared that police officers are liable whenever they use excessive force and that the standard they should use is objective reasonableness rather than substantive due process when they subdue suspicious persons. This is tantamount to a totality-of-circumstances test applied to discretionary actions of police officers in the field when they are dealing with situations in which only partial information exists that a crime may have been committed. The reasonableness of the situation and force used is determined on the spot, considering all circumstances.

Alabama v. White, 496 U.S. 325 (1990)

An anonymous tipster told police that White would be leaving her apartment at a particular time with a brown briefcase containing cocaine and that she would get in a particular type of car and drive to a particular motel. Watching her apartment, police saw White emerge and enter the described vehicle. They followed her to the motel and stopped her car. They advised her that she was suspected of carrying cocaine. At their request, she permitted them to search her vehicle, where they discovered the described briefcase. They asked her to open it, where they found some marijuana, and arrested her. A search of her purse incident to her arrest disclosed a quantity of cocaine. She was charged and convicted of possessing illegal substances. She appealed, arguing that the police lacked reasonable suspicion to stop her initially and therefore the discovered drugs were inadmissible as evidence against her. The U.S. Supreme Court disagreed, holding that the anonymous tip and the totality of circumstances of subsequent police surveillance more than satisfied the less demanding standard of reasonable suspicion contrasted with the more demanding standard of probable cause.

Minnick v. Mississippi, 498 U.S. 146 (1990)

A day after escaping from a Mississippi county jail, Minnick and an accomplice killed two men during the burglary of a trailer. Minnick fled to California, where he was arrested on Friday, August 22, 1986, by Lemon Grove police. On August 23, Federal Bureau of Investigation (FBI) agents advised Minnick of his right to counsel and his right not to answer their questions. Minnick made a partial confession to FBI agents, although he advised them to "come back Monday," when he would have an attorney present. The same day, Minnick was appointed an attorney, who advised him to say nothing to police. On Monday, August 25, Denham, a deputy sheriff from Mississippi, flew to the San Diego jail where Minnick was being held. Minnick was reluctant to talk to Denham, but jailers told him he "had to talk." Minnick related all the incidents following his jail escape and admitted committing one of the murders. He was subsequently convicted on two counts of capital murder and sentenced to death. He appealed, moving to suppress his statements to FBI agents and to Denham. The U.S. Supreme Court reversed Minnick's conviction and sentence and remanded the case to a lower court, reasoning that, once the Miranda warning had been given and an attorney appointed, further questioning by police might not resume without an attorney present, if the defendant had invoked the right to have counsel present.

Smith v. Ohio, 494 U.S. 541 (1990)

Smith, carrying a brown paper bag, was leaving a YMCA building with a companion in Ashland, Ohio, one evening. Two police officers observed him and his friend. Neither Smith nor his companion were known to police. They approached the two men and said, "Come here a minute." Smith was standing by his car and threw the brown paper bag on the hood of the car and turned to face police. They immediately seized his bag, which he attempted to protect, and opened it, discovering drug paraphernalia. They placed Smith under arrest for possession of drug paraphernalia, and he was subsequently convicted. Smith appealed. The police and the state reasoned that the discovery of the drug paraphernalia had given them probable cause to arrest Smith. They contended that the search of the bag and seizure of its contents were made incident to an arrest and so were properly admissible against Smith during his subsequent trial. The state further argued that Smith had abandoned his property (the bag) when he tossed it on the hood of his car. Thus the abandoned property fell within the purview of police to investigate it and its contents. The U.S. Supreme Court rejected these arguments and overturned Smith's conviction, holding that justifying a search by an arrest and an arrest by the search "will not do." A citizen who attempts to protect his private property from inspection has clearly not abandoned that property. The police had lacked probable cause to search the bag, and that drug paraphernalia was discovered was irrelevant and did not justify the arrest. Searches of areas in the immediate vicinity of persons arrested on the basis of probable cause are legitimately within the scope of police authority, but no search can be justified without probable cause. This case is a good example of how the U.S. Supreme Court treats the matter of the ends justifying the means. Finding illegal contraband without first having probable cause to make an arrest does not justify the search of a person or his personal effects, regardless of whatever is found.

Brower v. County of Inyo, 489 U.S. 593 (1991)

Brower was a suspect who had stolen a car, leading police on a twenty-mile chase down a major highway. In an effort to stop him, police caused an eighteen-wheel tractor-trailer rig to be placed across the highway ahead of him. Police headlights were turned toward Brower, thus preventing him from seeing the truck across the road. He crashed into the truck and was killed. His family filed a Title 42, U.S.C. Section 1983 civil rights action against police, alleging that Brower had been the subject of an unreasonable seizure. Liability was not decided by this case, but the U.S. Supreme Court declared that the roadblock established by police in this case was unreasonable and thus constituted an unreasonable seizure, violating Brower's Fourth Amendment rights. The police measures clearly exceeded the reasonableness necessary to stop a fleeing thief. It was a property crime, the punishment for which would probably have been a short prison term, certainly not the death penalty. Because the officers knew or should have known that the roadblock and blinding headlights would probably cause Brower's death, they were clearly using excessive force, which was unconstitutional.

California v. Acevedo, 500 U.S. 565 (1991)

Drug Enforcement Administration agents discovered a Federal Express package shipped from Hawaii to California that contained a large quantity of marijuana. They allowed Federal Express personnel to deliver the package to a house and placed the house under surveillance. Subsequently, a man entered the house and left later carrying a tote bag. The agents intercepted him and found about a pound of marijuana in the bag. Later they observed Acevedo arrive at the house and leave later carrying a brown paper bag about the size of the tote bag. Police officers stopped Acevedo's car thereafter, searched the brown paper bag without a warrant, and discovered marijuana. The police lacked probable cause to search the vehicle itself, although they did have probable cause to believe that the paper bag held marijuana. Acevedo was convicted and he appealed. The U.S. Supreme Court upheld Acevedo's conviction, saying that probable cause to believe that a container has contraband may enable officers to search that container, even if it is in a vehicle that they lack probable cause to search.

Illinois v. Condon, 507 U.S. 948 (1993)

Condon was suspected of dealing in cocaine. An informant provided police in Du Page County with sufficient information to obtain a warrant to search Condon's home. One evening, a team of police officers stormed Condon's home without knocking or announcing their presence and found a large quantity of cocaine, marijuana, and several weapons. At a later trial, Condon was convicted. He appealed, alleging that police had not knocked and first announced their intentions before conducting the search. Police countered that their unannounced entry and search were caused by exigent circumstances. Condon's conviction was overturned by the Illinois Supreme Court, which held that the unannounced entry had not been prompted by exigent circumstances and conflicted with the protocol to be followed in such instances of searches and seizures. The Illinois prosecutor appealed the ruling to the U.S. Supreme Court, which declined to hear Illinois's appeal in this ruling. However, some dissenting U.S. Supreme Court members suggested that, because of the present conflict among the states about search-and-seizure protocol, the U.S. Supreme Court should hear the case and resolve the conflict.

Minnesota v. Dickerson, 508 U.S. 366 (1993)

Dickerson emerged from a known crack house and was observed by police officers walking down an alley. When he saw the officers approaching him, he reversed direction and walked away from them. They decided to stop him for an investigative pat-down. They discovered no weapons, but one of the officers thrust his hand into Dickerson's pockets and found a small quantity of crack cocaine in a glassine envelope. The officer claimed that he had felt a small lump that felt like crack cocaine through Dickerson's clothing after the initial pat-down and frisk. Dickerson was charged with cocaine possession and convicted. He appealed, and the U.S. Supreme Court overturned his conviction on the ground that the search of Dickerson went well beyond the scope specified in *Terry v. Ohio*, where police officer pat-downs and frisks of suspects were used exclusively for the purpose of determining whether the suspects possessed a dangerous weapon that might be used to harm the police. This specific type of incident is directly on point and consistent with a U.S. Supreme Court ruling in another case involving excessive officer intrusion into a suspect's pocket in a search for contraband: *Sibron v. New York* (1968).

Withrow v. Williams, 507 U.S. 680 (1993)

Williams, an inmate in a Michigan prison, was suspected of a double murder. During the investigation, he was interrogated by police, who did not immediately tell him his Miranda rights. He made several pre–Miranda warning statements that were inculpatory and several more after the warning by police. Williams admitted to providing a weapon to the man who actually did the killing. A bench trial resulted in Williams's conviction and he was given two concurrent life sentences for the two felony-murder convictions. Williams appealed, alleging that his Miranda rights had been violated by police. Williams alleged that police had told him throughout all pre– and post–Miranda warning questioning that, if he confessed, he would be given lenient treatment and that that inducement was sufficient to overcome his will against giving incriminating information to them. Williams claimed that his admissions had been involuntarily made throughout the entire interrogation, and thus, the admissions should have been suppressed. The U.S. Supreme Court heard his case and ruled that Williams's statements to police were involuntary and thus excludable as evidence against him, in view of the violation of the Miranda warning.

Elder v. Holloway, 510 U.S. 510 (1994)

Elder was arrested without warrant by Idaho police because they believed he was wanted in Florida on a criminal charge. At first, they planned to arrest him in his workplace, which was a public area, where an arrest warrant is not required. However, they found that Elder had left work early and gone home. They continued to his home, where they surrounded the dwelling and ordered him out of the house. Authorities instructed Elder to crawl out of the house, but Elder, who suffered from epilepsy, walked out of the house instead and immediately experienced an epileptic seizure. He fell to the ground, where his head struck the pavement, causing him to suffer permanent brain trauma and paralysis. Subsequently, Elder filed suit against the police officers under Title 42, U.S.C. Section 1983, alleging that the officers had violated his civil rights by arresting him in his home without a suitable warrant. The U.S. District Court granted the officers a summary judgment on the grounds of their qualified immunity from such suits. Elder appealed. The U.S. Supreme Court overturned the summary judgment and ordered the case sent back to district court for a trial resolution of factual questions. However, the Supreme Court did not offer an opinion or ruling on the qualified immunity defense. Rather, it placed the matter in the circuit court of appeals to resolve the issue in light of all prevailing law and authority.

Arizona v. Evans, 514 U.S. 1 (1995)

Evans was arrested by Phoenix police during a routine traffic stop when it was discovered there was an outstanding arrest warrant against him. In the search incident to his arrest, police found marijuana in his trunk and charged him with marijuana possession. He was convicted. Later, it was determined that computer errors had implicated him wrongly by associating an outstanding arrest warrant for another person with a similar name. Thus, police officers had arrested the wrong man and had searched the wrong man's automobile trunk. Evans sought to have his conviction overturned, because, he said, his Fourth Amendment right against an unreasonable search and seizure had been violated. After various appeals to the state court and an appeal to the Ninth Circuit Court of Appeals, Evans's conviction was overturned. The government appealed to the U.S. Supreme Court, which reinstated Evans's original conviction, saying simply that the "good faith" exception to the exclusionary rule was in effect, inasmuch as arresting officers had been acting appropriately and not engaging in misconduct. The police had had no knowledge of computer errors. The significance of this case is that even if an arrest is later found to be illegal or unsubstantiated by the facts, such as computer errors, if police, acting in good faith, discover contraband or controlled substances incident to their arrest of the wrong person, the evidence they discover may be admissible against the suspect later in court. The primary function of the exclusionary rule is to guard against police misconduct. In this case, there was no police misconduct, only clerical error unattributable to police.

Bailey v. United States, 516 U.S. 137 (1995)

A police officer stopped Bailey's vehicle in the District of Columbia because it lacked an inspection sticker and a front license plate. When he failed to produce a valid driver's license, Bailey was ordered from the car. At that time, the officer saw something in plain view between the two front seats. A bag was produced, yielding 30 grams of cocaine. Bailey was subsequently convicted of drug charges. His sentence was enhanced by a federal district court judge when it was determined that during the discovery of the cocaine the police had found a firearm in the vehicle trunk. An appeal to the U.S. Supreme Court resulted in the sentence enhancement being overturned. The U.S. Supreme Court noted that the federal provision allowing enhancing sentences for using firearms during the commission of a federal crime refers to an active employment of the firearm by the defendant. In this case, the firearm, though loaded, was in a bag inside the locked vehicle trunk. Thus, the prosecution would have had to prove that Bailey was actively using his firearm during his possession and transportation of cocaine. The prosecution failed to show that Bailey intended such active employment of the firearm.

Johnson v. Jones, 515 U.S. 304 (1995)

Five police officers arrested Jones because they thought he was drunk, when in fact Jones was a diabetic suffering from an insulin seizure. Jones later found himself in a hospital with several broken ribs. He sued. His allegations that police officers had used excessive force when arresting him and beating him at the station house were substantiated by other collateral factual information. The police officers asked for a summary judgment in Jones's suit against them, and the motion was denied by a district court. The officers appealed. The U.S. Supreme Court affirmed the denial of the motion, holding that police officers may not appeal a district court's summary judgment order insofar as that order determines whether or not the pretrial record sets forth a "genuine" issue of fact for trial. Jones was therefore entitled to a trial on the issue of whether his Title 42, U.S.C. Section 1983 civil rights had been violated.

Koon v. United States, 518 U.S. 81 (1996)

Police officers Koon and Powell were convicted in federal court of violating constitutional rights of motorist King under color of law during arrest and they were sentenced to thirty months' imprisonment. A U.S. District Court trial judge used U.S. sentencing guidelines and justified a downward departure of eight offense levels from "27" to "19" to arrive at a thirty- to thirty-seven–month sentence. The government appealed, contending that downward departure of eight offense levels from "27" was an abuse of judicial discretion and that the factors cited for the downward departure were not statutory. An original offense seriousness level of "27" would have meant imposing a sentence of seventy to eighty-seven months. The Ninth Circuit Court of Appeals rejected all of the trial court's reasons for the downward departure and Koon and Powell petitioned the U.S. Supreme Court. The Supreme Court upheld the circuit court of appeals in part and reversed it in part. Specifically, the Supreme Court said that the primary question to be answered on appeal is whether the trial judge abused his discretion by the downward departure in sentencing. The reasons given by the trial judge for the downward departure from an offense level of "27" to "19" were that: (1) the victim's misconduct provoked police use of force; (2) Koon and Powell had been subjected to successive state and federal criminal prosecutions; (3) Koon and Powell posed a low risk of recidivism; (4) Koon and Powell would probably lose their jobs and be precluded from employment in law enforcement; and (5) Koon and Powell would be unusually susceptible to abuse in prison. The Supreme Court concluded that a five-level downward departure based on the victim's misconduct that provoked officer use of force was justified, because victim misconduct is an encouraged (by the U.S. Sentencing Commission) basis for a guideline departure. The Supreme Court said that the remaining three-level departure was an abuse of judicial discretion. Federal district judges may not consider a convicted offender's career loss as a downward departure factor. Further, trial judges may not consider an offender's low likelihood of recidivism, because this factor is already incorporated into the Criminal History Category in the sentencing guideline table. Considering this factor to justify a downward departure, therefore, would be tantamount to counting the factor twice.

The Supreme Court upheld the trial judge's reliance on the offenders' susceptibility to prison abuse and the burdens of successive state and federal prosecutions, however. The Supreme

Court remanded the case back to the district court, where a new sentence could be determined. Thus, a new offense level must be chosen on the basis of the victim's own misconduct that provoked the officers and on which offender susceptibility to prison abuse and the burden of successive state and federal prosecutions could be considered. The significance of this case for criminal justice is that specific factors are identified by the Supreme Court to guide federal judges in imposing sentences on police officers convicted of misconduct and violating citizen rights under color of law. Victim response that provokes police use of force, an officer's susceptibility to abuse in prison, and the burden of successive state and federal prosecutions are acceptable factors to be considered to justify downward departures in offense seriousness, whereas one's low recidivism potential and loss of employment opportunity in law enforcement are not legitimate factors to justify downward departure in offense seriousness.

County of Sacramento v. Lewis, 118 S.Ct. 1708 (1998)

Smith and another county deputy, Stapp, were on patrol in separate cruisers when they observed a motorcycle approaching at high speed, driven by Willard and carrying Lewis. Smith and Stapp attempted to stop the speeding motorcycle by flashing their cruiser lights and maneuvering their cruisers to pen the cycle in. However, Willard maneuvered between the two police cruisers and sped off. Smith and Stapp turned on their emergency lights and began a high-speed pursuit. The chase transpired through various neighborhoods and city streets at speeds in excess of one hundred miles per hour. The chase ended a few miles later when Willard crashed his motorcycle. Willard was thrown clear, but Lewis was thrown onto the road, into the path of the pursuing cruiser driven by Smith. Smith slammed on his brakes but could not prevent his vehicle from skidding into Lewis, killing him. Lewis's parents brought a Section 1983 suit against Sacramento County and the sheriff's deputies, alleging that the pursuit was undertaken with deliberate indifference and reckless disregard for the lives of Willard and Lewis. A federal court granted summary judgment in favor of Smith, but the Ninth Circuit Court of Appeals reversed, holding that the appropriate degree of fault for substantive due process liability for high-speed police pursuits is deliberate indifference to, or reckless disregard for, a person's right to life and personal security. Sacramento County and Smith appealed to the U.S. Supreme

Court, where the case was heard. The Supreme Court reversed the Ninth Circuit Court of Appeals by holding that a police officer does not violate substantive due process by causing death through deliberate or reckless indifference to life in a high-speed automobile chase aimed at apprehending a suspected offender. High-speed chases with no intent to harm suspects physically or to worsen their legal plight do not give rise to due process liability. Smith was faced with a course of lawless behavior for which the police were not to blame. They had done nothing to cause Willard's high speed in the first place, nothing to excuse his flouting of the commonly understood police authority to control traffic, and nothing to encourage him to race through traffic at breakneck speed. Willard's outrageous behavior was practically instantaneous, and so was Smith's instinctive response to do his job, not to induce Willard's lawlessness, or to terrorize, harm, or kill. Thus, Lewis's Fourteenth Amendment substantive due process rights were not violated by the officers' conduct.

Dickerson v. United States, 120 S.Ct. 2326 (2000)

Dickerson was indicted for bank robbery, conspiracy to commit bank robbery, and using a firearm in the course of committing a crime of violence. Federal Bureau of Investigation (FBI) agents interviewed Dickerson, who gave several incriminating statements voluntarily without a Miranda warning being given. Subsequently, the government sought to introduced Dickerson's statements against him in a criminal trial in a U.S. District Court. Dickerson moved to suppress the statements because they had been given before Dickerson received the Miranda warning from the FBI agents. Dickerson's motion to suppress the incriminating statements was granted. The government appealed, and the Fourth Circuit Court of Appeals reversed the district court's suppression order. Dickerson appealed to the U.S. Supreme Court, where the case was heard. The Supreme Court reversed the Fourth Circuit and allowed the suppression order to stand. The Court noted that Congress had passed a law, Title 18, U.S.C. Section 3501, which made the admissibility of statements such as Dickerson's turn solely on whether they were made voluntarily, regardless of whether or not a suspect had been given the Miranda warning. This law was interpreted by the U.S. Supreme Court as an attempt to overrule *Miranda* and its influence on confessions of suspects. The Supreme Court held that Congress may not legislatively supersede its decisions when interpreting and

applying the Constitution. The Miranda warning is constitutionally based on two grounds. First, it protects suspects by observing their right against self-incrimination. Second, the due process
clause of the Fourteenth Amendment probes the voluntariness of
confessions through a consideration of the totality of circumstances under which confessions are given. The Supreme Court
also stressed the principle of *stare decisis* and noted that the Miranda warning has become embedded in routine police practice
to the point where the warnings have become a part of the national culture. The U.S. Supreme Court declined to overrule *Miranda,* holding that any departure from precedent should be
supported by some special justification. In the Dickerson case,
such justification was not demonstrated.

Florida v. J. L., 120 S.Ct. 1375 (2000)

In October 1995 in Miami, an anonymous tip was received by police that a young black male was standing at a particular bus stop
wearing a plaid shirt and carrying a gun. Police arrived at the
scene and saw several black males standing at the bus stop, one
of whom was wearing a plaid shirt. The officers saw no firearm,
nor did they observe any illegal conduct. However, they approached one of the boys, J. L., fifteen, and made him put his
hands up, whereupon they conducted a frisk of his person. They
seized a gun from his pocket and arrested him for carrying a concealed weapon. Later at J. L.'s trial, J. L. sought to suppress the
weapon as the fruit of an unlawful search. The trial court granted
the motion and suppressed the weapon as evidence against J. L.;
however, the appellate court reversed the trial court. The Florida
Supreme Court reversed the appellate court, holding that tips
from unknown informants can form the basis for reasonable suspicion only if accompanied by specific indicators of reliability,
such as the correct forecast of a suspect's "not easily predicted"
movements. Because the tip leading to J. L.'s search and weapon
seizure did not provide any such predictions nor did it contain
any other qualifying indication of reliability, the police were not
justified in subjecting J. L. to a search or pat-down and frisk.
Florida prosecutors appealed to the U.S. Supreme Court, which
heard the case. The U.S. Supreme Court upheld the Florida
Supreme Court, holding that anonymous tips lacking any indicators of reliability do not justify stops and frisks whenever and
however they allege the illegal possession of a firearm.

6

Agencies and Organizations

Police misconduct has been prevalent throughout the United States since its inception. Both public and private agencies have been established to minimize or prevent police misconduct. Numerous commissions have been created to investigate allegations of misconduct among law enforcement officers at all levels and in most jurisdictions. Different law enforcement agencies at the federal, state, and local levels have been responsive to the demand for accountability among law enforcement officers by establishing organizations and regulatory bodies to deal with allegations of all types of misconduct.

This chapter presents descriptions and contact information regarding various public and private organizations that endeavor either to investigate police misconduct and control it or to educate and train law enforcement officers so that potential misconduct can be minimized or prevented. Many of these organizations have overlapping goals and objectives, although it is not necessarily the case that these organizations are especially competitive. If substantial duplication of function among different organizations is detected, it is likely coincidental.

Every attempt has been made to provide the most current information available. Some of these organizations have been in existence for many decades, whereas others have only recently been established. Some agencies and commissions have been created for short-term objectives. Internet websites are provided where available. Addresses, telephone numbers, and other relevant contact information are also provided.

Action for Police Accountability:
Community Control of Police (APA)
3128 16th Street
Box 127

San Francisco, CA 94103
(415) 487-5437
Internet: http://www.bayswan.org/APA.html

Originating in 1969 as the Committee to Combat Fascism, Action for Police Accountability (APA) was convened in Oakland, California, for people of diverse ethnicities and nationalities to discuss their struggles for justice throughout the world. One result of this meeting was the formulation and adoption of revisions to various city charters, specifically for San Francisco, Oakland, Berkeley, Richmond, and Alameda. These revisions were directed at heightening accountability of police by their being required to work in areas where they do their policing. Revisions suggested to city councils included requiring that police officers live in precincts where they are employed; seven commissioners would be appointed by a local police control council comprised of fifteen members who would be elected by the community; the councils would have disciplinary power over police officers; and the councils would be able to recall commissioners if they were no longer responsive to community needs.

American Civil Liberties Union (ACLU)
125 Broad Street
New York, NY 10004-2400
(212) 549-2500
Internet: http://www.aclu.org

The American Civil Liberties Union (ACLU) was founded in 1920 by Crystal Eastman and Roger Baldwin. The nonprofit, nonparticsan ACLU had nearly 300,000 members in 2001 with offices in all fifty-one states. Its mission is to fight civil liberties violations whenever and wherever they occur. Most ACLU clients are ordinary people who have suffered injustices because of their race, gender, or disability. The ACLU concerns itself with a variety of issues, including rights of people with AIDS; rights of people sentenced to the death penalty; lesbian, gay, bisexual, and transgender rights; immigrant rights; reproductive freedom; voting rights; women's rights; and workplace rights. The ACLU has approximately 2,000 volunteer attorneys nationwide who close more than 6,000 cases annually. ACLU attorneys appear before the U.S. Supreme Court annually more than any others with the exception of those from the Department of Justice. The ACLU is supported by membership dues and grants from private foundations and individuals.

Community Oriented Policing Services (COPS)
U.S. Department of Justice
Office of Community Oriented Policing Services
1100 Vermont Avenue, N.W.
Washington, DC 20530
(202) 514-2058
Fax: (202) 616-9249
Internet: http://www.usdoj.gov/cops/news_info/legislate/leg_
history.htm

Community Oriented Policing Services (COPS) was established
in 1994 by Attorney General Janet Reno. The enabling legislation
was the Violent Crime Control and Law Enforcement Act of 1994.
The goal of COPS is to promote community policing and create
100,000 new police officer positions throughout the United
States. Presently, the COPS program has funded more than
100,000 police officers with $8.8 billion during 1994-2000. COPS
provides grant monies for individual police departments
throughout the United States as a means of improving their effectiveness and crime prevention capabilities.

Community Policing Consortium (CPC)
1726 M Street, N.W., Suite 801
Washington, DC 20036
(800) 833-3085
Fax: (202) 833-9295
Internet: http://www.communitypolicing.org

The Community Policing Consortium (CPC) is administered and
funded by the U.S. Department of Justice, Office of Community
Oriented Policing Services (COPS). CPC was established in 1993
as a multiphased project. The CPC's primary mission is to deliver
community policing training and technical assistance to police
departments and sheriff's offices that are designated COPS
grantees. Training sessions are held at the state/regional and
county levels and use curricula reflecting the breadth of the
CPC's collective police knowledge. For agencies that need
overview training, the CPC offers orientation to community
policing as well as sheriff-specific sessions that address the individual agency's unique issues and obstacles. Training in problem
solving, developing strategies, managing calls for service and de-
ploying personnel, building community partnerships, and understanding cultural diversity, as well as train-the-trainer
workshops are available to agencies searching for more specific

courses. The CPC is comprised of five organizations: the International Association of Chiefs of Police (IACP); the National Sheriffs' Association (NSA); the Police Executive Research Forum (PERF); the Police Foundation (PF); and the National Organization of Black Law Enforcement Executives (NOBLE). These four organizations (1) researched and produced the CPC monograph entitled, *Understanding Community Policing: A Framework for Action;* (2) provided training and technical assistance to five community policing demonstration sites; and (3) conducted meetings of community policing leaders.

Fraternal Order of Police (FOP)
National Legislative Office
309 Massachusetts Avenue, N.E.
Washington, DC 20002
(202) 547-8189
Fax: (202) 547-8190
e-mail: natlfop@wizard.net
Internet: http://www.grandlodgefop.org

The Fraternal Order of Police (FOP) was formed on May 14, 1915 by two Pittsburgh, Pennsylvania, patrol officers, Martin Toole and Delbert Nagle, who were concerned about making life better for themselves and other officers in Pittsburgh as well as in other jurisdictions. They formed Fort Pitt Lodge #1, deciding on this name because of the anti-union sentiment prevalent at the time. They advised the current Pittsburgh mayor, Joe Armstrong, that the FOP would be the means to bring grievances before the mayor or city council. Before the formation of the FOP, no organization existed to present grievances to the city or initiate change through the legislature. In 2000, there were more than two thousand local FOP lodges, with a membership of 290,000 officers nationally. The FOP, the largest professional police organization in the United States, is dedicated to increasing confidence in the police to the benefit of peace, as well as protecting the public.

Human Rights Watch (HRW)
350 Fifth Avenue, 34th Floor
New York, NY 10118-3299
(212) 290-4700
Fax: (212) 612-4333
e-mail: hrwnyc@hrw.org
Internet: http://www.hrw.org

Human Rights Watch (HRW) is dedicated to protecting the human rights of persons around the world. HRW stands with victims and activists to prevent discrimination, to uphold political freedom, to protect people from inhumane conduct in wartime, and to bring offenders to justice. HRW investigates human rights violations and holds abusers accountable. HRW challenges governments and those who hold power to end abusive practices and respect international rights law.

Independent Police Auditor (IPA)
2 North Second Street, Suite 93
San Jose, CA 95113
(408) 794-6226
Fax: (408) 977-1053
Internet: http://www.ci.san-jose.ca.us/ipa/home.html

The office of Independent Police Auditor (IPA) was established in 1993 to audit investigations of citizen complaints of misconduct by San Jose, California, police officers. The IPA prepares public reports containing a summary of issues, problems, and trends. Also, the IPA makes recommendations regarding department policies and additional officer training. Information is made available to the public through radio, television, and presentations at community meetings.

Institute of Public Administration (IPA)
411 Lafayette Street, Suite 303
New York, NY 10003
(212) 992-9898
Fax: (212) 995-4876
e-mail: mp553@nyu.edu
Internet: http://www.theipa.org

The Institute of Public Administration (IPA) was established in 1906 in New York City and was originally named the Bureau of Municipal Research. During the next seven years, several such bureaus were established in several other cities. The IPA was established to create more effective public administration of governmental agencies and organizations. Various training programs have been sponsored by the IPA to train administrators to perform different supervisory functions in both the public and private sectors. Both state and federal government operations have been studied by the IPA, and numerous surveys have been conducted in order to evaluate, improve, and maximize the effectiveness of a variety of agencies. An early director of the IPA was Bruce Smith, who focused the attention of the IPA on police administration. Through Smith's guidance and interests, the IPA investigated ways of improving the effectiveness of police operations in municipalities both in the United States and abroad. The IPA has acquired a truly international focus in recent years, assisting various countries and major world cities in their planning and operations. A 1999 study was conducted of former New York City mayor Rudolph Giuliani's accomplishments, including his crime prevention efforts.

International Association of Chiefs of Police (IACP)
515 North Washington Street
Alexandria, VA 22314
(703) 836-6767
Fax: (703) 836-4543
e-mail: information@theiacp.org
Internet: http://www.theiacp.org

Founded in 1893, the International Association of Chiefs of Police's (IACP's) goals are to advance the science and art of police services; to develop and disseminate improved administrative, technical, and operational practices and promote their use in police work; to foster police cooperation and the exchange of information and experience among police administrators throughout the world; to bring about recruitment and training of qualified persons in the police profession; and to encourage adherence of all police officers to high professional standards of performance and conduct. Since 1893, the IACP has been serving the needs of the law enforcement community. Many historically acclaimed programs have been launched. Professionally recognized programs such as the Federal Bureau of Investigation Identification Division and the Uniform Crime Records System can trace their origins back to the IACP. The IACP was instrumental in forwarding breakthrough technologies and philosophies from the early years to the present. From spearheading the national use of fingerprint identification to partnering in a consortium on community policing to gathering top experts on criminal justice, the government, and education for summits on violence, homicide, and youth violence, the IACP has realized our responsibility to positively effect the goals of law enforcement. The IACP is a member of the Community Policing Consortium.

International Association of Women Police (IAWP)
Jan Taylor, Administrative Assistant
RR #1, Box 149
Deer Isle, ME 04627
e-mail: iawp@iawp.org
Internet: http://www.iawp.org

The International Association of Women Police (IAWP) was first organized as the International Policewomen's Association in 1915. The charter was adopted in 1916 in Washington, D.C. In 1956, a meeting in San Diego, California, of the International Policewomen's Association resulted in the change of its name to the International Association of Women Police. The IAWP promotes the idea of separate women's bureaus in order to foster equality of opportunity for the advancement of women in police ranks. The first biannual meeting was held in 1957 at Purdue University in Lafayette, Indiana. In 1963 the IAWP began holding three-day seminars, which subsequently were expanded to become training conferences for research conducted by universities and professional organizations. These seminars attract experts in diverse criminal justice fields who share their views and disseminate important information to the membership. Presently the IAWP includes members from fourteen different countries. Affiliate chapters of the IAWP have been formed in various countries, cities, states, and provinces in order to provide support and training to officers who cannot attend the IAWP training conferences. Although IAWP exists primarily to benefit female police officers, male officers have been permitted membership in the IAWP since 1976. Generally, the goals of the IAWP include increasing professionalism in police work; furthering the use of women in law enforcement/police service; and providing a forum for sharing developments in police administration.

International Foundation for Protection Officers (IFPO)
P.O. Box 771329
Naples, FL 34107-1329
(941) 430-0534
Fax: (941) 430-0533
Internet: http://www.ifpo.com

The International Foundation for Protection Officers (IFPO) was established as a nonprofit organization in January 1988 for the purpose of facilitating the training and certification needs of protection officers and security supervisors from both the commercial and proprietary sectors. The foundation has established a professional association, and associate and corporate memberships are available to individuals or organizations involved in the security industry. Two comprehensive distance delivery–styled courses are offered: the *Certified Protection Officer (CPO)* program, and the *Certified Security Supervisor (CSS)* program. Both programs are designed to be completed at a self-paced schedule of home study. Many corporations and institutions have adopted these programs and integrated them with their existing staff development process and training guidelines. A key objective is to keep professionals who perform private law enforcement functions current on trends within the security industry and enhance life safety and property protection.

National Association of Police Organizations, Inc. (NAPO)
750 First Street, N.E., Suite 920
Washington, DC 20002
(202) 842-4420
Fax: (202) 842-4396
e-mail: napo@erols.com
Internet: http://www.napo.org

The National Association of Police Organizations (NAPO) is a coalition of police unions and associations from across the United States that serves to advance the interests of law enforcement officers nationwide through legislative and legal advocacy, political action, and education. Founded in 1978, NAPO is now the strongest unified voice supporting law enforcement officers in the United States. NAPO represents more than 4,000 police unions and associations, 225,000 sworn law enforcement officers, 11,000 retired officers, and more than 100,000 citizens who share a common dedication to fair and effective crime control and law enforcement.

National Center for Women and Policing (NCWP)
8105 West Third Street
Los Angeles, CA 90048
(323) 651-2532
e-mail: womencops@feminist.org
Internet: http://www.feminist.org/police/ncwpContact.html

A division of the Feminist Majority Foundation, the National Center for Women and Policing (NCWP) promotes increasing the numbers of women at all ranks of law enforcement as a strategy for improving police response to violence against women, reducing police brutality and excessive force, and strengthening community policing reforms. The NCWP provides training, research, education, and action programs, focusing in three major areas: (1) educational campaigns to raise awareness among decision makers and the general public about the benefits of increasing the numbers of women in policing; (2) innovative leadership training and advocacy programs to increase the numbers of women in policing and policy-making positions, including strategies to increase recruitment, hiring, and promotion of women and eliminate sexual discrimination and harassment of women officers; and (3) promotion of specialized Family Violence Response Protocols within law enforcement agencies for more effective police response to family violence crimes, including police family violence.

National Coalition on Police Accountability (N-COPA)

59 East Van Buren, #2418
Chicago, IL 60605
(312) 663-5392
Fax: (312) 663-5396
Internet: http://websyr.edu/~nkrhodes/N-COPA.html

N-COPA is an organization of religious, community, and legal groups and progressive law enforcement representatives working to hold police accountable to their communities through public education, community organizing, legislation, litigation, and promotion of empowered independent oversight. N-COPA was established in 1996 by Citizens Alert, a nonprofit organization.

National Drug Enforcement Officers Association (NDEOA)

FBI Academy
P.O. Box 1475
Quantico, VA 22134-1475
(202) 298-9653
Internet: http://www.ndeoa.org

The National Drug Enforcement Officers Association (NDEOA) is dedicated to promote the cooperation, education, and exchange of information among all law enforcement agencies involved in the enforcement of controlled substance laws. The NDEOA also sponsors seminars to train law enforcement officers in law enforcement tactics and operations relating to drug enforcement. Information concerning the latest changes in U.S. drug laws is exchanged on a regular basis at national and regional events. This information includes ways in which the drug laws affect citizen rights in the enforcement process.

National Labor Relations Board (NLRB)
1099 14th Street
Washington, DC 20570-0001
(202) 273-1991
Fax: (202) 273-4270
Internet: http://www.nlrb.gov

The National Labor Relations Board (NLRB) is an independent federal agency created by Congress in 1935 to administer the National Labor Relations Act, the primary law governing relations between unions and employees in the private sector. The statute guarantees the right of employees to organize and bargain collectively with their employers or to refrain from all such activity. All local, state, and federal law enforcement agencies are within the jurisdiction of the NLRB. The NLRB investigates complaints made by individuals, employers, or labor organizations of unfair labor practices and engages in good faith bargaining to resolve issues. Bargaining issues include wages, hours, and other terms or conditions of employment.

National Organization of Black Law Enforcement Executives (NOBLE)
4609 Pinecrest Office Park Drive, Suite F
Alexandria, VA 22312-1442
(703) 658-1529
Fax: (703) 658-9479
e-mail: noble@noblenatl.org
Internet: http://www.noblenatl.org

The National Organization of Black Law Enforcement Executives (NOBLE) was founded in 1976 to address crime in urban low-income areas. With the recognition that black law enforcement executives could have a significantly more effective impact upon the criminal justice system through a unified voice, NOBLE was created. NOBLE's membership is located around the country, with more than thirty-five local chapters representing state, local, and federal law enforcement executives. NOBLE's mission is to work with communities to foster greater involvement and cooperation with criminal justice agencies, have a positive impact on crime and violence, unify the impact of black law enforcement officers at the executive levels, provide black law enforcement executives with a platform where ideas and opinions can be addressed, and disseminate information pertinent to minority law enforcement executives. NOBLE also provides training, research, and consultation on criminal justice issues. NOBLE is a member of the Community Policing Consortium.

National Sheriffs' Association (NSA)
1450 Duke Street
Alexandria, VA 22314-3490
(703) 836-7827
Internet: http://www.sheriffs.org/home.htm

The National Sheriffs' Association (NSA) is a nonprofit organization dedicated to raising the level of professionalism among law enforcement leaders across the nation. Since 1940, the NSA has been involved in numerous programs to enable sheriffs, deputies, chiefs of police, and others in law enforcement to perform their jobs in the best possible manner and to better serve the people in their counties or jurisdictions. NSA offers training, information, and recognition to sheriffs, deputies, and other policing officials throughout the nation and has forged cooperative relationships with local, state, and federal law enforcement. NSA, headquartered in Alexandria, Virginia, serves as a center of a vast network of information, filling requests for information daily and enabling criminal justice professionals to locate the information and programs they need. NSA recognizes the need to seek information from the membership, particularly the sheriff and the state sheriffs' associations, in order to meet the needs and concerns of individual members. NSA also assists sheriffs' offices and departments in locating and preparing grant applications for state and federal grant funding. The NSA is a member of the Community Policing Consortium.

National Sheriffs' Educational Foundation, Inc. (NSEF)
1450 Duke Street
Alexandria, VA 22314-3490
(703) 836-7827
Internet: http://www.sheriffs.org

The National Sheriffs' Educational Foundation (NSEF) is sponsored by the National Sheriffs' Association. It is registered in Washington, D.C. The concern, direction, and management of the affairs of NSEF is vested in the board of directors, which pursues such policies, programs, and principles as are authorized by the

Articles of Incorporation and the laws of the District of Columbia. NSEF is established for educational purposes and to encourage and promote fair and efficient administration of criminal justice throughout the United States and its territories. Additional objectives include (1) to encourage protection of the jurisdiction of the sheriff as a constitutional or statutory officer and to support sheriffs throughout the United States in their efforts to discharge their law enforcement, corrections, and judicial responsibilities in a fair, efficient, and professional manner; (2) to cooperate with public and private organizations dedicated to the reduction of crime and to the improvement of law enforcement and other criminal justice systems and programs; (3) to develop and encourage the practice of high standards of personal and professional conduct among sheriffs and other criminal justice practitioners; (4) to conduct such research, study, and investigation as may be necessary and advisable to develop information, knowledge, and data that would be useful in improving the administration of criminal justice; (5) to promote the law enforcement profession by providing appropriate educational courses in cooperation with institutions of higher learning; and (6) to conduct competitions and make awards for outstanding services to all areas of the criminal justice community.

National Sheriffs' Institute (NSI)
1450 Duke Street
Alexandria, VA 22314-3490
(703) 836-7827
Internet: http://www.sheriffs.org

The National Sheriffs' Institute (NSI) is an executive development program sponsored by the National Sheriffs' Association. It was established in 1972 to provide executive management and training for sheriffs and their command personnel. NSI is recognized as a source of essential information for both sheriffs and command officials in complex jobs. The NSI classes, usually held at the FBI Academy in Quantico, Virginia, and the National Academy for the National Institute of Corrections in Longmont, Colorado, are much sought after and held in high esteem by the thousands of sheriffs and command officials who have attended. Through the NSI and its classes, sheriffs and their command officials hear recognized experts in such diverse fields as jail administration, liability issues, crime prevention, budget preparation, and public and employee relations.

**October 22 National Day of Protest to
Stop Police Brutality, Repression, and the
Criminalization of a Generation (NDP)**
P.O. Box 2627
New York, NY 10009
e-mail: Oct22@unstoppable.com
Internet: http://www.october22.org

The October 22 National Day of Protest to Stop Police Brutality, Repression, and the Criminalization of a Generation (NDP) was formed on October 22, 1995. This coalition was established to protest police brutality in the United States. NDP founders have brought together numerous family members of police murder victims and survivors of police brutality to testify about how brutal police officers have affected their lives.

Peace and Justice Works (PJW)
P.O. Box 42456
Portland, OR 97242
(503) 236-3065
Internet: http://www.rdrop.com/~pjw

Peace and Justice Works (PJW), formerly known as Portland Peaceworks, is an Oregon nonprofit corporation established in 1992. PJW's main purpose is to educate the general public on important issues including but not limited to peace, justice, the environment, and human rights. PJW created the Portland Copwatch/People Overseeing Police Study Group (PCPOPSG), which investigates incidents in which police misconduct is alleged.

The Police Complaint Center (PCC)
(850) 894-6819
Fax: (850) 574-3256
Internet: http://www.policeabuse.com

The Police Complaint Center (PCC) is a national nonprofit organization that provides assistance to victims of police misconduct. Using available technology, the PCC documents and investigates alleged incidents of police abuse. The primary service is to assist victims of misconduct with reporting complaints to appropriate enforcement agencies. The PCC assists with the filing of complaints because it believes that accountability is critical to the public service mission of police organizations. PCC efforts are not intended to hinder the police nor to embarrass officers without cause. However, the PCC is sure that cases of misconduct and failure to receive complaints by the police must be publicized to prevent their reoccurrence.

Police Executive Research Forum (PERF)
1120 Connecticut Avenue, N.W., Suite 930
Washington, DC 20036
(202) 466-7820
Internet: http://www.policeforum.org/perfhome.html

The Police Executive Research Forum (PERF) is a national membership organization of progressive police executives from the largest city, county, and state law enforcement agencies. PERF is dedicated to improving policing and advancing professionalism through research and involvement in public policy debate. PERF was incorporated in 1977 to: (1) improve the delivery of police services and crime control nationwide; (2) encourage debate of police and criminal justice issues within the law enforcement community; (3) implement and promote the use of law enforcement research; and (4) provide national leadership, technical assistance, and vital management services to police agencies. PERF has published *Police Quarterly*, which was subsequently taken over by Sage Publications. PERF is a member of the Community Policing Consortium.

Police Foundation (PF)
1201 Connecticut Avenue, N.W.
Washington, DC 20036
(202) 833-1460
Fax: (202) 659-9149
e-mail: pfinfo@policefoundation.org
Internet: http://www.policefoundation.org

Founded in 1970 through a Ford Foundation grant, the Police Foundation (PF) has as its purpose helping police be more effective in doing their job, whether it be such duties as deterring robberies, intervening in potentially injurious family disputes, or working to improve relationships between the police and the communities they serve. To accomplish its mission, the PF works closely with police officers and police agencies across the country, and it is in their hard work and contributions that PF's accomplishments are rooted. The PF works as a catalyst for change and an advocate for new ideas, in restating and reminding the public about the fundamental purposes of policing, and in ensuring that an important link remains intact between the police and the public they serve. The PF is a member of the Community Policing Consortium.

**Portland Copwatch/People Overseeing
Police Study Group (PCPOPSG)**
P.O. Box 42456
Portland, OR 97242
(503) 236-3065
e-mail: copwatch@teleport.com
Internet: http://www.teleport.com/~copwatch

The Portland Copwatch/People Overseeing Police Study Group (PCPOPSG) is a grassroots group promoting police accountability through citizen action. It was formed as a project of Peace and Justice Works (PJW) in 1992. PCPOPSG also participates in community forums on police accountability, including meetings of Portland, Oregon's review board, also known as the Police Chief's Forum. The PCPOPSG publishes a newsletter, *People's Police Report,* which includes information about local and national police accountability efforts. Police behaviors are observed in different parts of Portland, and contacts are made and information is spread throughout the community. The goals of PCPOPSG are to (1) empower victims of police misconduct to pursue their grievances, with the goal of resolving individual cases and preventing future occurrences; (2) educate the general public, and in particular target groups of police abuse, on their rights and responsibilities; and (3) promote and monitor an effective system for civilian oversight of police.

Women Peace Officers Association (WPOA)
7355 Dayton Avenue
Hesperia, CA 92345
Internet: http://www.wpoaca.com/contact.html

The Women Peace Officers Association (WPOA) was founded in California in 1928. A cofounder was Alice Stebbins Wells, the first female police officer in the United States, who served as the WPOA's first president. The WPOA meets annually and convenes seminars focused on special topics of interest to women in law enforcement. One concern of the WPOA is the equal treatment of women who perform law enforcement functions. The WPOA works cooperatively with other organizations to further the interests of women in law enforcement.

7

Print and Nonprint Resources

Resource materials in print about police misconduct and its various forms are abundant. This chapter divides print resources into three types: (1) books, journal articles, and dissertations; (2) journals, magazines, bulletins, and newsletters; and (3) government documents and agency publications. Books include texts and trade publications featuring particular topics related to police deviance of all types. Journal articles are frequently research investigations of various aspects of police misconduct in diverse police departments and organizations throughout the United States. Also, doctoral dissertations or theses, which are usually empirical studies, are eventually converted into articles and published in journals or short books. It is believed important to include some of these dissertations in the listing below because of their relevance to police misconduct and easy accessibility through university microfilms.

The Bureau of Justice Statistics (BJS), a division of the U.S. Department of Justice, collects much information about all criminal justice topics, including police misconduct. Many government periodicals and other documents are available free to the public upon written request. When materials are purchased from the BJS or U.S. Government Printing Office, government charges are usually minimal, depending upon the size and number of documents requested. An annual publication containing some information about the police and different types of misconduct is the *Sourcebook of Criminal Justice Statistics*. This publication is also available in CD-ROM format, again for a nominal charge. The information on the CD-ROM may be downloaded and printed to facilitate one's research.

Books, Journal Articles, and Dissertations

Adams, Kenneth. **"Measuring the Prevalence of Police Abuse of Force."** In eds. William A. Geller and Hans Toch, *And Justice for All: Understanding and Controlling Police Abuse of Force.* Washington, DC: Police Executive Research Forum, 1995. Pages 61–97.

This chapter examines the extensiveness of the use of force among U.S. police. The etiology of the police use of excessive force is examined, and factors are investigated that contribute to its use. Administrative measures are outlined to minimize the use of excessive force against civilians. Included are internal and external measures to control excessive force by various types of punishment methods, including internal affairs and civilian complaint review boards.

Alpert, Geoffrey P. **"A Factorial Analysis of Police Pursuit Driving Decisions: A Research Note."** *Justice Quarterly* 15:347–359, 1998.

This article examines police pursuit driving, which has become an important public policy concern and topic of research. The study reported concerns the attitudes of police officers and supervisors from four different agencies concerning the continuation of a pursuit. The most influential factor on the officers' opinions is the offense for which the suspect is wanted. This one factor is more than twice as important as the environmental factors such as chase area, traffic conditions, and weather.

Amnesty International. *United States of America: Police Brutality and Excessive Force in the New York City Police Department.* New York: Amnesty International, 1996. 72 pages.

This report presents the results of an investigation into allegations of ill treatment, deaths in custody, and unjustified shootings by police officers in the New York City Police Department. Data are drawn from records, dating from the late 1980s to early 1996, of more than ninety cases of alleged excessive force by officers. Allegations include beatings with various instruments and shootings in violation of the department's own guidelines. Though the male, female, and juvenile victims had a variety of social, racial, and ethnic backgrounds, evidence suggests that the large majority were racial minorities, particularly African Americans and those of Latin American or Asian descent. In many of the cases, international standards as well as U.S. law appear to have been violated with impunity, a partial result of police officers' "code of silence." Recommendations are offered.

Babovic, Budimir. **"Police Brutality or Police Torture?"** *Policing: An International Journal of Police Strategies and Management* 23:374–380, 2000.

An essay on the use of force by the police distinguishes between police brutality and police torture. Police torture is a distinctive category of police brutality. It is committed when officers use force with a view to achieving a task or design, most frequently to extort confessions or to induce compliance. Distinguishing between brutality and torture is necessary because the two differ from each other in their sources and motivations, in the difficulties of their uncovering, and in the recognized and admitted indispensability of their repression. This distinction is useful for addressing the question of whether the relationship between brutality and military status and spirit of the police can be established. Accountability and oversight should be considered as particularly important issues in confronting police brutality.

Barkan, Steven E., and Steven F. Cohn. **"Racial Prejudice and Support by Whites for Police Use of Force: A Research Note."** *Justice Quarterly* 15:743–753, 1998.

Recent research suggests that whites' approval of police use of force may derive partly from racial prejudice against African Americans. A study tests this possibility using data from the 1990 wave of the General Social Survey, a national multistage probability sample of the noninstitutionalized English-speaking U.S. population. The 1990 wave included a special module and other items on racial prejudice. As predicted, negative stereotypes of African Americans contributed to whites' support for police use of excessive force. Theoretical and policy implications of this finding are discussed.

Beattie-Repetti, Cheryl Ann. *The Politics of Civilian Review: Police Accountability in Washington, DC and New York City, 1948–1974.* Ann Arbor, MI: University Microfilms International, 1996. 405 pages.

A study examines the historical development of the civilian review of complaints against police in Washington, D.C., and New York City from 1948 to 1973. A modified version of a structural contradictions theory of lawmaking provides the model; newspapers, government documents, and archival materials provide the data. Political conflicts concerning restraint of police brutality and the creation of civilian review boards did not emerge directly from the contradictions of policing, but were fostered by an interaction between these contradictions and those of race. The broader racial conflicts significantly affected African-American interpretations of police behavior. But civilian review did not ease conflicts between police and minority communities and has been limited by legal and bureaucratic constraints. Civilian review has symbolic value as a form of democratic accountability, and its use has mobilized African-American political resources. Though Washington's more independent form of civilian review does not appear to have reduced conflict over policing, its use has introduced new standards of police conduct and sustained a greater proportion of complaints.

Bonswor, Stephen E. *Police Criminal Misconduct: Its Effect on Management by the Year 2001.* Sacramento, CA: Peace Officer Standards and Training (POST), 1992. 96 pages.

A report that projects the impact of police criminal misconduct on the management of police agencies by the year 2001. Topics consider detection of criminal conduct, consequences of civil liability resulting from police misconduct, and the impact of external corruption controls. A strategic plan and transition management plan for law enforcement agencies are provided.

Brandl, Steven G., and David E. Barlow. *Classics in Policing.* Cincinnati, OH: Anderson Publishing Company, 1996. 378 pages.

This book provides students with easy access to actual words and ideas offered by scholars in classic contributions to police theory and research. Students can evaluate the writings directly and be challenged to construct their own interpretations regarding the significance of each work. Selections include articles about police discretion and its abuses, the history and role of the police in the United States, and selected instances of police corruption.

Burris, John L., and Catherine Whitney. *Blue v. Black: Let's End the Conflict between the Cops and Minorities.* New York: St. Martin's Press, 1999. 240 pages.

A journalistic study chronicles numerous incidents of police brutality against minorities in the United States from 1980 to the present. Newspaper files, court records, and interviews with police and members of minorities provide the data. Solutions for ending the cycle of police and civilian distrust are offered.

Chin, Gabriel J., and Scott C. Wells. **"The 'Blue Wall of Silence' as Evidence of Bias and Motive to Lie: A New Approach to Police Perjury."** *University of Pittsburgh Law Review* 59:233–299, 1998.

A legal essay and review explores types of police perjury, especially the "blue wall of silence," an unwritten code in which officers are unwilling to disclose perjury or other misconduct by other officers. The code of silence has been exposed through various police commissions, media coverage, and academic studies, but nonetheless remains a deeply ingrained problem throughout U.S. police forces. Breaking the code of silence will not be easy and cannot be accomplished until it is acknowledged and confronted by police departments and the courts. A suggested approach for the courts involves admitting extrinsic evidence about the code and issuing a jury instruction relating to suspect testimony by police officers.

Cordner, Gary W., and Robert Sheehan. *Police Administration.* 4th ed. Cincinnati, OH: Anderson Publishing Company, 1999. 517 pages.

An up-to-date comprehensive introduction, this revised text examines police administration from multiple perspectives, including a systems view as well as a traditional orientation. Topics include ways of improving police officer effectiveness through administration, improving police-community relations, and minimizing police deviance and misconduct.

Crank, John P., and Michael A. Caldero. *Police Ethics: The Corruption of Noble Cause.* Cincinnati, OH: Anderson Publishing Company, 2000. 275 pages.

This book provides an examination of "noble cause," how it emerges as a fundamental principle of police ethics, and how it can provide the basis for corruption. The noble cause—a commitment to "doing something about bad people"—is a central "ends-based" police ethic that can be corrupted whenever officers violate the law on behalf of personally held moral values. This book is about the power that police use to do their work and how it can corrupt the police at the individual and organizational levels. The book provides students of policing with a realistic understanding of the kinds of problems they will confront in the practice of police work. Developing their work from a broad scholarly and professional base, the authors challenge contemporary views of the police on topics such as hiring procedures, public order policing, police discretion, and fundamental ethical problems that underlie police work.

del Carmen, Rolando V., and Jeffery T. Walker. *Briefs of Leading Cases in Law Enforcement.* 4th ed. Cincinnati, OH: Anderson Publishing Company, 2000. 279 pages.

The fourth edition of this popular reference book briefs numerous cases dealing with topics of primary importance to law enforcement officials. Cases cited include those relating to lawsuits against the police alleging police misconduct, violations of civil rights, and police corruption.

Delattre, Edwin J. *Character and Cops: Ethics in Policing.* 3rd ed. Washington, DC: AEI Press, 1996. 371 pages.

The third edition of a textbook on police ethics examines the moral problems frequently faced by police officers and managers as they do their jobs. Chapter topics include: the police mission; discretion; public corruption for profit; authority and reform in controlling corruption; leadership and the character of a department; illegal narcotics—moral issues and public policy; the fundamentals of character and training; deliberation and moral problems in training; deadly force and guilt; ethical ideals, youth violence and gang enforcement; police, the O. J. Simpson trial, and race; and the spirit of public service and individual conscience.

Escobar, Edward J. *Race, Police, and the Making of Political Identity: Mexican Americans and the Los Angeles Police Department, 1900–1945.* Berkeley, CA: University of California Press, 1999.

A historical study, covering the period from 1900 to 1945, examines the changing relationship between the Los Angeles (California) Police Department (LAPD) and Mexican-American city residents. Data were obtained from law enforcement records, newspaper and journal articles, and other secondary sources. During this period, the relationship between the LAPD and Mexican Americans evolved toward extreme mutual hostility and suspicion. By the 1940s, police interactions with Mexican Americans, especially youths, led the police to believe that Mexican Americans were a criminally inclined group that required harsh treatment. Subsequently, Mexican Americans came to see police as regular violators of their rights and chronic abusers of their community. To end violations and the abuse, many people in the Mexican-American community came to believe they would have to politically organize themselves to combat police misconduct. The end result of such mutual suspicions were the Zoot Suit Riots.

Fogel, David. **"The Investigation and Disciplining of Police Misconduct."** *Police Studies* 10:1–15, 1987.

A study compares how three major western cities (London, Paris, and Chicago) respond to citizen complaints alleging police misconduct. In Britain, the new Police Complaints Authority (PCA) supervises police investigations of police misconduct. PCA may change a recommended discipline and seek indictments in cooperation with the director of Public Prosecutions. In the French system of police discipline, civilians (except for police union representatives) are not involved . The Paris International Geodynamics Service (police of the police) and the national Inspection Generale de la Police Nationale handle all complaints and disciplinary cases, although civilians investigate allegations. In Chicago, the police department's Office of Professional Standards (all civilians) investigates and recommends discipline in sustained cases against police officers.

Freeman, Alexa P. **"Unscheduled Departures: The Circumvention of Just Sentencing for Police Brutality."** *Hastings Law Journal* 47:677–777, 1996.

A legal essay argues that police brutality is an egregious crime, the harm of which extends beyond the physical and psychological injuries to victims. Situated in a social reality of acute racial divisions and radically different perceptions of the criminal justice system, police brutality serves as a lightning rod for widespread public fear and anger. Failure to control the police brings with it terrible social consequences and undermines the rule of law. In the United States, state and federal governments have long neglected the reality of police brutality. Freeman argues that it is incumbent on the U.S. Sentencing Commission to reaffirm its intent to maintain strong police brutality sentences by amending its guidelines.

Gaines, Larry K., Victor E. Kappeler, and Joseph B. Vaughn. *Policing in America*. 3rd ed. Cincinnati, OH: Anderson Publishing Company, 1999. 438 pages.

This comprehensive core text provides an overview of law enforcement topics, integrating major empirical findings and theory-based research findings in the field with a thorough analysis of contemporary policing problems. The issues-oriented discussion focuses on critical concerns facing American police, including personnel systems, organization and management, operations, discretion, ethics and deviance, civil liability, and police-community relations.

Geller, William A., and Hans Toch eds. *And Justice for All: Understanding and Controlling Police Abuse of Force*. Washington, DC: Police Executive Research Forum, 1995. 372 pages.

This collection of selected articles highlights different applications of the use of excessive force by police under diverse circumstances. Articles included examine the reasons why officers chose to use excessive force in those incidents and how they could have responded differently. Alternative strategies are provided and recommendations are made concerning administrative and policy changes in different police departments to developed more standardized and less injurious ways of effecting arrests of criminal suspects.

Geller, William A., and Hans Toch, eds. *Police Violence: Understanding and Controlling Police Abuse of Force*. New Haven, CT: Yale University Press, 1996. 379 pages.

An anthology of fifteen previously unpublished papers contains theoretical and practical perspectives on police abuse of force. Carl B. Klockars explores the implications of definitions of police use of excessive force for mechanisms appropriate to its control. Robert E. Worden connects theories of police behavior to new evidence on the use of force by police. Kenneth Adams discusses problems in measuring the prevalence of police abuse of force. Hans Toch examines the violence-prone police officer. Timothy J. Flanagan and Michael S. Vaughn address public opinion about police abuse of force. Hubert G. Locke considers the role of race in the abuse of police power. J. Douglas Grant and Joan Grant explore officer selection and the prevention of excessive force. James J. Fyfe describes training to reduce police-civilian violence. David Lester addresses officers' attitudes toward police use of force. George L. Kelling and Robert B. Kliesmet discuss police unions, police culture, and use of force. Douglas W. Perez and William Ker Muir explore administrative review of alleged police brutality. Wayne A. Kerstetter examines procedural justice and the review of citizen complaints. Mary M. Cheh ponders whether lawsuits are an answer to police brutality. David H. Bayley surveys police brutality abroad. William A. Geller and Hans Toch investigate ways of understanding and controlling police abuse of force.

Giordo, Michel. **"Undercover Probes of Police Corruption: Risk Factors in Proactive Internal Affairs Investigations."** *Behavioral Sciences and the Law* 16:479–496, 1998.

A study examines the role of cognitive and organizational factors in police managers' decisions to initiate internal undercover investigations of officer corruption. Questionnaires centering on three scenarios of police misconduct—conducting a "shakedown" of drug dealers, extracting sexual favors from a woman, and accepting free meals at a restaurant—were completed by 217 mid- to upper-level police managers. Although 90 percent of the managers endorsed an undercover investigation in cases of serious misconduct, only 45 percent supported an undercover probe of accepting free meals. Endorsing an undercover probe of minor misconduct was associated with a manager's Machiavellian and bureaucratic attitudes and was unrelated to familiarity with internal affairs or criminal undercover investigations. The study found that the absence of guidelines for invoking undercover internal investigations can lead to inappropriate use or overuse of those investigations.

Green, Mark. *Investigation of the New York City Police Department's Response to Civilian Complaints of Police Misconduct: Interim Report.* New York: Office of the New York Public Advocate and the Accountability Project, 1999. 37 pages.

This publication reports an investigation by the New York City Public Advocate's office into the city police department's response to civilian complaints of police misconduct. Data were obtained from the records of 283 cases of misconduct substantiated by the Civilian Complaint Review Board (CCRB) involving allegations against 420 officers between 1994 and 1997. Some 90 percent of the time the police department rejected, without conducting its own investigation, the CCRB's conclusion that legally sufficient evidence existed that the officer had engaged in misconduct. A series of cases suggested that the Public Advocate's Office may not have been adequately prepared to present the case or was insufficiently aggressive in pursuing it. More than 72 percent of officers whose cases were reviewed had a history of misconduct but were not disciplined. It may be that the Public Advocate's Office may have failed to prosecute cases because of institutional bias.

Greene, Judith A. **"Zero Tolerance: A Case Study of Police Policies and Practices in New York City."** *Crime and Delinquency* 45:171–187, 1999.

The police reforms introduced in New York City by Police Commissioner William Bratton during 1994 and 1996 have been hailed by Mayor Rudolph Giuliani as the epitome of "zero-tolerance" policing, and he credits those reforms for winning dramatic reductions in the city's crime rate. An essay and review examine the negative effects of the city's reliance on a highly aggres-sive, traditional law enforcement style. As the crime rate has gone down, the number of complaints filed before the Civilian Complaint Review Board has jumped skyward, as has the number of lawsuits alleging police misconduct and abuse of force. Comparison of crime rates, arrest statistics, and citizen complaints in New York City with those in San Diego, where a more problem-oriented community policing strategy has been adopted, gives strong evidence that effective crime control can be achieved while producing fewer negative impacts on urban neighborhoods.

Hall, John C. **"Due Process and Deadly Force: When Police Conduct Shocks the Conscience."** *FBI Law Enforcement Bulletin* 68:27–32, 1999.

Several different constitutional amendments are examined in this article, which seeks to determine conditions under which deadly force ought to be applied when subduing dangerous suspects. Recommendations relate to improved training to provide officers with the clearest possible guidance in deadly force situations. Constitutional rights of citizens must be considered, but these rights' considerations must be balanced against the jeopardy facing officers who are attempting to subdue dangerous suspects. The due process standard is examined and the conditions under which officer safety override the due process standard are described and considered.

Harrison, Bob. **"Noble Cause Corruption and the Police Ethic."** *FBI Law Enforcement Bulletin* 68:1–7, 1999.

Police officers are viewed as instruments of morality. This essay examines the moral underpinnings of police work and operations and the factors impinging upon law enforcement officers that may cause them to depart from their moral principles. Various conflicts of interest are described and scenarios presented with possible solutions for minimizing corruption and managing to remain true to noble intent. Conflicts arise that contribute to incidents of misconduct, as some police officers use unlawful means to achieve desired ends, such as criminal convictions. Several solutions to resolving ethical conflicts are presented.

Holmes, Malcolm D. **"Minority Threat and Police Brutality: Determinants of Civil Rights Criminal Complaints in U.S. Municipalities."** *Criminology* 38:343–367, 2000.

The conflict theory of law stipulates that strategies of crime control regulate threats to the interests of dominant groups; aggregate-level research on policing has generally supported this proposition. Police brutality constitutes an extralegal mechanism of control that has yet to be examined in this theoretical framework. A study tests the hypothesis that the greater the number of threatening acts and people, the greater is the number of police brutality civil rights criminal complaints filed with the U.S. Department of Justice. Data were gathered from the Department of Justice Police Brutality Study for 1985–1990, the U.S. *Uniform Crime Reports* for 1985–1990, and census reports for 1990. Consistent with threat hypothesis predictions, measures of the presence of threatening people (percent black, percent Hispanic [in the Southwest], and majority/minority income inequality) were positively related to average annual civil rights criminal complaints. Theoretical, substantive, and policy implications of the findings are addressed.

Human Rights Watch. *Shielded from Justice: Police Brutality and Accountability in the United States.* New York: Human Rights Watch, 1998. 440 pages.

A study examines police brutality in fourteen U.S. cities: Atlanta; Boston; Chicago; Detroit; Indianapolis; Los Angeles; Minneapolis; New Orleans; New York; Philadelphia; Portland, Oregon; Providence, Rhode Island; San Francisco; and Washington, D.C. Interviews and correspondence were carried out with attorneys who represented victims alleging ill treatment by police, representatives of police department internal affairs units, police officers, citizen review agency staff, city officials, and others. Police brutality is one of the most serious, enduring, and divisive human rights violations in the United States. The problem is nationwide and its nature is institutionalized. Police officers engage in unjustified shootings, severe beatings, fatal chokings, and unnecessarily rough physical treatment in cities, while their superiors fail to control them or even to record the full magnitude of the problem. A victim seeking redress faces obstacles at every point in the process. Minority groups have alleged that they are disproportionately targeted by police. Severe abuse persists because overwhelming barriers to accountability make it all too likely that officers who commit abuses will escape punishment and continue their conduct. Recommendations are offered for police administration, the use of civil remedies, local criminal prosecution, federal criminal civil rights prosecution, and federal data collection.

Jefferis, Eric S., Robert J. Kaminski, Stephen Holmes, and Daniel Hanley. **"The Effect of a Video-Taped Arrest on Public Perceptions of Police Use of Force."** *Journal of Criminal Justice* 25:141–165, 1997.

This article examines a highly publicized incident involving the use of excessive force that was videotaped. The videotape itself became evidence in a subsequent trial involving officers charged with using excessive force. The use of videotapes in patrol cars is increasing in popularity, in part because it provides an independent and objective view of incidents in which excessive force might be applied. Various implications for controlling police behavior and minimizing police misconduct are examined.

Jett, Monty B. **"Pepper Spray Training for Safety."** *FBI Law Enforcement Bulletin* 66:17–23, 1997.

This article examines the use of pepper spray as an alternative to deadly force or excessive physical force in subduing criminal suspects. Pepper spray, or oleoresin capsicum (OC), is considered a useful tool for police to use in subduing especially violent suspects. However, questions about the safe use of OC continue to be raised. In some instances, deaths occur as the result of using OC on certain suspects. The article examines several in-custody deaths that resulted from applying OC when effecting arrests. Various reasons for in-custody deaths are examined. Recommendations include educating officers as to which suspects are more likely than others to respond in negative ways and possibly die from OC. Circumstances are described and policy recommendations are made.

Kaminski, Robert J., and Eric Jefferis. **"The Effect of a Violent Televised Arrest on Public Perceptions of the Police: A Partial Test of Easton's Theoretical Framework."** *Policing: An International Journal of Police Strategies and Management* 21:15–30, 1998.

This article examines public reaction to a televised arrest involving excessive force. Public opinion is solicited concerning the justification officers have for using excessive force to subdue criminal suspects. Solutions are examined and ways of minimizing the use of excessive force are explored. Recommendations include departmental policy changes and greater administrative control and monitoring of officer conduct. Greater training in the exercise of discretion in police-citizen encounters is encouraged.

Kaminski, Robert J., Steven M. Edwards, and James W. Johnson. **"Assessing the Incapacitative Effects of Pepper Spray during Resistive Encounters with Police."** *Policing: An International Journal of Police Strategies and Management* 22:7–29, 1999.

This article examines ways of applying force to subdue suspects without risking permanent physical injuries that might be caused with violent excessive force. Although pepper spray is an irritant and can cause some physical harm, it is viewed as a less dangerous form of force to subdue persons considered dangerous to others or themselves. Comparisons are made between various types of excessive force and the incapacitative effects of pepper spray. Conditions under which to apply such means of control for subduing suspects are discussed.

Kappeler, Victor E., Richard D. Sluder, and Geoffrey P. Alpert. *Forces of Deviance: Understanding the Dark Side of Policing.* Prospect Heights, IL: Waveland Press, 1994. 308 pages.

This textbook illustrates how the development of U.S. law enforcement, with its insistence that police authority be subject to local political control, has fostered a climate in which misconduct is allowed to flourish. Chapter topics include organizing and structuring police deviance; the ideology and culture of police; motive and justification for breaking normative bonds; internal and external controls; and forging the boundaries of police behavior. Case examples include the Rodney King beating in Los Angeles, the investigation of serial killer Jeffrey Dahmer, and corruption in the District of Columbia's Metropolitan Police.

Kelly, Gerald E. *Honor for Sale: The Darkest Chapter in the History of New York's Finest.* New York: Sharon, 1999. 278 pages.

In 1998, more than five hundred pounds of narcotics disappeared from the New York City Police Department's evidence room. A journalistic study recounts allegations that the police were involved in theft and murder, but the case was never resolved. Reasons are explored for why this situation occurred, and recommendations are made for policy change to minimize police misconduct in the future.

Kelly, Martin A. **"Jesus and Police Brutality."** *International Journal of Comparative and Applied Criminal Justice* 23:137–140, 1999.

An essay describes how the ancient Roman police went "out of control" on the first Good Friday in their mistreatment of the prisoner, Jesus, and what lessons can be learned to help us cope with today's pandemic problem of police abuse. The organization of the criminal justice system in the ancient Roman provinces and the occupational pressures exerted on the individual police officer are described. Similarities are noted in the self-image of the ancient Roman police officer and his present-day counterpart. These parallels produce insights into today's incidents of police brutality and provide lessons for reducing their frequency. It is also noted that several Roman officers treated Jesus with respect and courtesy, and hence can serve as role models.

Klotter, John C. *Legal Guide for Police: Constitutional Issues.* 5th ed. Cincinnati, OH: Anderson Publishing Company, 1998. 212 pages.

This book examines today's law enforcement officers, who are required to be highly knowledgeable about the law. Students will find this revised guide to be a valuable tool, bringing them up-to-date with the latest developments in the laws of arrest; search and seizure; and police authority to detain, question suspects, and engage in pretrial identification procedures. Other topics include police power and its uses and abuses and the civil liabilities of police officers and agencies.

Lawrence, Regina Greenwood. *Defining Events: News Coverage of Police Use of Force.* Ann Arbor, MI: University Microfilms International, 1997. 312 pages.

A study analyzes how police use of force and police brutality are represented in the news. Adopting a social constructionist perspective on the news and on public problems, it seeks to understand how public definitions of use-of-force incidents are constructed in the news and when and why the news occasionally designates police brutality as a serious public problem. Content analysis of the *New York Times* and *Los Angeles Times* reveals that the typical news story about use of force is brief, episodic, and structured around claims provided to reporters by officials. The stories focus attention on deviant violent criminal suspects who threaten officers and the public and, occasionally, on "rogue cops" who cross the line between acceptable and unacceptable use of force. In contrast, the widely publicized beating of Rodney King thoroughly escaped the efforts of the Los Angeles Police Department (LAPD) to contain its public definition. The King beating became a major news event not simply because it was videotaped, but because the narrative the video suggested undermined official claims about that event, because other officials publicly challenged the LAPD's individualizing claims about the event, and because citizens in Los Angeles and beyond mobilized to define the King beating as part of a pattern of police abuse. A small number of incidents become occasions for news coverage that is less critical than that in the King case but more critical than that given to most use-of-force incidents. The analysis finds that particular "story cues" arising from some use-of-force incidents encourage more critical news reporting because they provide the raw materials for dramatic storytelling that identifies potential official wrongdoing. But the openings for critical discourse about policing created by these story cues are constrained by privileged official access to the news and a dominant discourse of crime control.

Leffler, Sheldon S. *Beyond Community Relations: Addressing Police Brutality Directly.* New York: New York City Council, Committee on Public Safety, 1998.

In 1997 the mayor of New York City appointed a special task force to investigate police brutality following the Louima beating incident in Brooklyn. The task force's 1998 report focused primarily on the nature of police-community relations. A dissenting report by the City Council staff suggests that police misconduct and brutality can be attributed to inadequate policies and procedures within the New York City Police Department (NYCPD) and offers specific recommendations. Recommendations include increased officer monitoring and a central clearinghouse to cross-reference complaints against police misconduct; more rapid and thorough response to all officer misconduct; supervision of all officers, but greater accountability for new ones; clear guidelines for physical and verbal confrontations during an arrest that preclude an arresting officer processing the arrest; annual reports of antibrutality and antimisconduct initiatives; and improved community interaction with the NYCPD.

Lersch, Kim Michelle. **"Exploring Gender Differences in Citizen Allegations of Misconduct: An Analysis of a Municipal Police Department."** *Women and Criminal Justice* 9:69–79, 1998.

A study addresses possible differences between male and female officers named in allegations of police misconduct. Data were acquired from 527 complaints filed with the internal affairs office of a large police department in the southeastern United States from 1992 to 1994. Male officers were more likely to find themselves named in citizen complaints. Although minority male officers were overrepresented among those accused of alleged misconduct, no significant racial difference emerged among accused female officers. Once an accusation of misconduct was made, males and females were equally likely to be accused of the misuse of force.

Lersch, Kim Michelle. **"Police Misconduct and Malpractice: A Critical Analysis of Citizens' Complaints."** *Policing* 21:80–96, 1998.

A study tests several hypotheses suggested by conflict theory about official complaints lodged against a large police department in the southeastern United States from 1992 to 1994. Because a single complaint of misconduct may include allegations against two or more officers, the 527 complaints translated into 682 allegations of wrongdoing. Data were drawn from agency personnel files. In support of the hypotheses, minority citizens and those with less power and fewer resources were more likely to file complaints of misconduct and to allege more serious forms of misconduct than those with greater power and more resources. There appeared to be some relationship between the complainant's race and the substantiation rate of complaints: when the bivariate relationship was examined, race was a significant predictor. Findings are consistent with conflict theory's view that policy brutality and misconduct are used by dominant groups to protect their hold on society's limited resources.

Littlejohn, Edward J. **"The Civilian Police Commission: A Deterrent to Police Misconduct."** *University of Detroit Journal of Urban Law* 59:6–62, 1981.

Citizen review boards, which were heavily advocated during the 1960s, did not work well. They were unsuccessful in investigating citizen complaints against the police and as deterrents of police misconduct principally because of their lack of power within the organizations they sought to influence. The review function, which begins only after misconduct has occurred, did not permit investigations into or control over police departments' policies, disciplinary practices, or other internal matters systematically related to police misconduct. The external character of review boards also caused massive resistance from police officers, who resented being investigated and judged by strangers. The history of the review board concept has demonstrated that its revival, which was attempted in at least two major cities, has little or no chance of succeeding. However, the Board of Police Commissioners (BPC) in Detroit demonstrates that a civilian commission can control a police department's internal complaint program and also conduct investigations independently. The BPC, in addition to managing a complaint system and monitoring departmental discipline with its own staff, has supervisory responsibility for the entire Detroit Police Department. Because of its substantial internal authority, the BPC is able to directly affect departmental policies and personnel practices that contributed to poor police-community relations and reinforced police misconduct. Nevertheless, there remains a great reluctance among police officials to punish "one of their own" when a citizen complains. An independent administrative body similar to the BPC, by focusing on the problems of police misconduct and citizen complaints, has unique opportunities for deterring misconduct, for promoting supervisors' accountability, and for fairly resolving both citizen dissatisfactions and police officer concerns over internal complaint investigations.

Lynch, Gerald W., ed. *Human Dignity and the Police: Ethics and Integrity in Police Work.* Springfield, IL: Charles C Thomas, 1999. 168 pages.

This textbook addresses the challenge of how best to control the police and eliminate their misuse of authority and excessive force against citizens. Chapter topics include agency efforts to prevent abuses; government responses to police abuse of power; the role of the press in police reform; course development and evolution; the experimental approach: the role of the trainer and its critical importance; the course as a change agent: the impact on instructor and participants; human rights as a component of coursework at the International Law Enforcement Academy; the importance of dignity training for emerging democracies in the newly independent nations of Eastern and Central Europe; and the future of law enforcement.

McAlary, Mike. *Good Cop, Bad Cop: Detective Joe Trimboli's Heroic Pursuit of NYPD Officer Michael Dowd.* New York: Pocket Books, 1994. 277 pages.

A journalistic account chronicles the downfall of New York City police officer Michael Dowd after a relentless pursuit by Detective Joe Trimboli. Dowd was arrested in 1992 for bribery and extortion in connection with sheltering a gang of drug traffickers. The Dowd case mushroomed into the worst police corruption scandal in New York City in twenty years.

McCafferty, Francis L., and Margaret A. McCafferty. **"Corruption in Law Enforcement: A Paradigm of Occupational Stress and Deviancy."** *Journal of the American Academy of Psychiatry and the Law* 26:57–65, 1998.

An essay and review, based on the principal author's more than thirty years of experience in psychiatric evaluation and treatment of law enforcement officers, explores the factors that contribute to police corruption. Law enforcement corruption has parallels in other agencies of government, in industry and labor, and in other professions. Among the many types of police corruption are extortion, accepting bribes, perjury, and premeditated theft. Remedies for combating corruption include instituting better hiring practices, mandating longer probation periods, ensuring better supervision, and regularly reevaluating officers.

More, Harry W. *Special Topics in Policing.* 2nd ed. Cincinnati, OH: Anderson Publishing Company, 1998. 331 pages.

This book provides thorough coverage of many of the critical issues that police officers deal with on a daily basis, including stress and burnout as policing becomes an increasingly dangerous profession. Other important issues treated include corruption, deviant behavior, use of deadly force, and abuses of discretion. Consideration is also given to policing in a free society, internal and external review of police conduct, and the reality of enforcing the law.

Nelson, Jill, ed. *Police Brutality: An Anthology.* New York: W. W. Norton, 2000. 264 pages.

An anthology of twelve previously unpublished essays provides historical, empirical, and personal accounts of police brutality in the United States dating back more than a century. The essays highlight the abusive and often violent relationship between the African-American community and the police.

Ogletree, Charles J. Jr., Mary Prosser, and Abbe Smith. *Beyond the Rodney King Story: An Investigation of Police Misconduct in Minority Communities.* Boston, MA: Northeastern University Press, 1995. 198 pages.

A joint study by the National Association for the Advancement of Colored People and the Criminal Justice Institute at Harvard Law School examined police misconduct with respect to minorities in the United States. Data were obtained at public hearings in six cities—Norfolk, Miami, Los Angeles, Houston, St. Louis, and Indianapolis—and from secondary sources. The study found all of the following: Racism is a central part of police misconduct. Police abuse of citizens has become more common and takes a variety of forms: excessive force during arrest, physical abuse, and, most frequently, verbal abuse and harassment in minority communities. Citizens who file complaints against the police are rarely victorious; procedures are often not widely publicized; complaints are discouraged; intrapolice investigations are not given wide credibility; and civil lawsuits are not often successful. A relation between the race of the officer and citizen and the incidence of abuse is apparent: minorities report greater violence by white officers, but black officers themselves are sometimes pressured to tolerate race-motivated police abuse in order to keep their jobs. Police have adopted an "us versus them" mentality with respect to community relations as well as a code of silence. However, some departments are now adopting a cooperative philosophy with the community. Although some departments have increased the number of minority officers, minorities remain underrepresented in both the higher ranks and specialized units. Recommendations cover the concept of policing, accountability, hiring diversity, recruitment and selection criteria, continuing training, promotion and advancement criteria, community-oriented policing, and civilian review.

Olson, Dean T. **"Improving Deadly Force Decision Making."** *FBI Law Enforcement Bulletin* 67:1–9, 1998.

This article deals with deadly force situations encountered by law enforcement officers and the discretionary decision making that precedes the application of deadly force. Various types of training strategies are described to improve an officer's decision-making powers for when and when not to use deadly force. The deadly force triangle model is described, which represents three factors—ability, opportunity, and jeopardy. All three factors must be present to justify deadly force. The article notes that many deadly force situations lack the clarity for officers to make clear-cut decisions. Different police department policies are inconsistent with their use of deadly force or do not depict accurately in which police-citizen encounters deadly force may be a consideration. Recommended are examinations of incorrect assumptions about the application of deadly force, survival stress management training, and the application of the dynamic training technique, in which various role-playing scenarios are used to give officers greater discretionary experience.

Owens, Tom, and Rod Browning. *Lying Eyes: The Truth Behind the Corruption and Brutality of the LAPD and the Beating of Rodney King.* New York: Thunder's Mouth Press, 1994. 282 pages.

A former Los Angeles police officer describes his experience investigating police misconduct in connection with the Rodney King investigation. The narrative depicts institutionalized racism, brutality, and systematic manipulation of evidence by the police department. A personal impression of Rodney King is also provided.

Pate, Antony M., and Lorie A. Fridell. *Police Use of Force: Official Reports, Citizen Complaints, and Legal Consequences, Vols. I and II.* Washington, DC: The Police Foundation, 1993. 242 pages.

This publication examines the general use of excessive force among selected police departments. Department policies are examined, and officer discretionary powers are described. Recommendations are made that call for administrative changes and policy modifications to govern in a more systematic way the conditions under which the use of force against citizens is applied. Implications, including civil and criminal liabilities, for police officers who use deadly force are examined.

Sandler, Ross, ed. **"Police Corruption, Municipal Corruption: Cures at What Cost?"** *New York Law School Law Review* 40:1–188, 1995.

Proceedings of a 1995 symposium on police corruption in New York City encompass eight symposium speeches and five articles. Editor Ross Sandler provides an introduction. Harold Baer and Joseph P. Armao provide an overview of the Mollen Commission, which in 1994 found that corruption centered on the narcotics trade represented a serious and alarming threat to the integrity of law enforcement in New York City. Additional speeches outline the views of the city council, the corporation counsel, the incumbent police commissioner, and four former city law enforcement officials. Annette Gordon-Reed discusses independent oversight of city corrections and police agencies. Strategies for reforming contracting in the city's construction industry are assessed by Thomas D. Thacher II, Frank Anechiarico, and James B. Jacobs. Mark Davies weighs the utility of government ethics laws.

Sechrest, Dale K., and Pamela Burns. **"Police Corruption: The Miami Case."** *Criminal Justice and Behavior* 19:294–313, 1992.

A case study explores how mandated changes in the screening, selection, and hiring of Miami, Florida, police officers in the early 1980s contributed to significant corruption. It is hypothesized that the corruption occurred as a result of both social (or community) changes as well as departmental problems. Data sources included official departmental data, summaries of official documents and newspaper reports, and interviews with supervisors within the department's personnel unit. The Miami Police Department faced personnel problems at the same time that the community experienced increased crime, especially greater drug trafficking, and major community social problems. These problems were not addressed adequately by community leaders.

Miami and Dade County lacked an immediate response to social changes brought about by the influx of Cuban refugees in the Mariel boatlift as well as several racially sensitive incidents involving law enforcement in the county and requirements for minority hiring within the department. Community problems led to mistakes in hiring, standards for supervision were lowered, and disciplinary actions dropped significantly. Implications of the Miami experience are addressed.

Skolnick, Jerome H., and James J. Fyfe. *Above the Law: Police and the Excessive Use of Force.* New York: Free Press, 1993. 313 pages.

A review explores the use of excessive force by police officers in the United States, with particular reference to the beating of Rodney King in Los Angeles. Part I describes the occasions for policy brutality. A success story is the marked decline in the brutalization of suspects while they are being interrogated. Part II concentrates on the causes of police brutality. There is a causal connection between excessive force and the traditional culture of policing, that is, the values and understandings that patrol officers learn from their peers. Two aspects of this culture encourage excessive force: (1) the idea that police are soldiers in wars on crime and drugs; and (2) the insularity, authoritarianism, and narrow-mindedness of some police administrators and departments. Part III explores remedies. These include accountability mechanisms, such as press monitoring, civilian review boards, and improved internal managements, as well as broader police reforms, such as community- and problem-oriented policing.

Souryal, Sam S. **"Personal Loyalty to Superiors in Criminal Justice Agencies."** *Justice Quarterly* 16:871–895, 1999.

This article examines the loyalties of police agency workers and how such loyalties may undermine conscientious obedience to bureaucratic rules. Some administrators and officers may engage in misconduct or corruption, but agency member loyalty may cause some persons to overlook the misconduct and not report it. Arguments are presented for and against employee loyalty to the organization and staff. A professional model is advanced based on organizational identification and individual accountability to minimize the incidence of misconduct and strengthen organizational effectiveness.

Stevens, Dennis J. **"Corruption among Narcotics Officers: A Study of Innocence and Integrity."** *Journal of Police and Criminal Psychology* 14:1–10, 1999.

A study examines factors associated with corruption among narcotics law enforcement officers. Questionnaire data were supplied by 255 members of the North Carolina Narcotics Law Enforcement Officers Association. Corruption was defined to include police brutality, personal use of contraband, and abuse of due process rights. Corruption existed among narcotics officers, and it was related to officers' lack of experience, innocence, and integrity. It is recommended that narcotics officers be selected based on their experiences, especially military service.

Vaughn, Michael S. **"Police Sexual Violence: Civil Liability under State Tort Law."** *Crime and Delinquency* 45:334–357, 1999.

An essay and review analyzes the civil liability, under U.S. state tort law, of criminal justice personnel who engage in police sexual violence (PSV). Vicarious liability under the doctrine of *respondeat superior* is described, and five theories are identified that courts use to decide whether criminal justice agents commit sexual violence within the scope of employment. Also discussed are PSV cases litigated pursuant to intentional and negligence torts. Governmental entities need to systematically collect data on the prevalence of PSV, and criminal justice agencies should monitor employees effectively.

Weitzer, Ronald. **"Citizens' Perceptions of Police Misconduct: Race and Neighborhood Context."** *Justice Quarterly* 16:819–846.

This article examines the controversial issue of allegations of police abuse of minorities. African-American citizens are the targets of three types of police misconduct: unjustified street stops of citizens; verbal abuse; and use of excessive force. Residents of Washington, D.C., are interviewed in depth, and findings support the idea that neighborhood context conditions residents' attitudes and reported experiences to the police. The roles of race, class, and neighborhood context in police-citizen relations are discussed, as well as the implications of increasing both police and citizen understanding of those roles.

Williams, George T. **"Reluctance to Use Deadly Force: Causes, Consequences, and Cures."** *FBI Law Enforcement Bulletin* 68:1–5, 1999.

This article describes the conditions under which deadly force is applied in police-citizen encounters. Fears of law enforcement officers are justifiably heightened by the fact that their work has become increasingly dangerous and greater numbers of officer deaths result from attempting to effect arrests of dangerous subjects. Some officers are reluctant to use deadly force, even when it is justified. Explanations for this reluctance are examined and ways of overcoming this reluctance are provided.

Wrobleski, Henry M., and Karen M. Hess. *Introduction to Law Enforcement and Criminal Justice.* Belmont, CA: Wadsworth Publishing Company, 2000. 500 pages.

This book includes a number of chapters dealing with police administration and operations. Included are sections dealing with police misconduct, including corruption, graft, and other forms of police deviance. The authors take a look at current and compelling issues, including brutality, community-based policing, and technology.

Journals, Magazines, Bulletins, and Newsletters

American Police Beat
P.O. Box 382702
Cambridge, MA 02238–2702
(800) 234–0056
Internet: http://apbweb.com

This journal is published ten times a year. It contains various articles and features dealing with various policing issues, including misconduct and corruption. Recent newspaper articles also are reported. Focusing primarily on U.S. police systems, this publication examines critical and timely issues relevant to police officers and the public.

Blue Line News Week
12A-4981 Highway 7 East, Suite 254
Markham, ON, Canada L3R 1N1
Internet: www.blueline.ca/home.htm

This magazine reports various articles dealing with policing, including police stress, training, ethics, and misconduct. It is a practical magazine, offering helpful tips to police officers for resolving various types of issues.

The Ethics Roll Call
Southwestern Legal Foundation
Southwestern Law Enforcement Institute
P.O. Box 830707
Richardson, TX 75083–0707
(972) 664–3471

This newsletter is published quarterly. It publishes short articles and contemporary news information concerning law enforcement officers and ethical issues. It raises questions about police ethics under different circumstances and poses various solutions. Short article submissions are requested from rank-and-file police officers as well as interested professionals. Occasional book reviews receive brief coverage.

FBI Law Enforcement Bulletin
FBI Academy
Madison Building, Room 209
Quantico, VA 22135
e-mail: leb@fbi.gov

This bulletin is published monthly by the Federal Bureau of Investigation. It solicits from academicians and interested practitioners, including police officers and law enforcement officers in all departments and agencies, articles concerning all aspects of policing and policing programs. It features periodic book reviews and law-related articles as they affect law enforcement. Each issue deals with selected topics that are up-to-date concerns for U.S. law enforcement officers.

Journal of Police and Criminal Psychology
University of Evansville
Department of Psychology
1800 Lincoln Avenue
Evansville, IN 47722
e-mail: bw6@evansville.edu
Internet: cep.jmu.edu/spcp/journal.htm

This journal is the official journal of the Society for Police and Criminal Psychology. It contains articles pertaining to research and theoretical issues in criminal justice. Some of the articles pertain to police misconduct and corruption and why officers become involved in these activities.

National Institute of Justice Journal
National Institute of Justice
National Criminal Justice Reference Center
P.O. Box 6000
Rockville, MD 20849–6000
(301) 519–5500
Internet: www.ojp.usdoj.gov/nij/journals

The *National Institute of Justice Journal* is published by the National Institute of Justice, the research arm of the U.S. Department of Justice, to announce the Institute's policy-relevant research results and initiatives. The attorney general has determined that publication of this periodical is necessary in the transaction of the public business required by law of the Department of Justice. Featured articles include police misconduct, community policing, and police ethical issues.

National Institute of Justice Research in Brief
National Institute of Justice
National Criminal Justice Reference Service
P.O. Box 6000
Rockville, MD 20849–6000
(800) 851–3420
Internet: www.ncjrs.org

This publication is distributed on the basis of the development of particular topics related to criminal justice research issues. It examines a wide variety of policing issues, including community policing and police misconduct and corruption. The research reported is mostly sponsored by the National Institute of Justice and reflects the findings of the investigators who are responsible for each issue's preparation.

Police: The Law Enforcement Magazine
21061 S. Western Boulevard
Torrance, CA 90501
(310) 533–2400
e-mail: info@policemag.com
Internet: http://www.policemag.com/index.cfm

This magazine covers a wide variety of topics of interest to the police and the public. It includes articles about police training and equipment. It features up-to-date issues that are of concern to new officers and offers strategies for problem-solving situations on the job. The magazine reports on forthcoming meetings of police professional organizations, job listings, investigative tools, and the location of police training centers.

Policing
MCB University Press
60/62 Toller Lane
Bradford, Weste Yorkshire
BD8 9BY UK
(01274) 777700

This journal is published quarterly. It features a wide variety of articles pertaining to police and policing issues, including but not limited to police misconduct and corruption. It caters to academicians in the social sciences who publish their research about the police in different departments throughout the world. Featured are articles from the United Kingdom and the United States.

**Policing and Society: An International Journal
of Research and Policy**
Department of Sociology
University of Durham
New Elvet, Durham DH1 3JT, UK
+44(0) 191 374 2311
e-mail: james.sheptycki@durham.ac.uk

This journal publishes articles from all countries and features research and theoretical pieces having to do with law enforcement issues. The journal provides much valuable research information on a quarterly basis and has relevance for line officers as well as police administrators interested in policy formulation and implementation. The journal is committed to a rigorous policy debate and the highest standards of scholarship dealing with social scientific investigations of police policy, legal analyses of police powers and their constitutional status, and management-oriented research on aspects of police organizations.

Government Documents and Agency Publications

Adams, Kenneth et al. *Use of Force by Police: Overview of National and Local Data*. Washington, DC: National Institute of Justice, Bureau of Justice Statistics, 1999. 76 pages.

Recent developments have heightened concern about police use of force. This government-sponsored research presents several high-profile incidents of police excessive use of force. One factor contributing to the excessive use of force by police is the zero-tolerance policies some police departments have established. It is reported that police use excessive force frequently. Various statistics are presented concerning the different forms of force police use to effect arrests of criminal suspects. Use of force occurs most frequently when suspects are under the influence of drugs or alcohol, and the use of force appears unrelated to the personal characteristics of police officers. A small proportion of police officers seem to be involved in excessive force situations more than other officers. Various reasons for excessive use of force by police are discussed.

Alpert, Geoffrey P. *Police Pursuit: Policies and Training.* Washington, DC: U.S. Department of Justice, National Institute of Justice, 1997. NCJ 164831. 86 pages.

This publication outlines conditions under which high-speed pursuit of criminal suspects are undertaken. Department policies are examined to determine when such pursuits are justified and can be controlled in order to minimize dangers to innocent civilians. There is widespread variation among police departments concerning police pursuit policies. Often police are untrained about when to engage in hot pursuit and when such pursuits are self-defeating, resulting in greater threat to life and damage to property than the offense itself. Strategies are considered for policy changes. Recommendations are made for establishing more reasonable policies and educating officers as to the conditions under which high-speed pursuits may be safely conducted.

Bayley, David H., and James Garofalo. **"Patrol Officer Effectiveness in Managing Conflict during Police-Citizen Encounters."** In *Report to the Governor, Vol. III.* Albany, NY: New York State Commission on Criminal Justice and the Use of Force, 1987. 88 pages.

This publication examines various methods to subdue criminal suspects, including physical force. Different forms of force are described, and excessive force is defined. Alternative strategies, for instance, using verbal judo and other nonviolent methods, are considered. Recommendations include providing officers with ample training and greater amounts of education to equip them with the verbal skills to defuse potentially deadly encounters in which deadly force or excessive force that might cause physical injuries could occur. Several strategies for subduing criminal suspects are considered that reduce considerably officer liability.

Garner, Joel, John Buchanan, Tom Schade, and John Hepburn. *Understanding the Use of Force by and against the Police.* Washington, DC: U.S. Department of Justice, National Institute of Justice, 1996. NCJ 158614. 71 pages.

This publication explores the different reasons why police respond to police-citizen encounters with excessive force. Factors are examined that contribute to police aggressiveness as well as citizen aggressiveness. Alternative solutions are proposed to regulate policies and control police conduct when making arrests.

Greenfeld, Lawrence A., Patrick A. Langan, and Steven K. Smith. *Police Use of Force: Collection of National Data.* Washington, DC: U.S. Department of Justice, Bureau of Justice Statistics and National Institute of Justice, 1997. NCJ 165040. 38 pages.

This publication describes different incidents in which police officers in various U.S. police departments have applied excessive force. Police liability is examined. The publication also reviews various research reports of incidents in which excessive use of force has occurred. Factors are examined that contribute to excessive use of force. Recommendations are made for controlling officer conduct and establishing policies that will minimize citizen injuries and police liabilities, improving generally the quality of officer discretion and decision making relative to the application of force when effecting arrests.

Independent Commission on the Los Angeles Police Department. *Report of the Independent Commission on the Los Angeles Police Department.* Los Angeles, CA: Independent Commission on the Los Angeles Police Department, 1996. 78 pages.

This publication examines the Rodney King incident in great detail. It also includes a discussion of the use of different types of force by Los Angeles police officers when arresting civilian suspects. Factors are examined that contributed to the incident initially and recommendations are made for controlling subsequent incidents. Practical measures are provided to enable police to make better decisions when applying their discretion in affecting citizen arrests.

Klockars, Carl B., Sanja Kutnjak Ivkovich, William E. Harver, and Maria R. Haberfeld. *The Measurement of Police Integrity.* Washington, DC: U.S. Department of Justice, Office of Justice Programs, 2000. NCJ 181465. 11 pages.

This publication explores police officers' understanding of police agency rules concerning police misconduct and the extent of the police officers' support for these rules. A survey considers officer opinions about the appropriate punishment for misconduct, their familiarity with the expected disciplinary threat, their perceptions of disciplinary fairness, and their willingness to report misconduct. The results of this survey have important implications for researchers and policymakers as well as for police practitioners.

Los Angeles Police Department Board of Inquiry into the Rampart Area Corruption Incident. *Public Report.* Los Angeles, CA: Los Angeles Police Department Board of Inquiry into the Rampart Area Corruption Incident, 2000. 600 pages.

This report examines incidents during 1997 and 1998 in which officers were identified as suspects in serious criminal activity, including bank robbery, false imprisonment and beating of an arrestee, and theft of cocaine from the department's property division. It is the board's view that the Rampart corruption incidents occurred because a few individuals decided to engage in blatant misconduct and, in some cases, criminal behavior. A series of 108 recommendations are presented for improving the testing and screening of police officer candidates; personnel practices; personnel investigations; corruption investigations; operational controls; anticorruption inspections and audits; ethics and integrity training; and job-specific training.

Major City Chief Administrators. *Maintaining Integrity in Law Enforcement Organizations: Selected Readings.* Washington, DC: FBI Academy, 1994. 182 pages.

A 1993 conference of large-city mayors and law enforcement administrators presented papers on personal and organizational integrity among law enforcement personnel in the United States. Topics are ethical concepts; police narcotics corruption; ethical issues in contemporary policing; entry-level screening of police candidates; excellence through the inspection process; investigating law enforcement corruption; reducing malfeasance; the sergeant's role in maintaining integrity; constraints in establishing ethics standards; and the police union's responsibility in maintaining organizational integrity. An appendix offers the Metro-Dade (Florida) Police Department Early Identification System on police conduct.

McEwen, Tom. *National Data Collection on Police Use of Force.* Washington, DC: U.S. Department of Justice, Bureau of Justice Statistics and the National Institute of Justice, 1996. NCJ 160113. 66 pages.

A compendium of information about the police use of force, this publication lists numerous articles and other documents that pertain to police violence and excessive use of force. Several studies are highlighted, and methods for controlling police deviance and excessive use of force are examined.

National Institute of Justice. *High Speed Pursuit: New Technologies around the Corner.* Washington, DC: National Law Enforcement Technology Center Bulletin. U.S. Department of Justice, National Institute of Justice, 1995. 78 pages.

Conditions under which high-speed pursuit of criminal suspects occurs are described and examined. Alternative means of subduing offenders are recommended. Different technologies are applied and suggested to reduce the liabilities accruing to officers involved in high-speed pursuits. Changing departmental policies relating to high-speed pursuits are discussed in light of changing technology. Implications for fleeing suspects and police are discussed. Methods for deciding when to engage in high-speed pursuits are examined.

Pinnizzotto, Anthony J., Edward F. Davis, and Charles E. Miller III. *In the Line of Fire: Violence against Law Enforcement.* Washington, DC: U.S. Department of Justice, Federal Bureau of Investigation and National Institute of Justice, 1997.

This publication examines citizen violence against the police. Although most publications focus upon excessive force used by police against citizens, police officers are exposed to greater threats from citizens annually. These threats are related in part to an increase in handgun possession by private citizens as well as the greater propensity of citizens to use physical force to resist arrest. Various explanations for such violence against the police are examined. Suggestions are made to educate and train police officers to minimize the incidence of citizen violence against them. Cooperative solutions are proposed.

Scrivner, Ellen M. *The Role of Police Psychology in Controlling Excessive Force.* Washington, DC: National Institute of Justice, 1994. NCJ 146206.

This publication examines how police officers can use verbal methods in the process of pursuing and subduing criminal suspects without having to resort to physical force or excessive force. Special programs are suggested as a part of the training that police receive through their law enforcement training academies. Greater use of psychology with particular types of suspects under different sets of circumstances suggests fruitful ways of minimizing personal injury and officer liabilities.

U.S. Department of the Treasury. *Department of the Treasury Report of the Good O' Boys Roundup Policy Review.* Washington, DC: U.S. Government Printing Office, 1996. 200 pages.

An annual retreat in Tennessee known as the "Good O' Boys Roundup" produced a policy review that was sparked by allegations of off-duty misconduct by agents of the Bureau of Alcohol, Tobacco and Firearms. The review (1) examines current departmental disciplinary and personnel policies; and (2) lists recommendations on disciplining, hiring, training, and evaluating and promoting.

U.S. House of Representatives Committee on the Judiciary. *Police Brutality.* Washington, DC: U.S. Government Printing Office, 1992. 323 pages.

This report contains proceedings of congressional hearings on police misconduct and the federal government response to the problem, examining issues related to police misbehavior within a broader context. Testimony is provided by representatives of police organizations, academia, civil rights organizations, organizations representing the interests of African-Americans, and others.

Videotapes

Arresting Prejudice
Type: VHS, color
Length: 32 minutes
Date: 1992
Cost: $399.00 (Item # GZ311)
Source: Insight Media

2162 Broadway
New York, NY 10024-0621
e-mail: cs@insight-media.com
Internet: www.insight-media.com

The Rodney King incident involving police brutality inflicted upon a motorist by officers from the Los Angeles Police Department has sensitized an already overcritical public about certain abuses by police officers against citizens. This tape is about two programs implemented in Houston, Texas, and Madison, Wisconsin. The programs are designed to heighten police awareness of cultural differences, especially where minority citizens are involved. In Houston, Texas, for instance, some police officers are being recruited and trained to speak Spanish in order to relate more effectively with the Hispanic community. In Madison, Wisconsin, minority police officers are overrepresented in relation to their proportionate representation in the city's racial/ethnic composition. The tape offers solutions to racial and ethnic tensions through improved public relations and interpersonal strategies implemented by these respective police departments.

Bad Lieutenant
Type: VHS, color
Length: 96 minutes
Date: 1992
Cost: $14.24 (Item # 276822)
Source: Movies Unlimited
3015 Darnell Road
Philadelphia, PA 19154-3295
(800) 668-4344
Internet: www.moviesunlimited.com

This is a feature film starring Harvey Keitel and Paul Calderone. Keitel is an out-of-control, burned-out police detective who abuses his authority by sexually assaulting female motorists and committing a variety of other offenses. He is addicted to drugs, gambles excessively, and is morally corrupt. Explicit examples of police misconduct by Keitel and some of his police officer associates provide students with insight into the inner workings of the police subculture. Although the film does not attempt to justify the misconduct portrayed, it does make it easy to see how such misconduct originates and is perpetuated over time by a police subculture that enforces a code of silence in very powerful informal ways.

Behind the Blue Wall: Police Brutality
Type: VHS, color
Length: 50 minutes
Cost: $19.95 (Item # AA-17757)
Source: A & E Television Networks
235 East 45th Street
New York, NY 10017
(888) 423-1212
Internet: www.AandE.com

Two notorious events are portrayed in this documentary. The New York Police Department has been involved in brutalizing minority citizens in different ways. The first case features Abner Louima. Louima was arrested without probable cause and taken to a New York City police station. While in police custody, Louima was brutalized by some of the officers. They inserted a toilet plunger handle into his rectum, causing severe internal injuries. The press sensationalized Louima's treatment by police and sensitized the public to various incidents of police brutality against the minority community. Another incident involved an African immigrant, Amadou Diallo. Diallo was gunned down by four police officers who were members of an elite New York police squad. New York City Police Commissioner Howard Safir and Alton White, a victim of police misconduct, are interviewed. The tape attempts to explain why such incidents occur and how police misconduct can be controlled.

Beyond the Blue: Life As a Female Police Officer
Type: VHS, color
Length: 25 minutes
Cost: $129 purchase, $75 rental (Item # DJR8572)
Source: Films for the Humanities & Sciences
P.O. Box 2053
Princeton, NJ 08543-2053
(800) 257-5126
Internet: www.films.com

This tape is about Angela Macdougal, who is a SWAT team member and sniper for a major police department. Interviewers follow her through her typical workday. Both Macdougal, who is a mother, and her husband are interviewed to determine their opinions and sentiments about the expectations others have of Macdougal and some of the problems female officers must confront in a traditionally male-dominated police environment. A high divorce rate among police officers suggests that these jobs involve a great deal of stress and burnout. The couple is interviewed as to how they cope with this stress and deal with the pressures of the job. Despite the high divorce rate among police officers, Macdougal and her husband believe that their marriage is solid.

The Choirboys
Type: VHS, color
Length: 119 minutes
Date: 1977
Cost: $14.99 (Item # 07-1628
Source: Movies Unlimited
           3015 Darnell Street
           Philadelphia, PA 19154-3295
           (800) 668-4344
           Internet: www.moviesunlimited.com

A fictional account of behind-the-scenes police activities by Joseph Wambaugh, former police officer with the Los Angeles Police Department. This tape portrays the dark side of policing and police humor, as police officers unwind after their shifts. This tape illustrates various forms of police misconduct, including sexual abuse, rape, and extortion. "R" rated, this movie describes "choir practice" as a euphemism for police rabble-rousing and misconduct off duty. It follows the lives of several officers through their workdays and the different encounters they have with citizens. It also shows the amount of discretion the officers exercise in whether or not to enforce the law.

Cop Land
Type: VHS, color
Length: 105 minutes
Date: 1997
Cost: $13.49 (Item # 112233)
Source: Movies Unlimited
           3015 Darnell Road
           Philadelphia, PA 19154-3295
           (800) 668-4344
           Internet: www.moviesunlimited.com

This feature film describes a controversial shooting by a New York City police officer that leads to an internal affairs investigation. Starring Sylvester Stallone and Robert DeNiro, the movie looks at local corruption and how the police are able to break down the wall of silence. One officer, Stallone, stands alone to expose the corrupt activities of the other officers. Stallone is punished by the other officers because of his honesty. The subculture of policing is accurately portrayed in this stunning drama. The code of silence is very much in evidence as Stallone reports the misconduct he observes to officers affiliated with internal affairs, the division that investigates officer corruption and misconduct.

Cops on Trial
Type: VHS, color
Length: 50 minutes
Cost: $29.95 (Item # AAE-17505)
Source: A & E Television Networks
235 East 45th Street
New York, NY 10017
(888) 423-1212
Internet: www.AandE.com

Why do police officers engage in misconduct and turn to corruption? These questions and others are examined in this tape. Experts from various police departments are interviewed to determine their views. Former Los Angeles Police Department chief Daryl Gates is interviewed. Gates defends his former police officers and rationalizes their conduct. He indicates that, although some of his officers were corrupt or engaged in misconduct, for the most part, the Los Angeles Police Department is a good organization, with the majority of officers being law-abiding, striving to serve and protect, and seeking to maintain a good public image. Bob Leuci, author of *Prince of the City*, is also interviewed. Leuci's book describes some of the most famous and controversial cases involving police assaults against citizens, including the Rodney King incident and the corruption case in New York City in which police detective Frank Serpico turned in corrupt officers. This tape reveals how justice is differentially applied when police officers are involved. Several legal strategies are explored about how to proceed against corrupt or dishonest police officers in court. Legal experts are interviewed and their opinions are given.

Cops or Criminals?
Type: VHS, color
Length: 50 minutes

Cost: $19.95 (Item # AAE-16069)
Source: A & E Television Networks
235 East 45th Street
New York, NY 10017
(888) 423-1212
Internet: www.AandE.com

The New Orleans Police Department (NOPD) has a history of being one of the most corrupt police departments in the United States. In the early 1990s, the U.S. Department of Justice gave serious consideration to having Federal Bureau of Investigation agents and the National Guard brought in to replace beat officers in the NOPD, believing that most NOPD officers were dishonest and violated the civil rights of citizens. This tape traces the history of NOPD corruption. Mayor Marc Morial is interviewed, and he provides some strategies for overcoming police corruption among the ranks of the NOPD. Admittedly, the long history of NOPD corruption is difficult to overcome. In one incident, an NOPD police officer, Len Davis, was convicted of murder and a host of other crimes. He involved a number of other officers in schemes ranging from protection for those engaged in drug trafficking to prostitution and other crimes. Another police officer was arrested and convicted of murder when she shot and killed an Oriental family in cold blood at their convenience store. Other family members who were hiding saw her kill their parents and other siblings. Later, the same officer returned to investigate these murders when they were reported. This ex–police officer is now on Louisiana's death row for her crimes. This incident does not help the public image of the NOPD. Some citizens have been advised that if they are ever stopped by the NOPD, they should keep driving and proceed to the nearest NOPD police station before stepping from their automobiles. Various programs and solutions to police corruption are proposed, including more extensive background checks when officers are recruited and trained. More careful screening of police candidates does much to control who becomes NOPD officers, and, as a result, police corruption and misconduct are minimized.

Cops under Fire
Type: VHS, color
Length: 50 minutes
Cost: $19.95 (Item # AAE-50102)
Source: A & E Television Networks
235 East 45th Street

New York, NY 10017
(888) 423-1212
Internet: www.AandE.com

Minorities have been the target of selective law enforcement by police for many decades. It seems that the white American public is generally unaware of police misconduct and excesses involving minority citizens. The Rodney King incident brought the treatment of minorities by police into sharper focus. This tape details the Rodney King beating and follows up the story by showing what happened to the police officers charged with violating King's civil rights under color of law. Television news reporter Mike Wallace interviews police and citizens to determine their views. Other incidents are described, including the New York City shooting of Amadou Diallo by four police officers. Some of the reasons for public mistrust of the police are examined. The tape also features racial profiling, situations in which police officers deliberately stop and harass those of color who are in the "wrong" neighborhoods or driving the "wrong" types of cars at the right times. Officer training programs are being revised and improved to reduce the incidence of racial profiling, which raises several constitutional issues.

Crooked Cops
Type: VHS, color
Length: 50 minutes
Cost: $19.95 (Item # AAE-21526)
Source: A & E Television Networks
235 East 45th Street
New York, NY 10017
(888) 423-1212
Internet: AandE.com

Virtually every large police department has several dishonest police officers who engage in various forms of misconduct. Often, because of the police code of silence and other factors, this corruption and misconduct goes unreported. Interviewer Mike Wallace examines police corruption and misconduct. Examined are various reasons for its emergence and persistence. Some police officers are taking an active role in drug trafficking, stealing drugs and other contraband from their own department evidence lockers and recycling these illicit products among drug dealers for sizeable profits. Law enforcement officers are profiled from New York City, Miami, Philadelphia, and New Orleans.

Professor Jim Fyfe from Temple University is interviewed. Fyfe is a former member of the New York Police Department and gives his professional insight and views concerning why corruption and misconduct exist and persist. He discusses the process whereby good cops go bad. Various solutions are proposed, including regulatory citizen complaint review boards, as a means of monitoring and punishing police misconduct whenever it is detected or reported.

Deadly Force
Type: VHS, color
Length: 50 minutes
Cost: $29.95 (Item # AAE-16012)
Source: A & E Television Networks
        235 East 45th Street
        New York, NY 10017
        (888) 423-1212
        Internet: www.AandE.com

This tape details the problems that led up to the tragic police bombing of a residence in Philadelphia. Several innocent victims are interviewed. The general issue of deadly force used against citizens is explored. Featured are police officers and law enforcement agencies at all levels, including the Federal Bureau of Investigation, Drug Enforcement Administration, and local law enforcement agencies. Incidents, such as the disastrous Waco, Texas, assault against the Branch Dividians, are featured. Whenever a citizen loses his or her life at the hands of a law enforcement officer, the public is increasingly wary of police and whether police should use deadly force in all but the most dire of life-threatening circumstances. The tape suggests that lethal force is becoming increasingly common. Various reasons for this increase in deadly force are examined, and several experts are interviewed and offer their views. Different incidents are examined and described, and possible solutions are offered as to how law enforcement officers could have approached these problems differently without inflicting substantial loss of life.

Dirty Harry
Type: VHS, color
Length: 102 minutes
Date: 1971
Cost: $13.49 (Item # 192584)
Source: Movies Unlimited

3015 Darnell Road
Philadelphia, PA 19154-3295
(800) 668-4344
Internet: www.moviesunlimited.com

This "R"-rated movie stars Clint Eastwood as Harry Callahan, a San Francisco detective. He has acquired the name "Dirty Harry" because of his highly unorthodox methods for catching criminals. Some of his methods cross the line and violate the constitutional rights of the criminals he is chasing. This story tells of a serial killer who uses his threats of sniping unsuspecting victims from a distance to extort a large sum of money from the city of San Francisco. Callahan eventually catches the serial killer, but the killer goes free because of constitutional rights violations committed by Callahan. Eventually, the killer kidnaps a busload of school children and holds them for ransom. A shootout at the end between the killer and Callahan resolves the issue. This is an excellent film for demonstrating the weight given to the constitutional rights of both criminals and victims and how the courts tend to weigh these rights. It also provides some interesting examples of how police officers can engage in creative investigations that cross the line and infringe upon one's constitutional rights.

Disorderly Conduct: Are the Police Killing Us?
Type: VHS, color
Length: 27 minutes
Date: 1997
Cost: $139 (Item # GZ849)
Source: Insight Media
2162 Broadway
New York, NY 10024-0621
e-mail: cs@insight-media.com
Internet: www.insight-media.com

This tape examines the topic of police subculture that seems to generate more than its fair share of violence. Archival footage is used to describe various incidents in which private citizens have been harassed by police officers under different circumstances. The history of police abuse in the United States is briefly examined, and police subculture is described. Explanations are given for why police officers tend to conceal wrongdoing by other officers, and the code of silence is explained. Various solutions are offered for how these problems can be dealt with constructively by an increasingly interested public.

Good Cop, Bad Cop
Type: VHS, color
Length: 60 minutes
Date: 1998
Cost: $109.00 (Item # GZ923)
Source: Insight Media
2162 Broadway
New York, NY 10024-0621
(800) 233-9910
e-mail: cs@insight-media.com
Internet: www.insight-media.com

What should citizens do to combat excessive force and misconduct by police? Law enforcement agencies at all levels have mission statements. A part of all law enforcement mission statements includes public protection and safety. Yet the very officers who are sworn to protect citizens are violating their civil rights and harassing them with seeming impunity. Should Americans tolerate this excessive force, particularly force directed largely toward minority citizens, who often find it difficult to contest police methods used against them? The police force of any city is a protective service, as interpreted by many interested observers. However, some of the conduct of the police crosses the line into misconduct. Should the public tolerate a degree of misconduct by police in exchange for their own protection? This is a Public Broadcasting Service (PBS) video that examines the uneasy relation between the public and police. A debate is conducted by a panel of experts and a studio audience who attempt to find solutions for combatting police brutality.

Inside the FBI: Surviving the Street
Type: VHS, color
Length: 52 minutes
Cost: $149 purchase, $75 rental (Item # DJR9176)
Source: Films for the Humanities & Sciences
P.O. Box 2053
Princeton, NJ 08543-2053
(800) 257-5126
Internet: www.films.com

The stresses and strains of police work are portrayed in this tape. Several police officers are interviewed regarding their views about the work they perform and its attendant hazards. Police officers, especially those officers who have beats in high-crime areas, are exposed to life-threatening situations almost daily. Drug dealers and other criminals engage in deadly exchanges of gunfire with police as law enforcement is attempted. Life from the standpoint of police officers is featured, and the stress and burnout of policing is described. Training programs sponsored by various agencies, including the Federal Bureau of Investigation (FBI), are described. One effect of these training programs is to prepare officers for many of the stress-producing encounters they will confront while performing their jobs. The FBI's Law Enforcement for Safety and Survival Program is featured. This program is designed to channel and control the human stress response through concentrated mental and physical preparation. Officers who have participated in this program are interviewed and their views are described.

Internal Affairs
Type: VHS, color
Length: 50 minutes
Cost: $29.95 (Item # AAE-16109)
Source: A & E Television Networks
235 East 45th Street
New York, NY 10017
(888) 423-1212
Internet: www.AandE.com

One of the most hated police divisions in any police department is internal affairs (IA), a department that investigates allegations of police misconduct and corruption. IA has the power to suspend officers from their jobs during such investigations. Those officers involved in IA are often regarded as turncoats or traitors by other officers, who see IA as a meddling, trouble-causing body. Further isolating regular officers from the IA division is the secrecy under which IA operates. IA uses informants, some of whom are other police officers. Thus, different forms of police impropriety and crime are investigated. When incriminating evidence of corruption or misconduct is found, the involved officers are disciplined in various ways. Some are suspended, whereas others are fired. In some instances, criminal or civil charges are filed against offending officers and their cases are heard in court. Cynthia White, a Chicago police officer, is interviewed. White informed on twelve other officers who were engaging in various forms of misconduct. Michael Dowd is also interviewed. Dowd is a police officer who was accused of dealing drugs. Marvin Hirsch, Dowd's attorney, also speaks about police misconduct and what can be done to prevent or control it. Charles Campisi, chief of internal affairs for the New York Police Department, is interviewed as well. Campisi describes some of the more notorious cases of police misconduct and corruption that have tarnished the police department.

L.A. Detectives: Homicide/Hate Crimes
Type: VHS, color
Length: 50 minutes
Cost: $19.95 (Item # AAE-16171)
Source: A & E Television Networks
235 East 45th Street
New York, NY 10017
(888) 423-1212
Internet: www.AandE.com

Jerry Beck and Rod Kusch are detectives interviewed in this tape. They are followed by reporters and interviewers as they attempt to solve the murder of a fifteen-year-old girl whose body was found in a dumpster beside a building. Someone reports that the girl's boyfriend was the perpetrator and shot her in their car. When these detectives interview the boyfriend at his apartment, they discover several incriminating pieces of evidence. Their investigation of the car that was the alleged site of the shooting reveals additional incriminating evidence, including the girl's blood and a bullet. An arrest of the boyfriend is made. In another incident, these detectives attempt to solve a drive-by shooting. Modern police investigative methods are portrayed. Thus, a good side of policing is depicted as a contrast to the misconduct and corruption depicted by other features and documentaries. Actual police footage of crime scenes and investigations supplements interviews and opinions offered by these detectives as they go about their daily routine.

The Life of a Black Cop
Type: VHS, color
Length: 22 minutes
Cost: $89.95 (Item # DJR10174)
Source: Films for the Humanities & Sciences
P.O. Box 2053
Princeton, NJ 08543-2053
(800) 257-5126
Internet: www.films.com

What is it like to be a black police officer in a predominantly white police department? This American Broadcasting Company (ABC)–produced tape features news correspondent David Turecamo, who interviews DeLacy Davis. Davis is a police officer in East Orange, New Jersey who has spoken out against police brutality and reported other officers to internal affairs. Because of his outspoken views and reports to internal affairs, Davis has been excluded by other officers from regular police activities. He has been given the silent treatment, and he and his family have been harassed. Davis believes that many other officers share his views and are basically honest. He advocates that they should band together and fight those who breed corruption and misconduct.

Magnum Force
Type: VHS, color
Length: 124 minutes
Date: 1973
Cost: $17.99 (Item # 191010)
Source: Movies Unlimited
3015 Darnell Road
Philadelphia, PA 19154-3295
(800) 668-4344
Internet: www.moviesunlimited.com

This "R"-rated movie is the consummate film about dishonest police officers. This is a sequel to *Dirty Harry* (described above). Clint Eastwood stars as "Dirty Harry" Callahan, a San Francisco detective who investigates several deaths of crime figures. The crime scenes lead Callahan to suspect that police officers are probably doing these execution-style killings. His investigations lead him to suspect four particular officers who are war veterans and police rookies who can shoot extremely well. Placing them under surveillance, Callahan eventually discovers a plot within the San Francisco Police Department to execute criminals who escape court convictions because of legal technicalities.

Memphis PD: War on the Streets
Type: VHS, color
Length: 48 minutes
Cost: $149 purchase, $75 rental (Item # DJR6643)
Source: Films for the Humanities & Sciences
P.O. Box 2053
Princeton, NJ 08543-2053

(800) 257-5126
Internet: www.films.com

This tape portrays a side of police life that is seldom seen by the public. The sensitive subject of police suicides is explored. Every year in the United States, police officers have a suicide rate that is nearly double that of the regular U.S. population. What factors trigger police suicides? Various officers are interviewed and offer their views about the stress and burnout generated by the dangerousness of police work. The Memphis, Tennessee, Police Department, where a number of police suicides have occurred, is featured in this documentary. Many officers are unable to cope successfully with the violence occurring around them, and suicide is sometimes chosen as a way of alleviating unrelenting job stress and tension. Both male and female officers are exposed to the hazards of police work, and they both are considered at high risk for suicide. Various programs are described in which counseling and other programs are offered to officers in an attempt to sensitize them to the pressures they will face while performing their jobs. Also covered are police alcoholism, illicit drug use, and spousal violence.

The New Centurions
Type: VHS, color
Length: 103 minutes
Date: 1972
Cost: $14.99 (Item # 02-1052)
Source: Movies Unlimited
3015 Darnell Road
Philadelphia, PA 19154-4344
(800) 668-4344
Internet: www.moviesunlimited.com

Starring George C. Scott, this film, based upon a Joseph Wambaugh novel, portrays the intimate lives of several police officers, including one played by Stacy Keach, who becomes so enamoured with his new position, that he loses his family in the process. The movie portrays the stresses of police life as seen through these officers' eyes, and it provides numerous examples of police misconduct both on and off the job. "R" rated, this movie is an excellent real-life portrayal of police work and the dangers that officers are subjected to in their daily encounters with the public.

Police
Type:　VHS, color
Length: 100 minutes
Cost:　$29.95 (Item # AAE-2156)
Source: A & E Television Networks
　　　　　235 East 45th Street
　　　　　New York, NY 10017
　　　　　(888) 423-1212
　　　　　Internet: www.AandE.com

Bill Kurtis examines the history of policing in U.S. society. Kurtis and his team of interviewers examine the history and growth of local and national law enforcement. The two-hour documentary begins with an examination of colonial militias and ends with a depiction of law enforcement in modern cities. Various critical incidents are described that are eventful in a historical sense. Kurtis interviews various police officers and police experts to determine their perceptions about contemporary U.S. policing and where it is headed. This documentary is an excellent portrayal of police history and provides insight into various types of problems with police departments today. Many of these problems are corruption- and misconduct-related.

Police
Type:　VHS, color
Length: 100 minutes
Date:　1980
Cost:　$99.00 (Item # GZ731)
Source: Insight Media
　　　　　2162 Broadway
　　　　　New York, NY 10024-0621
　　　　　(800) 233-9910
　　　　　e-mail: cs@insight-media.com
　　　　　Internet: www.insight-media.com

The history of U.S. policing is examined in this tape. Various police departments are featured, including the historical bases of their organization and operations. Events are described that have influenced police professionalism and the growth and development of different types of U.S. law enforcement agencies.

Police Pursuit: Policies and Practice
Type:　VHS, color
Length: 60 minutes (Item # NIJ 161836)

Date: 1997
Source: National Institute of Justice
National Criminal Justice Reference Service
Box 6000
Rockville, MD 20849-6000
(800) 851-3420
e-mail: askncjrs.org
Internet: www.ojp.usdoj.gov/nij

Police department policies about hot pursuit vary considerably among different departments throughout the United States. The typical standard justifies pursuits that do not jeopardize one's life. However, despite the training police officers receive, some officers are intent on engaging in hot pursuits of minor traffic offenders. Often, the results are deadly, and those pursued by police crash and are killed. Thus, in a sense, death penalties are imposed on some persons whose apprehension would have resulted in only a minor fine or limited jail time for eluding police. Various police officers are interviewed to describe the conditions under which they engage suspects in hot pursuits. Various rationales are provided. Policy changes are recommended, and program training methods are suggested.

Police Violence in the U.S.
Type: VHS, color
Length: 30 minutes
Date: 1991
Cost: $79.00 (Item # GZ844)
Source: Insight Media
2162 Broadway
New York, NY 10024-0621
(800) 233-9910
e-mail: cs@insight-media.com
Internet: www.insight-media.com

ABC Nightline features a documentary about police violence in the United States. The increasing number of incidents involving police violence perpetrated against innocent U.S. citizens is described and explained. The phenomenon of civilian complaints is examined, and civilian complaint review boards and other accountability mechanisms are described. Public reaction to police harassment against citizens is featured.

Racial Profiling and Law Enforcement:
America in Black and White
Type: VHS, color
Length: 44 minutes
Cost: $129.00 purchase, $75 rental (Item # DJR9370)
Source: Films for the Humanities & Sciences
P.O. Box 2053
Princeton, NJ 08543-2053
(800) 257-3767
Internet: www.films.com

Driving while black (DWB) is featured in this tape. Disproportionately large numbers of black motorists are stopped by police officers in cities throughout the United States. Often, the grounds for stopping these motorists cannot be articulated by officers easily. The only explanation seems to be DWB, or driving while black. Some officers contend that certain black motorists look like they might be engaged in drug trafficking or are drug couriers. The police refer to this practice of matching representative characteristics to a criminal as profiling, although the public calls it racial profiling because those most often targeted for special police harassment and investigation are minorities. Most of these persons stopped by police have committed no crime, yet they are badgered by police into permitting extensive automobile searches. Sometimes, money is seized and labeled as "drug money," when it may be the proceeds from someone's savings account or a recent bank withdrawal. Ted Koppel and Michael McQueen of American Broadcasting Company (ABC) television news interview various persons who have been stopped and harassed by police officers. These persons report being humiliated by police and want this practice to stop. Solutions to racial profiling are proposed. Also interviewed are O. J. Simpson, a law professor, and former Los Angeles assistant district attorney Christopher Darden.

The Rodney King Case: What the Jury Saw
in *California v. Powell*
Type: VHS, color
Length: 120 minutes
Date: 1992
Cost: $159.00 (Item # GZ160)
Source: Insight Media
2162 Broadway

New York, NY 10024-0621
(800) 233-9910
e-mail: cs@insight-media.com
Internet: www.insight-media.com

This tape details the prosecution and defense arguments in the case of the officers who were put on trial for the beating of Rodney King. Legal authorities are interviewed and trial testimony is presented to help account for why police officers engaged in their behavior toward King. The videotape of the Rodney King beating is featured. Viewers themselves have ample opportunity to review the beating and determine whether King was resisting arrest, as the officers have alleged.

The Rodney King Incident: Race and Justice in America
Type: VHS, color
Length: 57 minutes
Cost: $89.95 (Item # DJR8285)
Source: Films for the Humanities & Sciences
P.O. Box 2053
Princeton, NJ 08543
(800) 257-5126
Internet: www.films.com

The Rodney King beating in Los Angeles in 1992 set off numerous riots in various cities, including Los Angeles. Originally four officers were charged in his beating for his failing to stop promptly for a traffic offense. King's beating allegedly occurred because officers believed that King was resisting arrest. The amateur videotape of King's beating is featured, and various experts attempt to explain why police acted as they did. Rodney King is interviewed, as well as former Los Angeles Police Department chief Daryl Gates. Gates defends the officers who perpetrated the beating of King by noting certain aspects of the situation on the street that were not captured on the videotape. A diverse range of opinions about police misconduct and how it could have been prevented are presented.

Serpico
Type: VHS, color
Length: 129 minutes
Date: 1973
Cost: $14.99 (Item # 06-1102)
Source: Movies Unlimited

3015 Darnell Road
Philadelphia, PA 19154-3295
(800) 668-4344
Internet: www.moviesunlimited.com

Serpico is perhaps the best movie to depict police corruption. Frank Serpico, played by Al Pacino, begins his career as a New York City Police Department (NYPD) patrol officer. Over time, as he seeks advancement in the ranks, Serpico becomes overly familiar with a continuing pattern of corruption and graft stretching from the rank-and-file officers all the way to the higher administrative levels. Eventually Serpico becomes a detective and finds that corruption has extended into the narcotics division, where huge financial payoffs are made to police officers on a regular basis. Serpico attempts to report these incidents of misconduct, but no one seems to care. Worse, no one believes him. Eventually, however, he finds sympathetic ears in the higher ranks as he is transferred from one precinct to another because of his purist views. Serpico's reports about police misconduct led to the Knapp Commission (cited elsewhere in this book), which investigated allegations of police corruption in the NYPD. This movie is "R" rated and an excellent example of the different forms of police misconduct that continue unabated in the NYPD and other police departments throughout the United States.

Should We Fear the Police?
Type: VHS, color
Length: 30 minutes
Date: 1999
Cost: $99.00 (Item # GZ1381)
Source: Insight Media
2162 Broadway
New York, NY 10024-0621
(800) 233-9910
e-mail: cs@insight-media.com
Internet: www.insight-media.com

Police officers in New York City were involved in the shooting death of Amadou Diallo. Diallo was merely seeking entry into his apartment, when four police officers gunned him down. More than forty shots were fired at Diallo, and he was killed instantly. Diallo, black, was killed by white officers. The incident triggered extensive protest throughout the black community, whose members believed that the shooting was racially motivated. Police brutality charges were filed against the police officers involved in the shooting. A second case is featured involving a black contingent of New Jersey state troopers who sought to expose racial discrimination from white troopers within their ranks.

The Star Chamber
Type: VHS, color
Length: 109 minutes
Date: 1983
Cost: $14.99 (Item # 04-1657
Source: Movies Unlimited
           3015 Darnell Road
           Philadelphia, PA 19154-3295
           (800) 668-4344
           Internet: www.moviesunlimited.com

Criminals are being freed of criminal charges on technicalities in this feature film that depicts a group of corrupt vigilante judges who take the law into their own hands. Several judges meet regularly and conspire to kill particular persons who are believed to have escaped punishment through the criminal justice system. Several police officers have been recruited by this band of judges to execute certain criminals who have escaped punishment in criminal courts. Michael Douglas stars as the most recent member of this judicial band, but his own moral values cause him to put a stop to these illegal killings. "R" rated, this movie depicts many examples of police misconduct, extending to conspiracy and murder.

Suicide and the Police Officer
Type: VHS, color
Length: 39 minutes
Cost: $149 purchase, $75 rental (Item # DJR3103)
Source: Films for the Humanities & Sciences
           P.O. Box 2053
           Princeton, NJ 08543-2053
           (800) 257-5126
           Internet: www.films.com

One of the adverse consequences of police work is the considerable stress and burnout that are associated with law enforcement. The stresses of policing are highlighted in this tape. The New York City Police Foundation examines the causes of alcoholism, drug abuse, spousal abuse, and suicide that often are associated with the hazards and life-threatening work of the police. Solutions are proposed for minimizing police deaths attributable to suicide, including various forms of counseling and other interventions. Police officers are targeted for such programs if they exhibit certain signs of stress and are considered suicide-prone. The factors that are associated with such stress are examined and different intervention programs are described.

The Tarnished Shield: When Cops Go Bad
Type: VHS, color
Length: 52 minutes
Cost: $149 purchase, $75 rental (Item # DJR5298)
Source: Films for the Humanities & Sciences
          P.O. Box 2053
          Princeton, NJ 08543-2053
          (800) 257-5126
          Internet: www.films.com

Barbara Walters interviews Frank Serpico, a former detective with the New York Police Department (NYPD). Frank Serpico was the police detective who in the late 1960s reported extensive police corruption to his superiors. Other police officers retaliated by setting him up in a suspicious drug raid and shooting him. Serpico's testimony led to the formation of the Knapp Commission, which investigated police corruption. Corruption was found to be widespread, and various actions were taken to eradicate it. Although corruption still exists in the NYPD, it is less visible than in past decades. Walters also interviews a police officer whose arrest for dealing drugs led to the 1993 investigation of the New York Police Department. One of the interesting aspects of Walters's interview with this officer is that it shows his personal view that, as a police officer, one feels that one is above the law in many respects and is entitled to violate it anytime. The officer discloses the ease with which illicit monies are generated through police corruption, particularly drug trafficking and the protection of drug traffickers. Much insight is given into the personality of this police officer, and some of the factors that caused him to become a corrupt officer are examined.

The Thin Blue Line
Type: VHS, color
Length: 101 minutes
Date: 1988
Cost: $9.99 (Item # 441572)

Source: Movies Unlimited
3015 Darnell Road
Philadelphia, PA 19154-3295
(800) 668-4344
Internet: www.moviesunlimited.com

Filmmaker Errol Morris describes the saga of a man who was wrongfully convicted of murder in Texas. Randall Adams was convicted of murder and sentenced to life imprisonment for killing a police officer. Adams was innocent of the crime, although circumstantial evidence indicated that he was somehow involved. Subsequently it was determined that some of the evidence against Adams was actually fabricated by police investigators and that his prosecution was conducted in a malicious fashion. Police misconduct is amply illustrated in this tape, which also depicts the perjured testimony given at Randall Adams's trial by police and other officials who investigated the murder. Dennis Johnson stars as Randall Adams. Randall Adams was subsequently pardoned for his alleged crime.

Unlawful Entry
Type: VHS, color
Length: 107 minutes
Date: 1992
Cost: $9.99 (Item # 042596)
Source: Movies Unlimited
3015 Darnell Road
Philadelphia, PA 19154-3295
(800) 668-4344
Internet: www.moviesunlimited.com

This "R"-rated, suspenseful feature film, starring Ray Liotta and Madeline Stowe, highlights the corrupt activities of a police officer. The officer (Liotta) answers a call from a couple who have been burglarized. In the process, the investigating officer becomes attracted to the woman and obsessed with her. He stalks her in different ways and assaults her. The officer will do anything, including murder, to have this woman. Examples of police misconduct are illustrated graphically.

Use of Force by and against the Police
Type: VHS, color
Length: 60 minutes (Item # NCJ 158614)
Date: 1996

Source: National Institute of Justice
National Criminal Justice Reference Service
Box 6000
Rockville, MD 20849-6000
(800) 851-3420
e-mail: askncjrs.org
Internet: www.ojp.usdoj.gov/nij

A force continuum has been devised to measure the amount of force police officers apply when affecting someone's arrest. This tape examines excessive force and illustrates different types of force police use to subdue criminal suspects. Circumstances are described that depict conditions under which particular kinds of force should be used. The tape also illustrates force used against the police by citizens who attempt to avoid arrest. Officer injuries often result. Several solutions are offered as options to physical force, including verbal judo, a way of talking suspects into submitting to police arrest. This nonviolent method of defusing otherwise volatile police-citizen encounters is explained.

When Cops Kill
Type: VHS, color
Length: 50 minutes
Cost: $29.95 (Item # AAE-16050)
Source: A & E Television Networks
235 East 45th Street
New York, NY 10017
(888) 423-1212
Internet: www.AandE.com

The issue of deadly force is raised in this tape, which examines the conditions under which deadly force should be applied. Two cases involving the use of deadly force are portrayed. One is the Eleanor Bumpurs case. Bumpurs was a mentally ill grandmother who was shot to death in her Bronx, New York, home by police. Another case involved the shooting death of an unarmed suspect in Detroit. What justification do police officers provide for shooting grandmothers and unarmed suspects? The cases are examined in great detail, and experts and witnesses are interviewed. Various types of weapons and physical techniques as alternatives to deadly force are described.

Glossary

accountability and control   Created organizational subunits and work environments that greatly inhibited personal discretion and lower-echelon decision making; a disciplinary structure within which ordinary people could be hired for an exacting job and where they could be trained, equipped, and motivated to function effectively.

arrest rates by race   Numbers of persons per 1,000, 10,000, or some other common standard who are arrested according to racial characteristics.

back-to-the-people movement   Community-oriented policing focusing on foot patrols and neighborhood beats; proactive policing stressing community wellness.

basic car plan   Method to prevent and control crime; car teams consisted of nine officers: a lead officer; five senior officers with two to three years experience, accompanied by three probationary officers; operated on workload analysis factors that provided a minimum radio car plan (basic car plan) for all watches.

beat patrolling   Police patrol style originating in early 1900s designed to bring officers into closer physical contact with area residents; beats arranged for small geographical areas of neighborhoods or cities that are patrolled by individual officers, usually on foot.

Black Police Officers Association   Formed in 1971 and comprised of officers who "have put their color ahead of their duty as police officers."

blue curtain   Reluctance among police officials to punish "one of their own" when a citizen complains; when police agencies "investigate their own," the very language used in such investigations is telling.

Bow Street Runners   A small organization of paid police officers who attempted to apprehend criminals; originated in England in 1754.

British Crime Survey   Annual compilation of victimization figures for both England and Wales; comparable to the *National Crime Victimization Survey (NCVS)* published in the United States.

cadet programs   Programs designed to bring underage but otherwise qualified individuals into police service; applicants undergo preservice screening such as oral, physical, and background investigations and are generally accepted upon solid recommendations.

career integrity workshops   In-service training program initiated by Los Angeles County Sheriff's Department; in-house instructors trained in methods of leading small groups of deputies into creating "questionable conduct" scenarios and facilitating group discussions that delved into possible causes of actions or inactions and possible results. Students experience inappropriate behaviors more directly and see more realistic situations when they actively participate in the scenario than when it is presented in a predetermined way.

centurions   Commanders of units used as either military or paramilitary units for policing purposes in early Roman times, from about 100 B.C. to 200 A.D.; usually commanded units of one hundred men who were used for both policing and combat.

chancellors   King of England's agents who settled disputes on the king's behalf between neighbors; settled disputes involving property boundary issues, trespass allegations, and child misconduct; early equivalent of the chancellor with similar duties and responsibilities was the justice of the peace, dating back to about 1200 A.D.

Chinese Exclusion Act   Passed by Congress in 1882, this act barred Chinese laborers from entering the United States for ten years and subsequently was expanded to impose a head tax and exclude whole categories of people such as convicts and the mentally ill; for the first time there were real limits on European immigration.

Civil Rights Institute   Established by the Birmingham Civil Rights Institute in Birmingham, Alabama, in 1992, this museum tells the story of the 1960s civil rights movement that helped change the nation and the world; centerpiece in the city's historic Civil Rights District.

civil rights movement   Multiracial movement commenced in 1960s to combat racial injustice and inequality.

civilian complaint review boards   Panels of citizens that judge acts of misconduct committed by police officers and recommend appropriate sanctions.

code of silence   Negative and potentially self-destructive informal arrangement among police officers that discourages whistle-blowing regarding misconduct of other officers.

community-based policing   An umbrella term encompassing any law enforcement agency–, community citizen–, or group-initiated plan or program to enable police officers and community residents to work cooperatively in creative ways that will (1) reduce or control crime, fear of crime, and the incidence of victimizations; (2) promote mutual understanding for the purpose of enhancing police officer/citizen coproduction of community safety and security; and (3) establish a police-citizen communications network through which mutual problems may be discussed and resolved.

Community Patrol Officer Program (CPOP) A problem-oriented community policing effort commenced as a pilot project in 1984 in New York City to determine the feasibility of permanently assigning police officers to foot patrol in fairly large neighborhood beat areas; officers required to perform a variety of nontraditional tasks besides their normal law enforcement duties, to be full-service police officers, and to serve as community resources; additional tasks included helping residents to organize community groups, attending community meetings, making service referrals, and helping to devise strategies to deal not only with local crime and order-maintenance problems, but also with social needs; officers assigned to foot patrols for sixteen- to sixty-block beats; seventy-five precincts used the CPOP by 1989; most important function of CPOP was the prevention of street-level drug problems.

community policing A proactive, decentralized approach—a philosophy rather than a specific tactic—designed to reduce crime, disorder, and fear of crime by intensely involving the same officer in a community for a long term so that personal links are formed with residents.

community wellness A proactive collaborative effort between police departments and community residents to initiate watch and alert programs to inform police about possible criminal activities; as neighborhood residents take a more active role in preventing crime, observed crime decreases substantially in those neighborhoods over time.

Community-Police Educational Program Implemented by the Philadelphia Police Department in 1980; designed to educate citizens by explaining the necessity for certain police actions and to reduce their criticism of police performance.

conservative policing ideals The position that individuals act upon free choice and upon their free will; individuals are seen to be rational beings responsible for their actions or inactions; conservatives are concerned with maintaining the status quo and believe that although change may be evolutionary, it should be gradual.

constables Favored noblemen of the English king; commanded neighborhood groups and were the forerunners of modern-day police officers.

Crime Stoppers A Canadian program established in 1976 that uses the mass media to encourage the public to anonymously report criminal activity in exchange for a reward; has been somewhat helpful in combatting crime.

Crime Watch A crime reduction and control program; facilitated through greater police presence in neighborhoods and use of neighborhood observers.

crime watch programs Any program using a cooperative alliance between police and citizens to prevent and/or control crime.

cultural diversity Multiethnic and multiracial agencies and organizations intended to equalize employment and treatment of all ethnicities and races by police officers; the condition of being ethnically diverse.

day watch Day or night watch duties that English citizens were obligated to perform on a rotating basis, comparable to modern-day shift work; watchmen would be expected to yell out a hue and a cry in the event they detected crimes in progress or any other community disturbance, such as a fire or other emergency situation.

deadly force Use of force resulting in death of suspects.

"defense-of-life" standard Standard set by *Tennessee v. Garner* (1985) whereby police officers may shoot fleeing felons only if their own lives or the lives of others are directly threatened by suspects attempting to avoid apprehension or resisting arrest.

dropsy testimony Perjured testimony by police officers attempting to solidify a weak case; defendants are often alleged to have "dropped" illegal substances, for example, drugs on the ground during an automobile stop for a traffic violation; more prevalent after exclusionary rule became search and seizure standard after case of *Mapp v. Ohio* (1963).

emotional numbing Condition in which officers distance themselves from a stressful incident and make an effort not to feel anything; a denial of having an emotional component and often giving the appearance that the officer is in a state of shock; officers usually say, however, that they are in control and are having no problems dealing with the situation.

empowerment The essence of both organizational mission and values statements; permits employees the latitude to perform at their highest levels.

ethics Codes of honor tacitly or overtly observed by law enforcement officers; upholding both the spirit and letter of the law and fulfilling the mission statement of police agencies.

excessive force Any exceptional force extending beyond that necessary to disable suspects or take them into custody through arrest.

exigent circumstances Circumstances in which quick action is necessitated, such as searches for drugs and other contraband that might be destroyed easily; exception to exclusionary rule.

FLETC model Gradated or escalated amounts of force, applied in accordance with the nature of suspect cooperation or resistance; cooperative suspects are given verbal orders by officers, whereas other suspects might require varying degrees of force to subdue them.

foot patrols Officers patrolling on foot, presumably to bring them in closer touch with citizens; originating in Flint, Michigan, and elsewhere, have been moderately successful in bringing community residents into closer touch with patrolling officers.

golf cart patrolling Patrolling in golf carts; combined with sector patrolling, has been instrumental in bringing police officers closer to community residents.

"good faith" exception Exception to exclusionary rule and whereby police officers conduct search and seizure on basis of faulty warrant; acting in "good faith" presumably excuses conduct.

graft Gratuities accepted in the course of one's police role in exchange for favors or concessions usually involving violations of the law.

hate crimes Crimes motivated by bigotry against a social group.

hue and cry Warning shouted by day and night watchmen in England if crime was observed.

human relations School of organizational behavior stressing personal qualities of those in roles such as police officers; sees persons as personality systems with emotional components.

incident-driven policing A technocratic product whereby police officers have traditionally responded or reacted to calls for service.

internal affairs Department within police agencies that is charged with the responsibility to investigate misconduct and possible criminal behavior on the part of police officers; comprised of other police officers.

Law Enforcement Assistance Administration (LEAA) An outgrowth of the President's Crime Commission during 1965 to 1967, a time of great social unrest and civil disobedience and when racial and political tensions were exceptionally high; allocated millions of dollars to researchers and police departments over the next decade for various purposes; many experiments conducted with these monies led to innovative patrolling strategies in different communities.

legalistic model Emphasized the importance of written procedure and limited individual officer discretion; promoted a rigid bureaucratic mentality among law enforcement officers.

letter of the law Strictly legalistic approach to law enforcement; zero-tolerance interpretation of the law.

liberal policing ideals An ideology, a political philosophy, and related policies aimed at social reform designed to increase equality and democratic participation in governance; liberals advocate the use of state power to aid disadvantaged individuals and groups; they support a position that much criminal activity has roots in the social fabric.

mala in se **crimes** Illegal acts that are inherently wrong.

mala prohibita **crimes** Illegal acts that have been codified in law.

mentally ill Phrase describing persons who have a mental disease or defect that can prevent them from understanding the difference between right and wrong and who might not be able to conform their conduct according to the law.

Metropolitan Police Act of 1829 Act that empowered Sir Robert Peel to select and organize the Metropolitan Police of London.

Metropolitan Police Force Project Act of 1981 Toronto complaint review authorized by act to investigate citizen complaints against police.

Metropolitan Police of London A police department organized in 1829 by Sir Robert Peel, a prominent British government official; included duties that emphasized close interaction with the public and maintenance of proper attitudes and temperament.

military syndrome Propensity of police organizations to organize and operate police departments according to military organization and protocol, including use of ranks and similar hierarchies of authority.

mini-stations Small police stations strategically located in high-crime-rate neighborhoods; staffed by one or more police officers.

mission statements Goals and orientation statements of organizations; designed to disclose the purposes and responsibilities of the organizations and used to vest employees with direction and motivation.

National Advisory Commission on Criminal Justice Standards and Goals Promulgated several important goals for police departments in order to clarify their policing functions, including maintenance of order; enforcement of the law; prevention of criminal activity; detection of criminal activity; apprehension of criminals; participation in court proceedings; protection of constitutional guarantees; assistance to those who cannot care for themselves or who are in danger of physical harm; control of traffic; resolution of day-to-day conflicts among family, friends, and neighbors; creation and maintenance of a feeling of security in the community; promotion and preservation of civil order.

National Commission on Law Observance and Enforcement Commission created by Herbert Hoover in 1929; designed to investigate law enforcement practices and standards.

National Crime Victimization Survey (NCVS)   Annual survey of crime victims.

negative reinforcements   Punishments administered by superior officers to their subordinate police officers to curb particular kinds of undesirable conduct.

negligent hiring and selection   Basis for civil lawsuit alleging that incompetent persons have been selected to perform important tasks, such as police work, and alleging that injuries to victims are caused by such incompetent persons.

negligent retention   Basis for civil lawsuit against public officials alleging that ineffective or poorly trained personnel are retained despite their poor work record.

negligent training   Basis for civil lawsuit alleging that training of employees (e.g., to use firearms) is lacking.

neighborhood team policing   Cooperative enterprise between neighborhood citizens and police officers to maintain continuous vigil in communities and to report suspicious behavior or criminal activity.

Neighborhood Watch   Program using neighborhood residents as observers, particularly during evening hours, for criminal conduct.

night watch   Early English watchman program in which the watchman would report observed crime.

Operation Blockade   A U.S. Immigration and Naturalization Service experiment launched with $250,000 in extra overtime funds and agents shifted from inland posts in El Paso, Texas, to prevent the influx of illegal aliens into the United States.

Operation CLEAN   In Dallas, Texas, for example, a seven-phase program known as Operation CLEAN was implemented in March 1989. Specific areas of the city were targeted for Operation CLEAN, and concerted action among several municipal departments (police, fire, streets and sanitation, housing and neighborhood services departments, and the city attorney's office) resulted in a major effort leading to a 71 percent reduction in street crime. However, community involvement in this clean-up effort was required. Citizens established Crime Watch programs and increased their cooperation with police officers. Thus, crime reduction and decreased fear of crime in those affected neighborhoods were sustained through police-resident efforts.

organizational values   Standards imparted by organizations to membership designed to instill in them work motivation and goals.

participative management   Theory of organizations by which employees have some input regarding departmental operations.

patrol car video cameras Videotape units in police vehicles; used for various purposes (e.g., to tape arrests of suspected drunk drivers, to illustrate causes for stops and arrests of motorists for various charges).

Peace Officer Standards and Training (POST) Generally recognized criteria used to select and train persons for police work.

perjury Lying under oath in court.

plain view rule Exception to exclusionary rule whereby illegal contraband may be seized because it is in plain view; to use this rule, officers who seize contraband must be in places where they are permitted to be.

Police and Criminal Evidence Act of 1984 British act authorizing the establishment of an independent Police Complaints Authority in 1985.

police brutality Any unnecessary physical force used by police officers against arrested citizens that causes injuries to citizens.

Police Community Awareness Academies The formation of a citizens' police academy originated in England, specifically from the Devon and Cornwall Constabulary, Middlemoor Exeter; the idea was formulated when local citizens asked their constables how the agency operated. In 1977, two small British municipal police agencies established a police night school, a concept that in the United States has come to be known as the citizens' police academy.

police-community relations A generic concept including any program designed to promote or make more visible the law enforcement strategies that are aimed at crime prevention and control and in which varying degrees of proactive citizen involvement are solicited.

Police Complaints Authority An independent British investigative body to examine the validity of citizen complaints against police and capable of imposing appropriate administrative sanctions against the offending officers.

police discretion Choices by police officers to act in given ways in citizen-police encounters; selection of behaviors among alternatives.

police misconduct Any one of several different types of illegal and/or improper behavior of police officers; examples are acceptance of graft, falsifying police reports, and perjury.

police mission Either implicit or explicit statements about general goals and objectives of police departments and officers.

positive reinforcements Rewards given by administrators to lower-level police officers for good conduct or performance according to the requirements set forth in the police mission.

posttrauma strategies Officer help programs designed to provide individual or group counseling to officers involved in stressful events, such as shootings.

Precinct Community Councils (PCCs)   Established as liaisons between police officers and local residents; face-to-face councils that have done much to foster better police-community cooperation and create better conditions of community crime control.

problem-oriented policing   Citizen involvement in defining community crime problems and suggesting solutions for them.

productivity   Either measured or unmeasured output by officers; includes numbers of arrests, time on duty, tickets issued, participation in public events, etc.

professionalization movement   Efforts by various interests to encourage higher standards of selection for police officers, including more formal education and training.

psychological screening   Administration of tests or assessment devices designed to exclude police candidates whose personal behaviors and personalities are unsuitable for police work.

public disclosure   Information about police agencies and officers disseminated by a public relations officer.

public relations   Persons or bureaus involved in creating more effective and pleasant interactions and working associations between citizens and police officers.

quality circles   An application of total quality management, an approach that encourages workers classified similarly (e.g., dispatchers, detectives, patrol) to interact with one another in group settings to resolve problems common to their particular work specialties; acting as a team, these personnel can often offer recommendations that lead to savings in labor and time, enhanced service, and/or improved working conditions.

Retired Senior Volunteer Program   A national effort that places retirees in community volunteer positions; has been received in many quarters as one approach to augment decreasing police personnel shortages.

Section 1983 actions   Title 42, Section 1983 of the U.S. Code, setting forth grounds for legal actions involving civil rights violations by police officers against citizens.

selective enforcement   Act by police officers of prioritizing particular offenses and enforcing some laws and not enforcing others.

sense of community   Psychological milieu established between police officers and citizens in which citizens acquire a sense of security and safety in their own neighborhood.

service model Designed to meet community needs and expectations and therefore shaped by them.

sexual harassment Unwanted sexual advances or remarks, especially by one in a superior position or in authority. When refusing to submit to such behavior directly threatens a person's employment status, it is called "quid pro quo" harassment. When it is a repeated pattern by a coworker, it is called "hostile environment" harassment.

shouts and rattles Warning system of early New Yorkers who were equipped with rattles and were expected to shout and rattle their rattles in the event they observed crimes in progress or fleeing suspects; were paid forty-eight cents per twenty-four-hour shift.

situationally based discretion Options exercised by police officers during police-citizen encounters; may or may not include letter-of-law interpretations of events.

spirit of the law Efforts by police officers to exhibit leniency when law violations are observed; usually first offenders might receive leniency because of extenuating circumstances.

station house adjustments Decisions by police officers to deal informally with arrestees, often at the police station; actions often do not involve arrests, but warnings.

stress versus nonstress training Training received by police officers in which they are subjected to situations involving role strain and conflict generating stress; process involves how to cope with stress and reduce its adverse effects.

subculture Social cliques and behavior patterns of selected groups, such as gangs.

team policing Investigative teams of police officers, detectives, and other personnel are assigned to a particular community area to work as a team in solving crimes that occur in that area.

thief-takers Persons who were "fleet of foot" in early England; selected to pursue and apprehend fleeing criminals for a fee.

total quality management Similar to participative management, quality control, "management by objectives," and a host of other civilian industry managerial concepts.

totality of circumstances Exception to exclusionary rule, whereby officers may make warrantless searches of property and seizures of contraband on the basis of the entire set of suspicious circumstances.

Traffic Enforcement and Management System (TEAMS) Principles include (1) continuous training, (2) genuine employee participation throughout the organization, (3) change of the role of the manager or sergeant from "cop" to "facilitator," and (4) the encouragement of risk taking. An evaluation of this program suggests favorable results for improving staff morale, work satisfaction, and job effectiveness as well as reducing traffic fatalities.

Uniform Crime Reports (UCR)   Document published annually by the Federal Bureau of Investigation detailing reported crimes in the United States by state, county, and other variables.

volunteerism   In regard to policing, propensity of citizens to become actively involved in various auxiliary police functions, such as Neighborhood Watch.

warrantless searches and seizures   Any search of a person or one's car and/or premises that is not preceded by a valid search warrant issued by a judge based on probable cause and under oath.

watchmen   Citizens in early England who were paid to observe in their neighborhoods for possible criminal activity.

Index

About the Author

Dean J. Champion is professor of criminal justice at Texas A & M International University in Laredo, Texas. Dr. Champion has taught at the University of Tennessee–Knoxville, California State University–Long Beach, and Minot State University. He earned his Ph.D. from Purdue University and B.S. and M.A. degrees from Brigham Young University. He also completed several years of law school at the Nashville School of Law.

Dr. Champion has written more than twenty-five texts and/or edited works and maintains memberships in eleven professional organizations. He is a lifetime member of the American Society of Criminology, Academy of Criminal Justice Sciences, and the American Sociological Association. He is former editor of the ACJS/Anderson Series on *Issues in Crime and Justice* (1993–1996) and the *Journal of Crime and Justice* (1995–1998). He is a contributing author for the *Encarta Encyclopedia 2000* for Microsoft. He was the visiting scholar for the National Center for Juvenile Justice in 1992 and is president of the Midwestern Criminal Justice Association.

His published books for Prentice-Hall include *Basic Statistics for Social Research* (1970, 1981); *Research Methods for Criminal Justice and Criminology* (1993, 2000); *The Juvenile Justice System: Delinquency, Processing, and the Law* (1992, 1998, 2001); *Corrections in the United States: A Contemporary Perspective* (1990, 1998, 2001); *Probation, Parole, and Community Corrections* (1990, 1996, 1999); *Policing in the Community* (with George Rush) (1996); and *The Administration of Justice Systems* (2001). Works from other publishers include *The Sociology of Organizations* (McGraw-Hill, 1975); *Research Methods in Social Relations* (John Wiley & Sons, 1976); *Sociology* (Holt, Rinehart, and Winston, 1984); *The U.S.*

Sentencing Guidelines (Praeger, 1989); *Juvenile Transfer Hearings* (with G. Larry Mays) (Praeger, 1991); *Measuring Offender Risk* (Greenwood Press, 1994); *The Roxbury Dictionary of Criminal Justice: Key Terms and Leading Supreme Court Cases* (Roxbury Press, 1997, 2001); and *Criminal Justice in the United States,* 2nd Edition (Wadsworth, 1998). Dr. Champion's primary research interests relate to attorney use in juvenile justice proceedings and plea bargaining.